HANNS AND RUDOLF

HANNS AND RUDOLF

The German Jew and the Hunt for the Kommandant
of Auschwitz

Thomas Harding

WILLIAM HEINEMANN: LONDON

Published by William Heinemann 2013

2 4 6 8 10 9 7 5 3

First published in Great Britain in 2013 by
William Heinemann
Random House, 20 Vauxhall Bridge Road,
London SW1V 2SA

www.randomhouse.co.uk

Addresses for companies within The Random House Group Limited can be found at:
www.randomhouse.co.uk/offices.htm

The Random House Group Limited Reg. No. 954009

A CIP catalogue record for this book
is available from the British Library

ISBN 9780434022366 (Hardback)
ISBN 9780434022373 (Trade Paperback)

The Random House Group Limited supports The Forest Stewardship
Council® (FSC®), the leading international forest-certification organisation.
Our books carrying the FSC label are printed on FSC®-certified paper.
FSC is the only forest-certification scheme supported by the leading
environmental organisations, including Greenpeace. Our
paper procurement policy can be found at
www.randomhouse.co.uk/environment

Typeset by Palimpsest Book Production Ltd, Falkirk, Stirlingshire
Printed and bound in Great Britain by Clays Ltd, St Ives plc

For Kadian

CONTENTS

LIST OF ILLUSTRATIONS

Unless otherwise stated, all photographs courtesy Alexander Family Archive

GREAT BRITAIN 1945

FINLAND

Leningrad

ESTONIA

Riga
LATVIA

LITHUANIA

Moscow

...AST
...USSIA

USSR

Treblinka

Warsaw

POLAND

Krakow

...KIA

UKRAINE

...RY

ROMANIA

Caspian Sea

...IA

Black Sea

BULGARIA

Istanbul

...NIA

TURKEY

GREECE

CRETE

CYPRUS

Baghdad

Al-Kut

Jaffa
Jerusalem

Prees Heath,
Whitchurch
Shropshire

OCTU Lincolnshire

WALES

ENGLAND

Chalfont-St-Peter

Oxford/Woodstock

Newbury

Portsmouth

Weymouth

Isle of
Wight

St Ives

LONDON

Finchley
Golders
Green

Alexandra
Palace

Belsize Square

Kensington

Croydon

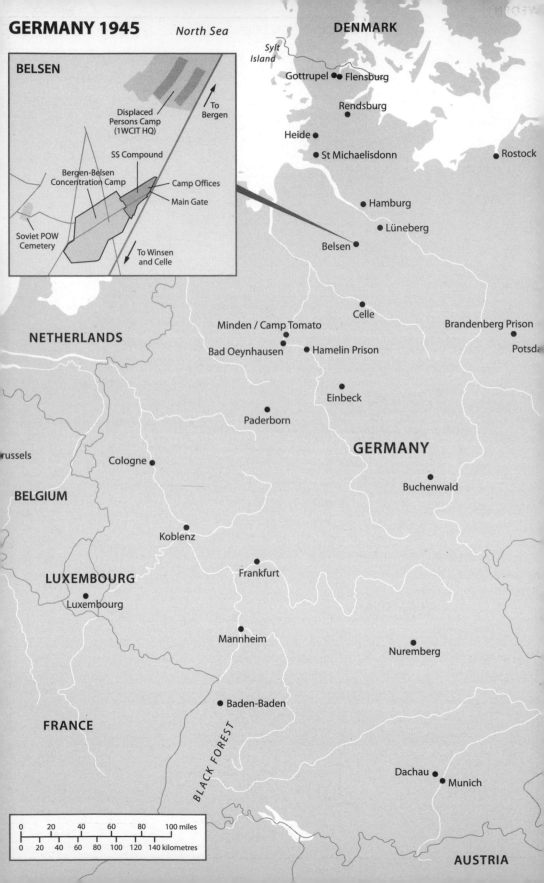

GERMANY 1945

North Sea

DENMARK

Sylt Island

BELSEN

Displaced Persons Camp (1WCIT HQ)

To Bergen

SS Compound

Bergen-Belsen Concentration Camp

Camp Offices

Main Gate

Soviet POW Cemetery

To Winsen and Celle

Gottrupel ●● Flensburg

Rendsburg

Heide ●

St Michaelisdonn ●

● Rostock

● Hamburg

● Lüneberg

Belsen ●

● Celle

NETHERLANDS

Minden / Camp Tomato

Bad Oeynhausen ● ● Hamelin Prison

Brandenberg Prison ●

Potsda

● Einbeck

● Paderborn

GERMANY

russels

Cologne ●

BELGIUM

● Buchenwald

Koblenz ●

Frankfurt ●

LUXEMBOURG

Luxembourg ●

Mannheim ●

Nuremberg ●

● Baden-Baden

FRANCE

BLACK FOREST

Dachau ● ● Munich

| 0 | 20 | 40 | 60 | 80 | 100 miles |

| 0 | 20 | 40 | 60 | 80 | 100 | 120 | 140 kilometres |

AUSTRIA

WEDEN

Baltic Sea

POMERANIA

Ravensbrück

achsenhausen

erlin

Oder

ANNEXED
POLISH
TERRITORY

LOWER
SILESIA

UPPER
SILESIA

POLAND

Oświęcim/
Auschwitz

● Krakow

Prague ●

CZECHOSLOVAKIA

BERLIN

Neue
Synagogue

Deutsches
Theater

Tiergarten

Opernplatz

Zoo

Reichstag

Fasanenstrasse
Synagogue

Prinz-Albrecht-Strasse
(Himmler's offices)

Kaiserallee
apartment

Sportpalast

Achenbachstrasse
(clinic)

Groß Glienicke
Lake

Potsdam

AUSCHWITZ 1

Gravel Pits

Crematoria

Rudolf's
office

Gates

Gallows

Barracks
(with numbers)

4

Höss
Villa

9
10
11

Black Wall

Sola River

AUSCHWITZ CAMPS

Vistula River

Dwory
Station

Oświęcim Station
and Rail Yard

Dwory
Rail Yard

DWORY

Sola River

OŚWIĘCIM

FG Farben plant

Auschwitz II
Birkenau

Auschwitz I

Auschwitz III
Morowitz

Solahütte (further
south of Auschwitz)

| 0 | 0.5 | 1 | 1.5 miles |
| 0 | 1 | 2 kilometres | |

Now write down this song and teach it to the Israelites and have them sing it, so that it may be a witness for me against them. And when many disasters and calamities come on them, this song will testify against them, because it will not be forgotten by their descendants.

Deuteronomy 31:19 and 21

AUTHOR'S NOTE

The Kommandant of Auschwitz's name can be spelled in different ways. Perhaps the most authentic is 'Rudolf Höß', which is how the Kommandant himself spelled it. This uses the letter ß, affirming the Kommandant's conservative Swabian heritage. The more common English spelling is 'Rudolf Hoess'. However, the Kommandant never spelled his name this way, and it also has the danger of being confused with Rudolf Hess, Hitler's secretary. I have chosen to use the contemporary German spelling, 'Rudolf Höss', which was not only the way that the SS typed his name, but also the way it was written by Hanns Alexander.

One more point. By calling Hanns and Rudolf by their first names I do not mean to equate them. Indeed, it is important to me that there be no moral equivalence. Yet both of these men were, self-evidently, human beings, and as such, if I am to tell their tales, I should begin with their first names. If this offends, and I understand why it might, I ask for your forgiveness.

PROLOGUE

ALEXANDER. Howard Harvey, lovingly known as Hanns, passed away quickly and peacefully on Friday, 23rd December. Cremation on Thursday, 28th December, 2.30 p.m. at Hoop Lane, Golders Green Crematorium, West Chapel. No flowers please. Donations, if desired, to North London Hospice.

Daily Telegraph, 28 December 2006

Hanns Alexander's funeral was held on a cold and rainy afternoon three days after Christmas. Considering the weather, and the timing, the turnout was impressive. More than three hundred people packed into the chapel. The congregation arrived early, and in full force, grabbing all the seats. Fifteen people from Hanns' old bank, Warburg's, were in attendance, including the former and current CEO. His close friends were there, as was the extended family. Hanns' wife of sixty years, Ann, sat in the front row, along with the couple's two daughters, Jackie and Annette.

The synagogue's cantor recited Kaddish, the traditional Jewish prayer for the dead. He then paused. Looking down upon Ann and her two daughters, he delivered a short sermon, saying how sorry he was for their loss and how Hanns would be missed by the entire community. When he had finished, two of Hanns' nephews stood to give a joint eulogy.

Much was familiar: Hanns growing up in Berlin. The Alexanders fleeing the Nazis and moving to England. Hanns fighting with the British Army. His career as a low-level banker. His commitment to the family and his half-century of schlepping for the synagogue.

But there was one detail that caught nearly everyone off guard: that at the war's end Hanns had tracked down the Kommandant of Auschwitz, Rudolf Höss.

This piqued my interest. For Hanns Alexander was my grand-mother's brother, my great-uncle. Growing up we had been cautioned not to ask questions about the war. Now I learned that Hanns may have been a Nazi hunter.

The idea that this nice but unremarkable man had been a Second World War hero seemed unlikely. Presumably, this was just another of Hanns' tales. For he was a bit of a rogue and a prankster, much respected for sure, but also a man who liked to play tricks on his elders and tell dirty jokes to us youngsters, and who, if truth be told, was prone to exaggeration. After all, if he had really been a Nazi hunter, wouldn't it have been mentioned in his obituary?

I decided to find out if it was true.

We live in an age when the waters are closing over the history of the Second World War, when we are about to lose the last remaining witnesses, when all that is left are accounts retold so many times that they have lost their original veracity. And so we are left with cari-catures: Hitler and Himmler as monsters, Churchill and Roosevelt as conquering warriors, and millions of Jews as victims.

Yet Hanns Alexander and Rudolf Höss were men with many sides to their characters. As such, this story challenges the traditional portrayal of the hero and the villain. Both men were adored by their families and respected by their colleagues. Both grew up in Germany in the early decades of the twentieth century and, in their way, loved their country. At times, Rudolf Höss, the brutal Kommandant, displayed a capacity for compassion. And the behaviour of his pursuer, Hanns Alexander, was not always above suspicion. This book is therefore a reminder of a more complex world, told through the lives of two men who grew up in parallel and yet opposing German cultures.

It is also an attempt to follow the courses of the two men's lives, and to understand how they came to meet. And the attempt raises difficult questions. How does a man become a mass murderer? Why does a person choose to confront his persecutors? What happens to the families of such men? Is revenge ever justified?

Even more, this story is an argument that when the worlds of these two men collided, modern history was changed. The testimony that emerged proved particularly significant in the war crimes trials at the end of the Second World War: Höss was the first senior Nazi to admit to executing Himmler's and Hitler's Final Solution. And he did so in great and shocking detail. This testimony, unprecedented in its description of human evil, drove the world to swear that such unspeakable atrocities would never again be repeated. From this point forward, those suffering from extreme injustice could dare to hope for intervention.

It is also the story of surprise. In my comfortable north London upbringing, Jews – and I am one – were cast as the victims of the Holocaust, not its avengers. I had never really questioned that stereotype until I fell into this story. Or, to be more accurate, it fell to me.

This is a Jew-fighting-back story. And while there are some well-known examples of resistance – uprisings in the ghettos, revolts in the camps, attacks from the woods – such examples are few. Each should be celebrated, as an inspiration to others. Even when faced

with profound brutality, hope for survival – and perhaps revenge
– is still possible.

This is a story pieced together from histories, biographies, archives,
family letters, old tape recordings and interviews with survivors. And
it is a story that was, for reasons that I think will become clear, never
fully told by the men at its heart: Hanns and Rudolf.

I

RUDOLF
BADEN-BADEN, GERMANY
1901

Rudolf Franz Ferdinand Höss was born on 25 November 1901. His mother, Paulina Speck, was twenty-two years old, and his father, Franz Xaver, was twenty-six. Rudolf was their first child. They lived at 10 Gunzenbachstrasse, a small white-washed house with a red-tiled roof, situated in a wooded valley on the outskirts of Baden-Baden.

In the early 1900s, the medieval town of Baden-Baden was rushing to catch up with the twentieth century. Located in south-west Germany, Baden-Baden sat along the banks of the gently meandering Oos River, at the bottom of a lush green valley full of well-tended vineyards. Five hills overlooked the town, and beyond them, the Black Forest stretched to the horizon.

For centuries Baden-Baden's natural springs and glamorous nightlife had drawn Europe's glitterati. Dostoevsky had researched his novel *The Gambler* at the casino there, and Queen Victoria, Napoleon III and Johannes Brahms all spent time in the city which, for a while, had been known as Europe's summer capital. With these tourists came great wealth, and during the first few years of the early 1900s major modern-isation efforts were under way. New tunnels had been carved out of the limestone seam supporting the town's Roman foundations to increase the capacity of the public baths; an electric funicular railway had been built up to Mount Merkur, offering magnificent views of the surrounding valley from its summit; and the wrought-iron gas street lights around the main square had recently been switched over to electricity.

Höss family house (centre), Baden-Baden

Yet in the Höss family's small house on the edge of town, life remained much as it always had. Franz Xaver had served as an officer with the German Army in Africa, until his career was ended by a poison arrow wound to the chest. He had returned to Germany to become a teacher at the military school in Metz, before retiring as a merchant to Baden-Baden. But for the hint of romanticism attached to his African exploits, he was in all respects unexceptional: a patriotic German and devout Catholic on the edge of middle-class respectability; a family indistinguishable from its neighbours. Three years after Rudolf's birth a daughter, Maria, was born; another daughter, Margarete, followed in 1906.

Rudolf spent most of his early childhood playing by himself. In his rural community the local children were mostly older and his sisters too young to be of interest. His mother was busy with the chores of children and house. Almost of necessity, Rudolf's favourite pastime was to wander away from the house into town towards the water tower that stood above the neighbourhood. Here he would sit, ear pressed against the walls, listening to the water rushing and gurgling. At other times, he ventured into the dark recesses of the Black Forest, whose edges fell only a short distance from his home.

Rudolf passed endless hours in the woods. But it was not as idyllic a location as it seemed. When he was five, he was kidnapped from the forest's fringes by a band of Gypsies. They carried him to their caravan, perhaps planning to sell him to another family or to put him to work in one of the local coal mines. Luckily for Rudolf a local farmer recognised him just as the Gypsies were leaving and came to his rescue.

After the kidnapping, Rudolf was not allowed to walk far. He was, however, permitted to visit the neighbours' farms, where he mucked out the stables and brushed the horses. It was during this time that Rudolf discovered he had an instinctive feel for these animals. He was small enough to creep under the horses' legs, but he was never kicked or bitten. While he was also fond of bulls and dogs, he truly fell in love with horses, a passion that would remain with him for the rest of his life.

When Rudolf turned six, the family took an important step towards solidifying its claim to respectability, moving to a larger house in the suburbs of Mannheim. Located sixty miles north of Rudolf's first home, and fifty miles south of Frankfurt, Mannheim was a much larger city than Baden-Baden, with a population of over 300,000 and an industrial base that served the entire region. While Rudolf missed the animals and the expansive beauty of the Black Forest, there was a silver lining to the move: on his next birthday he was given a coal-black pony, which he named Hans. He went for frequent rides in the nearby Haardt Forest and groomed the pony for hours when he returned home from school. He loved the animal so much that he would smuggle it into his bedroom when his parents were away. Any spare time that he had was spent with Hans, a pony so faithful that it followed Rudolf like a dog. They became inseparable.

★

Rudolf was captivated by his father's stories of his military career. He was particularly keen to hear about the Africa campaigns, his battles with the local populations, their strange religions, their exotic practices. But despite the fact that both Rudolf's father and grandfather had served in the military, Rudolf was more attracted to becoming a missionary than a soldier fighting in some foreign land.

It was from his father that Rudolf learned about the traditions and principles of the Catholic Church. Franz Xaver took his son on pilgrimages to holy sites in Switzerland and to Lourdes in France. Rudolf became a fervent believer; he later recalled that he 'prayed with a child's earnest gravity, and was ready and willing to act as an altar boy', and he took his 'religious duties very seriously'.

From the earliest age, Rudolf was given numerous tasks to perform as a member of the household, which he was expected to complete without complaint. For every misdemeanour Rudolf was severely punished. Even a small unkindness to one of his sisters – a harsh word or teasing remark – resulted in kneeling for long periods of time on the cold hard floor, seeking God's forgiveness.

Upon the birth of his first daughter, Franz Xaver swore an oath that his three-year-old son would become a priest: he would go to a seminary, he would be celibate, and he would pledge himself to prayer, learning and community. Rudolf's education was planned with the sole purpose of preparing him for a religious life. He later remembered:

> Great emphasis was always laid on my duty to obey and imme-diately comply with all the wishes and orders of my parents, my teachers, priests, indeed all adults, even including the serv-ants, and to let nothing divert me from that duty. What adults said was always right. Those educational principles became second nature to me.

Living in the suburbs meant Rudolf was surrounded by children of his age, and he enjoyed roughhousing with the other boys. His consideration of future missionary work in no way blunted his enthusiasm for these contests, and he proved no less ruthless when it came to exacting revenge. If another boy hurt him in any way he was relentless until he had paid him back. Thus Rudolf was feared by his playmates.

However, when Rudolf was eleven years old, one fight went too far. He and his friends had been involved in a light-hearted skirmish, during which one of the boys had fallen down a flight of stairs and broken his ankle. Horrified, Rudolf went straight to church and confessed to the priest, who was also a friend of the family. The priest promptly told Franz Xaver, who in turn punished Rudolf. This betrayal of the confessional code deeply upset Rudolf, destroying his belief in the trustworthiness of the profession.

> For a long, long time I went over all the details of what had happened again and again, because such a thing seemed to me so monstrous. At the time — and even today — I was and still am firmly convinced that my father confessor had broken the seal of the confessional. My faith in the sanctity of the priesthood was gone, and I began to have religious doubts. After what had happened I could no longer think the priest trustworthy.

Rudolf painted a dismal picture of his childhood: a father who was a fanatic and a bigot, and whom he therefore feared and despised, and a distant mother, who was either taking care of his two small sisters or was in bed recuperating from some sickness. Indeed, Rudolf recalled not being close to anyone in his family. He might shake somebody's hand or say a few words of thanks, but he was not a child who enjoyed physical touch. As a result, Rudolf did not share his problems with those around him: 'I dealt with all these difficulties by myself.'

On 3 May 1914, a year after the incident with the priest, Rudolf's forty-year-old father died at home. The cause of death was not recorded.

> I do not remember whether I was particularly affected by that loss. But I was still too young to see all its far-reaching consequences. And yet my father's death was to set my life on a course very different from the one he had wanted it to follow.

However, Franz Xaver's death did have an impact on the rest of the family. Rudolf's father had been the sole income earner and, with three children to feed, it was difficult for Rudolf's mother to make ends meet. But the death freed the son from his father's shadow; the young Rudolf would forge his own path sooner than he might otherwise have been allowed.

On 28 July 1914, the Archduke Ferdinand of Austria was assassinated in Sarajevo, and the Austro-Hungarian Empire reacted by invading Serbia. This aggression triggered retaliation by the other European powers – Russia, Britain, Germany, France and the Ottoman Empire – and within weeks they were embroiled in the First World War. The hostilities were initially focused in the Western European countries of Germany, France and Belgium, but the conflict soon spread east and south, through Europe and then to the colonies in Africa, Asia and the Pacific. The fighting was particularly fierce in the Middle East, which became a strategic battleground, partly because of its supply of oil, and partly for the symbolic value of its holy sites.

When war broke out Rudolf was twelve years old and the Höss family was still living on the outskirts of Mannheim. The city was only a two-hour train ride away from eastern France, and Rudolf was thrilled to be living so close to the conflict. He stood on the local train platform to witness the first groups of boys being sent off to the front line, excited about the war, but also desperate to be among them.

A year later, and after much pleading with his mother, Rudolf joined the Red Cross as an auxiliary. After school he spent as much time as he could working in the Red Cross hospital, distributing tobacco, food and drink to the injured. Horrified by the terrible traumas of modern warfare, Rudolf was nonetheless impressed by the wounded soldiers' bravery and resolute in his wish to fight for his country.

So it was that, in the summer of 1916, Rudolf left home, telling his mother that he intended to visit his grandparents. As soon as he was outside the town limits, he contacted a local captain, an old friend of his father's, and, lying about his age, enlisted. He was just fourteen years old.

It was not that rare for such a young person to join the army. Officially, the minimum age of enlistment in Germany during the First World War was seventeen. This limit had been in place since the creation of the German Constitution of 16 April 1871, which stated that every male was liable for military service, from his seventeenth until his forty-fifth birthday. Yet, since the declaration of war in 1914, boy soldiers had flooded the German Army. While the number of adult recruits dropped considerably in 1915 and 1916, as the vast majority of eligible men had by this time enlisted, most young lads – if healthy enough to pass a medical exam and willing enough to carry a rifle – were eagerly accepted, even if looks betrayed their age. As a consequence, hundreds of thousands of boy soldiers fought for the Germans during the Great War.

On 1 August 1916, with the help of his father's friend, Rudolf joined the 21st Baden Regiment of Dragoons, the same cavalry regiment in which both his father and grandfather had once served. He underwent a cursory medical inspection, and was given the standard uniform for a private in the German cavalry: knee-length black leather boots; grey woollen trousers; a wide black belt with an eagle-embossed buckle, the symbol of his home state; a pocketless grey jacket with brass buttons; and a *Feldmütze*, a grey flat woollen hat that sloped to one side and had a small silver rosette sewn onto the front. Best of all, he was now the proud owner of a brass-handled cavalry sword and a black scabbard which, when resting on the ground, reached as high as his hip. With only two weeks of training, Rudolf and his regiment set off on their long trek towards the Middle East. Their mission was to provide reinforcements to the Turkish troops who were battling the British for control of the south-eastern part of the Ottoman Empire.

On his way south, Rudolf sent his mother a letter telling her that he had gone to war. She had earlier 'with endless, truly touching patience and kindness, tried to make me change my mind', recalled Rudolf, wanting him to finish school and then to join the priesthood. But now that his 'father's strong, guiding hand' was missing, Rudolf felt able to defy her orders.

The Dragoons travelled by train from Mannheim through Hungary, Romania and Bulgaria, and on to Turkey. After a short rest period in Istanbul, the regiment rode south on horseback for over fifteen hundred miles, towards the Mesopotamian front line, to what is today known as Iraq. Rudolf, who had never before been outside Germany, spent the next month camping rough and surviving on meagre military rations. 'The secret training, together with my constant fear of being found out and taken home, as well as the long journey through many countries to Turkey, all left a great impression'; the exotic landscape and peoples were both new and profoundly shocking.

When Rudolf and his comrades finally arrived at the front line they found themselves in the middle of a year-long struggle for control of the oil fields between the Tigris and Euphrates Rivers. At the centre of this impasse was Al-Kut, a dusty town situated a hundred miles southeast of Baghdad, where for months the Turks had been laying siege to British forces. The Allies had attempted to break out of Al-Kut but were repeatedly repelled; each side had suffered high numbers of casualties. In April 1916, the Allies surrendered control of the town and more than 13,000 Allied troops were taken prisoner and pressed into hard labour. The British high command viewed the incident as a humiliating defeat and, concluding that the Mesopotamian Campaign should be a higher priority within their overall global war strategy, they replaced the Indian regional commander with an Englishman, reinforced the railway lines and sent in an additional 150,000 troops. The Central Powers responded to the Allies' changes by replacing the Turkish officer in command with a German general and bringing in fresh troops from Germany, including Rudolf's Dragoons from Baden-Baden.

At the end of 1916 Rudolf's unit joined the Turkish 6th Army on the outskirts of Al-Kut. Just as his cavalry unit was receiving its initial orders, a brigade of Indian soldiers attacked. Rudolf jumped off his horse and dived onto the rocky ground among some ancient ruins, his carefully starched cavalry uniform immediately caked in fine yellow desert dust. There was no battle plan and no complete orders had been given.

As the intensity of the shooting increased, the Turkish soldiers ran away, leaving the Germans to fend for themselves. Rudolf began to panic. The explosions from the enemy's grenades grew louder; all around him German soldiers were being hit. To his left, a man fell wounded and the soldier on his right didn't respond when Rudolf called his name.

> When I turned to look at him, I saw that he was bleeding from a large head wound and was already dead. I was overcome by horror worse than I ever knew in my life, and by a dreadful fear of suffering the same fate. If I had been alone I would certainly have run away like the Turks.

As Rudolf debated joining the Turkish retreat he saw his captain crouching behind a large boulder, firing steadily at the Indians in a disciplined and orderly fashion. A change came over him. Now calm and focused, he saw a tall Indian man with a black beard come racing forward, his British Lee–Enfield .303-inch rifle pointed straight ahead. Taking a deep breath, Rudolf raised his gun, set his sights and fired. It was his first kill.

After a few moments, he raised his gun again and started shooting, rapidly, round after round, 'as if the spell was broken'. Rudolf had discovered within himself a new skill: he could kill, efficiently and quickly, in the heat of battle.

Rudolf's captain had been watching, and now called out his name with encouragement. After a short time the Indian soldiers realised they were faced with stiff resistance, halted the attack and were driven back across the desert. By the end of that day, the German unit was in control of the ancient ruins. Rudolf and his comrades dug in to prepare for what was to become the daily task of defending this small piece of territory.

Rudolf recalled feeling mixed emotions during his first battle. He had found it 'exciting', but when he later walked across the field he had 'hesitantly and timidly' looked at the Indian soldier that he had killed and felt a 'little queasy'. When he told his captain that he had been scared, the man simply laughed and said that he should not worry. Over the coming months, Rudolf grew to love and trust this man, who came to be 'like a father' to Rudolf, and an authority figure he revered. Rudolf felt that the captain treated him as if he were a son, showing pride when Rudolf was promoted and ensuring that he wasn't assigned the most dangerous missions. For the first time in his life, he realised that somebody was looking out for him. As he confessed: 'it was a far closer relationship than I had had with my real father'.

In early 1917, Rudolf and his regiment were deployed to Palestine. Their first task was to defend the critical Hejaz railway line, which ran between Damascus, in Syria, and Medina, in Saudi Arabia. Later that year, the Dragoons found themselves at the front lines of Jerusalem. While the Mesopotamian Campaign had focused on the strategic supply of oil, the battles around Palestine were partly about destabilising British control of the Suez Canal and partly about capturing the venerated biblical cities.

It was during this battle for Jerusalem that Rudolf received a painful shot to the knee, and was taken to a German field hospital near Jaffa. There he became delirious with malaria, a relapse from an infection caught earlier in the campaign, and experienced bouts of fever so violent that he had to be watched closely by the medical staff.

While convalescing in the hospital, Rudolf was cared for by a young German nurse. She was gentle with him, propping him up carefully in bed and ensuring that he didn't hurt himself during one of his malarial episodes. At first he found her caresses confusing, but soon, 'spellbound by the magic of love, I saw her with new eyes'. In later weeks, once Rudolf could walk again, they found a quiet spot, away from the busy wards. 'She initiated me into every stage of love-making, leading to full sexual intercourse,' he remembered. 'I would never have summoned up the courage of my own accord. This first experience of love, with all its sweet affection, became a guideline for me all my life.' This was not only the fifteen-year-old boy's first sexual encounter, but the first time that he had experienced any type of physical intimacy: 'This tenderness was a wonderful experience such as I had never known before.' Rudolf swore to himself, somewhat naively, that he would have sex only if it involved true warmth and he would never, as his fellow soldiers did, visit prostitutes or conduct affairs with other men's girlfriends or wives.

Once he had recovered from his injuries, Rudolf was told to return to his unit. It must have been hard to say goodbye, but he had received his orders. He would never see the nurse again.

★

Over the course of the next few months Rudolf was wounded twice more: on 17 November 1917, a few days before his sixteenth birthday, with a bullet embedded in his thigh; and on 28 February 1918, with wounds to his hands and knees. None of these injuries prevented his participation in continued action.

For his wartime service Rudolf was awarded the Iron Cross Second Class by the German government, and the Iron Half Moon and the Baden Service Medal by the state of Baden-Baden for his efforts in Iraq and Palestine. The war had transformed him from a frightened and innocent young schoolboy into a toughened soldier. In Rudolf's eyes, the war 'had matured me, both outwardly and inwardly, far beyond my years'.

He was by now fully grown. At five feet six inches he was not tall, nor was he bulky like some of the other men in his unit. Instead he was thin, battle-hardened, with piercing brown eyes and a head of short-cropped fair hair. His was a soldier's body. For Rudolf had become accustomed to the pain and hardships of war, possessing the emotional wherewithal – a numbness, perhaps – to withstand injuries, and then to return to the fight. Even more, he had learned what he saw as leadership skills: displaying knowledge rather than rank, showing 'icy, imperturbable calm' in the face of adversity, and endeavouring to 'set an example all the time and never lose face, whatever one's real feelings'.

However, the spring of 1918 brought him sorrow that even he found difficult to hide. The captain that he had so looked up to over the previous year was killed during the Battle of Jordan. His death proved a heavy blow: 'I felt it painfully, and grieved for him.'

Once more Rudolf was alone.

2

HANNS
BERLIN, GERMANY
1917

Hanns Hermann Alexander was born on 6 May 1917, fifteen minutes before his twin brother Paul, at his parents' expansive apartment on the Kaiserallee, in West Berlin. The two boys were wartime babies, conceived when their father, Dr Alfred Alexander, was on leave from the military hospital he ran in the town of Zabern in German Alsace.

Shortly after their births, Alfred sent for his family – his wife, Henny, his two young daughters, Bella and Elsie, and his new twin sons – to join him at the front. It was a dangerous decision, with the hospital so close to the battlefield, but Alfred insisted. The family was reunited for eighteen months, enough time for both girls to attend a local school. At the end of October 1918, with the war's end fast approaching, Alsace partisans threatened to storm the hospital. The doctor had only a few hours to transport all of his patients and his family to the railway station. It was exhausting work, but Alfred and his hospital staff proved up to the task, and not a single patient was left behind. They were aboard the last train heading back to Berlin.

The family only made it as far as Ulm, sixty miles east of Stuttgart. Inspired by the revolution that had swept Russia the year before, workers' committees had taken over the Ulm railway lines and were calling not only for the end of the war but for Kaiser Wilhelm II's abdication. Similar violent protests had erupted around the country: sailors mutinied in the northern port of Kiel, refusing to set sail for battle; a left-wing council had forced the King of Bavaria to step down and a people's republic had been declared; and thousands of workers were staging violent protests across Berlin. The train was backed out of the station and shunted towards Frankfurt, where the family took refuge with Henny's parents until the way was clear.

When the Alexanders finally reached the capital in early December, they were greeted with scenes of chaos. Three weeks earlier, on 9 November 1918, Kaiser Wilhelm's abdication had been announced and the German Empire officially came to an end. Since then, a loose alliance between Social Democrats and members of the armed forces had filled the political vacuum, led by the Social Democrat Friedrich Ebert. But this provisional government was unable to maintain order for long. Left-wing radicals took to the streets seeking a swifter pace of change, while right-wing groups, angered at the loss of the war, formed informal units and fought battles with the Communists and workers' committees. In response, the military created brigades of recently demobilised veterans to suppress the left-wing uprising; their brutality did little more than fan the flames of revolt.

It was too dangerous to go out at night, food was scarce and Alfred was unable to resurrect his medical practice given the violence erupting across the city. To make matters worse, the economy, already ruined by four years of war, looked set to collapse.

The external situation felt like a pressurised drum ready to explode, but inside the Alexander apartment, all was calm and in good order. It didn't take Henny long to remove the sheets from the furniture, to wipe down the walls and to restock the pantry as best she could. Within a few days it once again felt like home. For the nineteen-month-old Hanns and Paul the apartment was the centre of their world and, regardless of the volatility outside, they set about exploring it.

The Alexander residence took up the entire first floor of 219/220 Kaiserallee, mid-way between Schaperstrasse and the junction of Spichernstrasse and Regensburger Strasse. The Kaiserallee was one of the smartest addresses in Berlin, and a road that served as a main artery of the city, running as it did from the working-class Friedenau district in the south all the way to the affluent Wilmersdorf district in the north-west. The apartment was vast, even by the generous standards of the area. In total, it had twenty-two rooms, including five bedrooms, three living rooms, one bathroom, two rooms for the maids, and a large kitchen. The apartment doubled as Dr Alexander's consultancy rooms, and it was in the new year that he started seeing his patients in the salon, just off the front hallway. The front room was as wide as the entire apartment, large enough to comfortably seat forty people for dinner, and had two balconies overlooking the Kaiserallee.

Berlin-Wilmersdorf   Kaiser-Allee, Ecke Spichern- und Regensburger Straße

The front door of the building was two storeys high and made of thick brown oak, and, as with most Berlin structures built in the mid-nineteenth century, possessed a courtyard at its centre, allowing light to stream into the apartment's interior. Behind the building was a communal garden with a small lawn and a few trees. Here Bella, Elsie, Hanns and Paul played with the other children from the neighbouring apartments.

Their home was ideally situated in the heart of the west Berlin Jewish community. And it was with this community that the Alexanders spent most of their time, chatting in one of the department stores that lined the Kurfürstendamm, having picnics on the manicured lawns of the Tiergarten park or visiting the animals at the Berlin Zoologischer Garten, all of which were only a short walk from their apartment.

Although he came from a comfortable, upper-middle-class family of doctors and lawyers, Hanns' father was no stranger to hardship. When Alfred was just five his own father had died of leukaemia and his sister had succumbed to pneumonia. Then, when he was in his twenties, his mother had suffered a severe asthma attack, and died shortly afterwards. Despite these setbacks, Alfred had managed to graduate as a doctor from one of Germany's most prestigious universities and set up his own practice in Berlin. He was a moody man, at times prone to shouting at his wife and withdrawing to his library and his collection of well-thumbed detective novels; at others ebullient and affectionate. He was also sentimental, perhaps even a soft man, often to be seen with his lips trembling and tears running down his cheeks, when overcome by the emotion of an aria playing on the gramophone or during a heartfelt speech delivered at a birthday party.

His wife, Henny, in contrast, had a far easier upbringing, as the descendant of two of Europe's most successful Jewish families. Her father, Lucien Picard, was a highly respected banker and the Swiss consul in Frankfurt, while her mother, Amalie, came from the wealthy Schwarzschild clan, a family so well known in their home town that the local children sang a song about them:

In Frankfurt, in Frankfurt, if you can't be as rich as the Rothschilds,
You can always hope to be as rich as the Schwarzschilds.

Henny was a buxom woman with a round face and strong arms. Though neither slim nor fashionable she cast an attractive figure and was possessed of a keen sense of humour. She was known for her kindness and willingness to help others. She was also a committed smoker, more often than not to be seen with a cigarette dangling almost vertically from her lower lip, even in the kitchen, where she liked to meddle with the cook's dishes. It was not unknown for Henny to tap the end of her cigarette butt on a saucepan and for the ash to end up in whatever happened to be cooking. Strong-willed and opinionated, she was the matriarch and heart of the family.

While Hanns and Paul spent much of their time with their parents and siblings, they were cared for, day to day, by their beloved nanny, Anna. Though from the conservative south-western region of

Germany, Anna believed that children should be allowed to develop their individual personalities, taking a more liberal attitude than the fixed regimen of many of her contemporaries.

Calm lasted until the twins could walk. By the age of five 'the boys', as they had become known, had already developed a reputation for childhood high jinks, driving their red Hollander, a kind of go-kart, at great speed along the passageway into the dining room, around the table, through to the living room, back up the passageway, running into walls as they went, chipping off the plaster, damaging the paint and screaming at startled servants.

Hanns and Paul were also quick to take advantage of their similar appearance. When guests visited, the twins were expected to wait in the hallway and welcome them. Instead, just one of the twins would

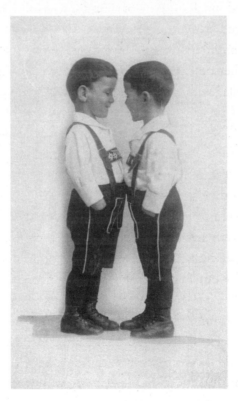

stand on duty in an apron, shake a visitor's hand, leave the room, remove his apron, and then double back to shake another person's hand. The other brother would meanwhile be in the kitchen, gorging on whatever delights Hilde the cook had prepared that day.

One of the boys' favourite books was *Max und Moritz*, a popular children's story in which two naughty boys play increasingly outrageous pranks on their friends and neighbours. They partially cut the planks of a bridge, and laugh when a tailor falls through and is washed downstream. They sneak into their teacher's house, fill his pipe with gunpowder, and watch as it explodes and singes his hair.

This book inspired the boys to ever more audacious behaviour. They let the bathwater overflow, flooding their father's consultancy room; they set off firecrackers in the kitchen, causing Hilde to spill the perfectly roasted lunch on the floor; and they built a fire in the living room and danced around it like Native Americans, until their sister, Elsie, smelled the smoke, rushed in and put the fire out with a bucket of water. At other times they simply enjoyed making mischief, particularly with Bella, who considered herself mature and sophisticated, and liked to put on airs. When she invited guests over for tea, Hanns and Paul would hide under the table, reach up and steal the expensive chocolates and slices of cake and, when they could, sneak a look up the girls' skirts. The girls would shriek and Bella would shoo the boys away, but in no time at all they would be back.

The twins were never severely punished for their bad behaviour. Instead they were indulged. Beyond the occasional outburst, Dr Alexander left discipline to his wife, and Henny, feigning shock at her sons' pranks but failing to check them, encouraged more and more outlandish acts.

When not causing trouble, Hanns liked to spend time exploring the apartment, seeking out relics from his father's time in the First World War. In the salon, he flipped through the photograph albums: Alfred astride a cavalryman's horse; posing in a trench during a field

Dr Alfred Alexander, 1917

trip to the front line; outside the hospital in Alsace. He examined his father's army uniform – neatly pressed grey jacket and trousers, a shiny silver pike helmet and knee-high leather boots – which hung in the hallway cupboard. But his favourite object of all was his father's Iron Cross First Class, a bronze medal attached to a black-and-white-striped ribbon, which was kept in a small green box on top of his father's desk. When nobody else was around Hanns liked to open the green box and, hoping that no one would see him, he would place the ribbon around his neck and imagine what it was like to be a German wartime hero.

By 1922, Dr Alexander's practice had grown sufficiently for extra space to be needed to accommodate his business. Although worried about his finances, he decided to invest in a large new medical building. He found a suitable property at 15 Achenbachstrasse, a four-storey structure that stood off the Rankeplatz, just round the corner from the apartment. He commissioned an architect and, borrowing funds from Henny's parents, converted the property into a sanatorium furnished with the very latest equipment, including X-ray machines, a laboratory and a roof garden where clients could convalesce in the open air. He invited three other doctors to join him in the venture, along with a team of nurses and technicians, and officially opened the doors in 1923. Within a short time each bed was full. He made a habit of conducting rounds every day and the nursing staff always knew where they could find him, as he would leave his cigar burning in the ashtray outside a patient's door.

This was a risky time to be making large investments. The economy was in turmoil after the war. By the early 1920s, the currency had undergone a dramatic devaluation: one gold mark was worth ten paper marks in late 1921; a year later a gold mark was worth 10,000 paper marks; and by late 1923 the rate was one to one hundred million. This hyperinflation led to the exponential rise in the price of goods, making it virtually impossible to carry out day-to-day shopping. Like everyone else, the Alexanders had to adjust to this reality, which affected both their income – as the doctor struggled to keep his prices in line with inflation – and their expenses.

Dr Alexander was soon feeling the strain. Many of his patients had died or moved away during the war and, increasingly afterwards, a large number of those who remained were unable to settle their debts. The doctor still treated them, in what he called a *Harachaman*, or 'act of mercy', believing that nobody should be denied medical attention because of lack of funds. However, such charity did not help to pay the bills. Dr Alexander's solution was to work still harder, dedicating long hours to his practice and rarely eating meals with his children.

As he was growing up, Hanns became increasingly aware of his Jewish identity. Like many other Berlin Jews, the Alexanders were not

Neue Synagogue, Berlin

particularly religious, calling themselves 'Three-Day-a-Year Jews'. They attended the Neue Synagogue in the centre of Berlin for the most holy of days: the two days of Rosh Hashanah and the one day of Yom Kippur, and visited their local synagogue on Fasanenstrasse for the occasional Saturday-morning Shabbat service.

The Alexanders also celebrated Christmas, each year driving to Frankfurt to spend the holidays with Henny's parents, Lucien and Amalie Picard. The Picards tended to orthodoxy, and so the Berlin family had to be diplomatic when it came to Christmas, which Alfred had always celebrated as a child. A compromise was struck under which Dr Alexander was allowed to purchase a modestly sized Christmas tree and install it upstairs, in the staff quarters, away from his in-laws' disapproving eyes. Once it was in place, Hanns and his siblings decorated the tree with beautifully carved wooden figures — a reindeer, an elf, a sledge, glass balls filled with snowmen and angels, chocolate money wrapped in gold, bright-coloured velvet boxes that hung from red ribbons — as well as a delightfully shiny silver star that sat on the tip of the very highest branch.

It was during these early years that Hanns was told about the family Torah, or the 'Alexander Torah' as it was known, which was stored in a cupboard in his father's library. After Alfred died, according to family custom, the scroll would be passed down to Hanns as the oldest son.

The Alexander Torah had been commissioned in 1790 by Hanns' great-great-great-grandfather, Moses Alexander, while he was living in Thalmässing, a small town near Nuremberg. Every aspect of its manufacture was specifically prescribed by Jewish tradition. Each day, before he picked up his quill, the scribe would have washed his hands, put on the leather straps of his tefillin, and then spent a few minutes in meditative silence. As he copied each of the 304,805 Hebrew characters from another Sefer Torah, he would have spoken each and every letter. When he made a mistake, he would have to scratch away the dried ink with a knife. However, if he had erred when writing the word 'God', he would have been obliged to cut out that entire section of parchment and start again. Typically, the writing of a Sefer Torah took six to twelve months, but given the intricate calligraphy used by this particular scribe – the ornate swirls, the perfection of the lines, the neatness of the parchment's stitching – the creation of the Alexander Torah would have taken longer. The production of the Torah was a holy task, or *mitzvah*, which brought a blessing upon the man who commissioned it, along with the entire family through the ages. It also meant, rather unusually for Jews in Berlin, that the Alexander family and not the synagogue owned the Torah.

Once a year the whole family travelled to their local synagogue on Fasanenstrasse to take part in the Simchat Torah service, a ceremony which celebrates the community's religious texts. Dr Alexander stood in line with the other men holding Torahs on their shoulders, with Hanns, Paul and the rest of the children trailing behind. The men paraded around the synagogue as the congregation bellowed out jubilant songs, and the men and women bowed as the scrolls were carried past. After the service, the rabbi handed sweets to the children and wished them a good holiday.

As the tumultuous 1920s tolled by, so Alfred Alexander's practice recovered and grew, with Alfred quickly recognised as one of Berlin's finest society doctors. Being gregarious and appreciative of good company, Alfred invited many of his patients home, where they were entertained by Henny at one of her sumptuous dinner parties. They now spent less time with members of the synagogue and community acquaintances, and more time mingling with some of Germany's most famous scientists, artists and film stars.

As their milieu evolved, the Alexanders' affluence, financial security and opportunities improved. But as their fortunes changed, so another side of post-war Germany was beginning to emerge.

3

RUDOLF
BERLIN, GERMANY
1918

On 30 October 1918, the Ottoman Empire agreed to a cessation of hostilities. Austria–Hungary followed suit on 3 November. Then at 5 a.m., on the morning of 11 November, the Germans finally agreed to an armistice in a railway carriage parked in a French forest. The war was finally over. It had lasted four years, had involved more than seventy million people and cost the lives of over nine million combatants.

When news of the armistice broke, Rudolf was leading his own platoon in long-range reconnaissance missions in Damascus. The German Army Corps advised him to surrender, but Rudolf vowed that he would never be captured, and was determined to avoid the prisoner-of-war camps. By this time Rudolf was a sergeant – indeed one of the youngest officers in the army – and informed the men in his cavalry platoon about his plans to make it home. The band of experienced soldiers, mostly in their twenties and thirties, immediately swore allegiance to their sixteen-year-old commander and committed themselves to fighting their way back to Germany, come what may.

It took Rudolf and his colleagues three months. From Syria they travelled through Turkey, where they hitched a ride on a decrepit boat from Istanbul across the Black Sea, to the little port of Varna in Bulgaria. From there, they headed west and fought against Allied troops still active in Romania. Travelling by horse, mostly by night, to avoid military police and mobs of vigilantes, they drove their horses through the deep Transylvanian snows and alpine peaks into Hungary and Austria, before finally reaching Mannheim.

When Rudolf arrived back in Mannheim, however, he discovered that everything had changed. His mother had succumbed to an unspecified illness a year before, on 8 April 1917, dying at the relatively youthful age of thirty-seven, and his uncle and guardian had sent his sisters to a convent, sold the family home and disposed of all of Rudolf's personal belongings. Rudolf was shocked, but could hardly be surprised. He had been overseas for two years, and maintained infrequent contact with his family, who fully expected the headstrong youth to embark on a long-planned religious career upon his return. He was not left destitute. The sale of the family house had generated some funds, of which a portion had been set aside to support Rudolf's stay in the seminary. Such an option should not have been unattractive given the precarious state of Germany's post-war economy. Yet Rudolf had no intention of following the family's wishes by becoming a priest. The man who Rudolf had become during the war didn't have the temperament for study and prayer. He walked away from what little inheritance there might have been, looking for something more familiar.

A little later, he heard from one of his old army comrades that some German veterans had formed a Freikorps and were still fighting the Russians in Latvia. If he wanted to join, then he should travel to Berlin and find Gerhard Rossbach.

The Freikorps were paramilitary units, independent of government control, composed of armed men espousing doctrines of nationhood and discipline. The Freikorps promised to bring stability back to the country. If they were successful, its members would be able to keep any land they conquered. By year's end the Freikorps would include over 200,000 men.

Rossbach himself epitomised the right-wing reactionary of that time: a veteran of the First World War embittered by the terms of the armistice, fearful of Bolsheviks taking over the country, and thirsty for the violence of warfare to restore the rightful place of his cherished motherland. Despite being only twenty-five years old and hailing from a small village in Pomerania, now north-west Poland, Rossbach was highly admired by the young urban recruits who surrounded him. They considered him to be an 'ideal man' – brutal, ruthless, swaggering and inexorably tough – someone who enjoyed getting drunk, smashing windows and brawling.

It was Rudolf's first trip to Berlin. He arrived to find the city in turmoil. A mob of disgruntled workers had occupied the newspaper district. Barricades were erected blocking many of the major streets, manned by armed left-wing activists. A series of strikes and mass marches had brought the city to a standstill. Trains filled with meat and vegetables stood rotting at the city's outskirts. Each day there were reports of murders, and bodies of political leaders had been found floating in the city's canals. The reformist government, still run by Friedrich Ebert and his Social Democrats, maintained control by deploying First World War veterans to violently suppress the revolutionaries.

It is not clear when Rudolf and Rossbach first met, but eventually, in the early months of 1919, they did, and Rudolf was soon informed of the Freikorps' next misson. The brigade was preparing to travel over seven hundred miles to the Baltic coast, partly by train, partly on foot. There they would relieve the Iron Brigade, another Freikorps group, who were trying to prevent the Russians from taking control of Latvia. For most Freikorps members, the real mission was to assist their German-speaking cousins in Latvia and to reassert German authority in a part of Europe which had been lost during the war. For others, it was a

chance to take out their aggression on the Bolsheviks. Rudolf quickly
signed on.

Rossbach's 3,000-strong brigade left Berlin and headed north, via
the free city of Danzig on the Baltic Coast, then north-east across
Lithuania and on to Riga, the capital of Latvia. It was an epic and
exhausting journey, but for Rudolf, it was a coming home.

> I became a soldier again. Once more I had a homeland, and a sense
> of security in the friendship of my comrades. Strange to say I, a
> loner who had to deal with all my internal turmoil for myself,
> was always drawn to a kind of companionship in which men could
> depend unconditionally on each other in distress and danger.

In Riga, Rossbach's Freikorps joined up with the Iron Brigade and,
together with the local partisans, managed to hold off and then to
push back the Red Army. As soon as they had beaten off the Russians,
the Freikorps marched on the city and, on 23 May 1919, wrested
control from the Latvians. Their intent was now clear for all to see:
they were there to regain the Baltic region for the local German
population.

The Freikorps were accused of horrendous massacres during this
time, including the killing of three hundred Latvian citizens in the
small town of Jelgava, another two hundred in Tukums, and over
three thousand in Riga. Now that the Russians had been forced out
of their land, the Latvians turned against their former German allies
and requested aid from their Estonian neighbours. For the next
month it was not clear who was fighting whom. The Latvians seemed
to be fighting everyone: the Russians, the Germans, even their own
people.

Rudolf had never experienced warfare like this, not even during
the most vicious battles of the Mesopotamian Campaign. He noted
the difference – civilians were now being caught up in the conflict.

The Latvians took cruel revenge on their own countrymen who allowed German or White Army soldiers into their homes and provided them with supplies. They set fire to their houses and burned the people who lived there alive. I often saw terrible sights: burnt-out huts and the bodies of women and children, charred or partly consumed by the fire. The first time I saw such things, I thought that the deranged human desire to destroy could go no further. Although later I was faced with much worse images, I can still see, in my mind's eye, those half-burnt houses, in which whole families had died, on the outskirts of the forest on the River Daugava. At that time I could still pray, and I did.

The Freikorps exposed Rudolf to brutality and violence on a scale he had not seen before. Yet it was also here that he witnessed men pledge deep personal allegiance to a cause and, more importantly, to a leader. These pledges were reinforced by secret vigilante courts instituted to try those they considered traitors. If found guilty, such men were immediately shot.

Eventually the Latvians succeeded in stemming the imperial ambitions of the Freikorps and, with British support, pushed the Germans westwards, back towards Prussia. The Freikorps had managed to curb the Bolshevik ambitions in the Baltics, but they had failed to retain any land for themselves.

While Rudolf was fighting the Russians and the Latvians, the German populace had elected a new assembly, dominated by German centre-right politicians. They adopted a new constitution, which would be the foundation of the Weimar Republic. The leaders of this new republic were fickle when it came to supporting the Freikorps' campaign in the Baltics. Sometimes they provided them with armaments and funds in their attempt to regain the Baltics and East Prussian lands, but at others, publicly denounced them. At the last,

when Rossbach's Freikorps needed help the most, the republic prof-
fered no assistance at all. This was the biggest lesson for Rudolf,
Rossbach and the other members of the Freikorps: their greatest
enemy was no longer the Bolsheviks or the Latvians; it was the
German republic.

After being pushed out of Riga, Rossbach's Freikorps kept fighting
for another two years, sometimes acting like a police force, sometimes as a private army – against the Poles, the French, and the
Communists, in southern Poland and in northern and western
Germany.

In 1921, the Rossbach Freikorps were finally outlawed by the
German government. Their unrestrained violence and anti-republican
ambitions had become too much of a liability. Rossbach quickly
adapted, opening the Tiergarten nightclub in Berlin, at 18 Hohen-
zollernstrasse, and staffing it with former members of his brigade.
The club acted both as a headquarters and as a front for the collection
and storage of weapons. He dispersed the rest of his men around the
Baltic region and Poland, where they worked on large estates owned
by men sympathetic to the Freikorps ideology, waiting for the next
chance to follow their leader into action. Rudolf found himself on
a farm in Silesia, in what is today southern Poland, as an apprentice
agriculturalist. Ever since his boyhood, Rudolf had loved animals
and the outdoors, and cherished the opportunity to live simply and
work in the fields.

A few months later, in November 1922, Rudolf headed south to
Munich, where he was reunited with his fellow soldiers celebrating
the fourth anniversary of the Rossbach Freikorps. The main star at
the party was Gerhard Rossbach himself, who had just been released
from prison after having been arrested for conspiring to overthrow
the republic. During the party, Rossbach declared that they would
create a new 'power organisation' that would 'end the present nonsense'

using 'blackjacks and bayonets'. Later that evening Rossbach, Rudolf and the others crossed Munich to hear a speech by a young man named Adolf Hitler, a rising star in the National Socialist movement.

Originally formed as the German Workers Party (DAP) in January 1919, the Munich-based National Socialist German Workers Party (NSDAP) was one of dozens of *völkisch* organisations – literally 'folk organisations', but in practice right-wing nationalist organisations – active in post-war Germany. Basing their appeal on ideals of national supremacy and ethnic purity (and by extension being anti-Slav and anti-Semitic) these groups attracted widespread support. The NSDAP was slow to build, however. When Hitler attended his first meeting in September 1919, there were only forty other people present. By 1921, largely due to Hitler's extraordinary gifts as a public speaker, the party had over three thousand members and, by 1922, its reputation had grown sufficiently to attract the attention of Rossbach and his men.

As the group walked through the doors of a large L-shaped building at number 18 Rosenheimer Strasse, down a flight of stairs, and into the cavernous Kindlkeller, they found a crowd of four thousand men and women gathered before them.

Sitting on a chair on a platform at the front of the beer cellar was the thirty-three-year-old Adolf Hitler, wearing heavy boots, a dark suit, a leather waistcoat and a semi-stiff white collar. After a few introductions, Hitler stood up and gave a brief summary of recent German history: losing the war, the fall of the Kaiser, the battles between nationalists and socialists, the founding of the republic, the betrayal at Versailles. As the audience warmed, Hitler began gesturing emphatically with his arms, praising Italy's prime minister and leader of the National Fascist Party, Benito Mussolini, for marching his supporters into Rome three weeks earlier when he came to power, and repeatedly thanking the veterans for their bravery and courage during the war. He attacked war profiteers and

Jews for their black-marketeering, and mocked the Communists' lack of respect for German ways and customs. When he concluded, the audience gave him a standing ovation.

Rudolf had never seen anything like this. He agreed with what Hitler was saying, but he rejected the mass propaganda and what he saw as the appeal to the crowd's basest instincts. Yet those in the room felt like his kind of people. Along with many of Rossbach's soldiers, he joined the queue of young men and women waiting to sign up with the National Socialists. When his turn came, he wrote down his details, signed his name and was handed a card with his party number: 3240.

As an early member of the National Socialist Party, Rudolf could have pursued a career within the organisation. Instead, he returned to his job as an agricultural officer, working on estates in Silesia and Mecklenburg. For the time being all he wanted was to be close to the land.

Believed to be Martin Bormann (left) and Rudolf Höss (right)

On 31 May 1923, six months after hearing Hitler's Munich speech, Rudolf met his friend Martin Bormann, a farm supervisor, for dinner at a restaurant in Parchim, a small town in Mecklenburg, 150 miles north of Berlin.

It was a warm spring evening. Bormann and Rudolf and two other friends stayed late at the restaurant, drinking beers and becoming increasingly rowdy. They then spotted a former brother-soldier, Walter Kadow, eating at a table nearby. Kadow had left the Freikorps with a black cloud hanging over his name: he was believed to have betrayed another member, Albert Leo Schlageter, to the French, who in turned accused Schlageter of blowing up bridges in the French-occupied Ruhr. Five days before the meeting at the Parchim restaurant, the French had taken Schlageter onto Golzheimer Heath, near Düsseldorf, read out his sentence and shot him.

Rudolf, Bormann and the others joined Kadow at his table, pretending to be eager to catch up with their old Freikorps colleague. After they were all fairly drunk, they suggested that they go for a drive, not telling Kadow where they were headed. A short while later they were outside town and entered some dark woods. There they beat Kadow with clubs until he could not stand. When he was half dead and covered with blood, one of the men cut his throat and another then shot him twice in the head with a revolver at close range. They buried the body in the woods and then drove back to town. Later, Rudolf described this killing in clinical tones: 'I was firmly convinced then, and I still am, that as a traitor he deserved to die.'

A few days after the killing, one of the participants called *Vorwärts*, the Berlin-based newspaper of the Social Democratic Party, and told a journalist what had happened. Soon afterwards, Rudolf and Martin Bormann were arrested. It was quickly agreed that Rudolf would protect Bormann — it is unclear if he offered or was asked, but either way it was an act of loyalty — taking full responsibility for the crime.

Rudolf had been unworried about his arrest. He was convinced that his case would be dismissed, and that the government had an unspoken agreement to release any arrested member of a right-wing paramilitary group in return for their support on the streets. However, this deal was soon to be broken.

On 9 November, Hitler led a crowd of National Socialists – including Gerhard Rossbach – into a Munich beer hall where Gustav von Kahr, the acting commissioner of Bavaria, was preparing to make a speech to three thousand people. Hitler jumped onto the platform and, shooting into the air, declared that the Bavarian government had been overthrown: 'The day for which I have been waiting with such longing for five years has arrived! I will make Germany a glorious state.' Skirmishes took place throughout the night and into the early hours, ending with a confrontation in Munich's city centre, where Hitler and his armed supporters came face-to-face with soldiers from the state police. During the fight that followed, sixteen Nazis were killed. Hitler was later arrested, taken into custody, and sentenced to five years for high treason. The unspoken agreement between the paramilitary groups and the government was swept away: no longer could political prisoners expect early release.

In the middle of Hitler's very public trial, Rudolf was found guilty of manslaughter. In the end he was not found guilty of murder, as even though the prosecutor had Kadow's badly damaged skull, he had been unable to prove whether the victim had died from a cut to the throat, blows to the head or bullet wounds. Rudolf was sentenced on 15 March 1924 to ten years of hard labour. For his part Bormann was sentenced to one year in prison.

As Rudolf and the other prisoners were escorted out of court, their supporters sang old battle songs of defiance, calling out their names and wishing them well. Rudolf was then driven from Leipzig to Brandenburg near Berlin, where he was handed over to the guards outside the ancient five-storey brick prison block on Neudorfer Strasse.

Only twenty-two years old, Rudolf was totally unprepared to face the prospect of a decade of incarceration.

Conditions were harsh. The prison had a reputation for appalling hygiene and widespread violence, with inmates ranging from petty criminals such as pickpockets, to gamblers, murderers and renowned safe-crackers. The main currency in this alternate criminal universe was tobacco, and even though it was illegal to smoke in prison, the smokers protected themselves by sharing cigarettes with the guards.

As a political prisoner, Rudolf was fortunate to be given a cell to himself. This allowed him privacy and control over his immediate environment, and for this he was grateful. He kept his cell immaculately clean and was proud that he was never faulted during inspections.

His day-to-day life was one of routine and monotony: brief periods exercising in the yard and performing his tedious duties as a supply clerk, though most of his time was filled by reading, something he had been unable to do while on active duty. The prison housed a small library, which was augmented by books sent by friends on the outside. Rudolf became a voracious reader, particularly of books on agricultural techniques, history, ethnology and genetics. He studied English, so that by the time he left prison he could speak fluently. He was able to keep up with the news on the outside world by exchanging letters with his military friends, though he was restricted as to how many pages he could write, and could send only one letter each month.

When not reading in his cell he listened in on conversations between other prisoners. Rudolf remembered one conversation in which an inmate bragged of robbing a game warden's house and killing a servant with an axe, before murdering the game warden's wife and four children by smashing their heads against a wall. Rudolf was so shaken by this story that he could not sleep. And though he would be told many such terrible stories in prison, this one upset him the most because the prisoner had 'described this dreadful deed in such vile and shocking terms'.

Rudolf became accustomed to carrying out his prison duties 'willingly, and without any unspoken protest', and would even let out a 'silent chuckle' at some of the more ridiculous orders. But he was repulsed by the vulgar speech of other inmates, and could '*never* get used to the way the prisoners spoke in coarse, risqué and vile terms of all that is fine and good and to many people sacred in life'. He was also distressed by the frequent brawls that erupted, as well as the violent punishment which was inevitably meted out by the guards.

Even though he was alone in his cell, he was able to meet other inmates in the courtyard or when he picked up supplies for work, had his hair cut or when he took a shower. During these chance encounters, Rudolf became fascinated with the prisoners' psychology, separating them into different types: the hard-nosed violent professionals, the politically motivated offenders and the unpopular prisoners – either the weak or informants who had to be protected. Until now, Rudolf had considered himself worldly, but prison made him realise how limited his horizons had been.

The authorities deployed a number of methods to pacify the inmates, but Rudolf's favourite was the concert they put on every Sunday morning in the prison chapel. One day, a famous female singer from Berlin performed 'Ave Maria', by the French Romantic composer Charles Gounod. Rudolf noticed how even the most hardened inmates were moved by her voice, and that during these brief few moments, the prison was quiet and calm. Only a small number were unaffected, and he saw that these men were quick to discuss their next nefarious deed as soon as the music had stopped.

In 1926 German penal policy was changed. The authorities now embraced the belief that prisoners could be reformed while behind bars. Rudolf was selected to join eight hundred other prisoners in a three-step recovery programme that focused on good behaviour, education and hard work. He excelled and, as one of a handful who successfully navigated the course, naturally expected to receive parole. Those hopes were dashed, however, by a letter from his lawyer, telling him that because he was a political prisoner, any parole would have to be approved at the very highest levels of state, which was highly unlikely given the currently calm political climate.

These were the golden years of the Weimar Republic. A new currency had been introduced and the economy had stabilised. This had been further underpinned by large loan agreements negotiated between the new government and American banks. Soon after, with the government agreeing not to challenge its western borders by force, Germany was accepted back into the international community, even joining the League of Nations. A sense of calm and order had descended on the country. The right-wing nationalists were deprived of their political oxygen, thereby removing any incentive that the government may have had to approve Rudolf's parole. After all, why allow the early release of a known troublemaker, a self-confessed murderer?

Devastated that he would have to serve out his ten-year sentence, Rudolf fell apart.

> I couldn't eat any more. Every morsel that I forced down came up again. I couldn't read or put my mind to anything. I paced my cell like a wild animal. I could not sleep, although I had always been able to sleep deeply and almost dreamlessly all night. I had to get up and go on pacing around the cell, unable to rest. If I did drop on my bed, overcome by exhaustion, and fall asleep, I would wake after a short time, bathed in sweat, from confused and fearful dreams. In those dreams I was always being pursued, struck down or shot, or else I fell into an abyss. Those were nights of torment. I heard the clock in the tower strike the hours, and the closer morning came, the more I feared the next

day, the people I would see again, and I wished I need never see another living soul.

Lying on his cot he began to hallucinate, seeing and speaking to his dead parents, as if he were a child. He confessed to breaking with the Church and that he had forgotten how to pray. When he was working, he felt like he was exerting more effort than he ever had before, but was still unable to meet his quotas. One day, a prison guard caught Rudolf tipping his lunch into the garbage and immediately took him to see the prison doctor. After a brief examination, the physician diagnosed 'prison psychosis' – a temporary psychotic state induced by the harsh surroundings – injected him with sedatives, and told the guards to put him in solitary confinement and wrap him in cold towels. For the next few days, he fell into a deep sleep, occasionally waking to eat the food that was left for him and which had been laced with more sedatives.

After his condition had improved somewhat, Rudolf was returned to his prison cell. The warden then intervened and increased his privileges: he was allowed to have his light on for longer than other inmates and to keep flowers in his room. As he regained his strength, he started to interact more with other prisoners, read newspapers, and on Sundays played chess. Perhaps best of all, he was permitted to write and receive additional letters from friends and former colleagues in the Freikorps. In this way he was kept up to date with the outside world, and with the seismic changes taking place in Germany.

Following the inconclusive general election of 1928, an unstable 'grand coalition' cobbled together from an array of right-wing and left-wing parties had seized power. With a sense that politics had achieved a modicum of security, the new government announced an amnesty for all political prisoners. This was the good news that Rudolf had been waiting for. Only four years into his ten-year sentence, at the age of twenty-six, Rudolf was released back into society, on the morning of 14 July 1928. A guard at the main entrance to the Brandenburg Prison handed him a small bag of possessions, opened the front gate and pointed him in the direction of the railway station.

4

HANNS
BERLIN, GERMANY
1928

By 1928, Dr Alfred Alexander's hard work had started to pay off. His practice had grown substantially, and Henny was able to hire an impressive domestic staff to help run their Berlin household. She employed a cook, two maids, a chauffeur, a washerwoman, an ironing lady, and even a man to come and wind the clocks.

Meanwhile, Dr Alexander had purchased a dark blue open-topped S-model Mercedes-Benz, and it wasn't long before the family was being driven out of their Wilmersdorf neighbourhood, through the Grunewald Forest, out to the countryside west of Berlin to Frankfurt to visit Henny's parents and south to Stuttgart, where they picnicked in the Black Forest.

They had also acquired a weekend house near the small village of Groß Glienicke, a bolt-hole fifteen miles west of Berlin where they might escape the bustle of the city and where the boys could run about without causing trouble. It was a charming one-level log structure that stood close to the lake shore. It had three small bedrooms, a tiny kitchen, and a living room with exposed log walls. White-and-blue Dutch tiles featuring various types of windmills were plastered in above the fireplace. A smaller cottage had also been built for a caretaker so that the property could be supervised and maintained when the family was away. Most excitingly of all, the children learned how to waterski, a sport that had been invented only a few years previously. His father bought a motorboat and built a dock at the end of the garden, and by the time he was eleven years old Hanns had become an expert skier.

Alexander weekend house, Glienicke

The family used the cottage as a party venue, with many of the children's birthdays celebrated next to the lake. At one such party, Hanns invited all his classmates for a springtime picnic. Sometime during the afternoon Henny pulled him aside and asked about a missing boy called Löwenstein. Hanns sheepishly admitted that the boy was tied up to one of the garden's cherry trees. Seeing his mother in a rare display of anger, Hanns ran over to Paul – whose idea it had probably been in the first place – and together they untied their friend.

Hanns and Paul attended the Waldschule, or forest school, located next to the Grunewald Forest at the western edge of Berlin. Each day the twins caught a tram outside their apartment and then an aboveground S-Bahn train from the zoo to Heerstrasse. From there they walked five minutes along the cobbled Lötzener Allee to the two-level school that stood at the end of the road. Hanns was proud that his parents trusted him and his brother to travel so far without adult supervision, and these trips fostered a sense of self-reliance and independence.

The Waldschule was an all-boys non-denominational school. The students were taught not only the typical classes of a German gymnasium – mathematics, classics, French and science – but also woodworking, cooking and agriculture. The school had been built on pastoral ideals and was committed to introducing country values and skills to its upper-middle-class students. To cope with the twins' obvious unruliness, the principal decided to separate them into different rooms. However, Hanns and Paul frequently swapped classes: Hanns, who was good at French, stood in for Paul; while Paul, who was the more competent at mathematics, stood in for Hanns. The teachers never knew the difference and Hanns thought it wonderful that he could so easily bamboozle the adults. In terms of their studies, neither twin was very successful.

Hanns never enjoyed reading, and performed badly at school tests – he would joke that although he and his brother were 'half-witted, together we made up a whole'. But he was better than most of his contemporaries at navigating Berlin's crowded streets. Some people might call what he had 'common sense'; it is perhaps more accurate to describe his self-reliance as nous: a nose for avoiding pitfalls and for solving the everyday puzzles that confronted him. He was equally comfortable traversing the wide thoroughfares and the dark alleyways. While Paul might be intimidated by having to ask an adult for help if lost, Hanns was comfortable seeking assistance to find his way home.

Throughout his childhood, Hanns was surrounded by some of the most famous and powerful people in Berlin. His father had by now become one of Berlin's eminent doctors, and his well-known patients could often be found at the family's apartment on Kaiserallee. To Hanns it would have been normal to see the Nobel Prize-winning scientist James Franck walking out of his father's consulting rooms or Albert Einstein eating at their dinner table. Equally, he would have been unfazed to have seen the director of the Deutsches Theater, Max Reinhardt, or movie stars such as Max Pallenberg or Marlene Dietrich greet him at the front door when he returned from school. The high profiles of the house guests did not, however, prevent Hanns from playing a prank or two. For instance, when his parents invited the composer Richard Strauss for dinner, he crept up behind him and flicked pieces of bread roll onto his bald head.

Hanns also mixed with his parents' friends when they attended the Alexanders' annual New Year's Eve party. In 1928 the more than two hundred partygoers posed for a photograph: all wore fancy dress and all looked somewhat the worse for wear as they stared at the camera. It was not easy to tell who were the real stars and who were the commoners dressed up as celebrities: one woman looked like Greta Garbo, another like Marlene Dietrich, while a third had come as a white-hatted milkmaid. There was a man dressed like a Zulu warrior, two or three like American cowboys, and at least two Charlie Chaplins. At the front of the crowd lay Hanns and Paul – dressed up like two of Aladdin's thieves in black puffy silk trousers and shirts, and long pointy shoes – looking triumphant as though they had just pulled off some mischief, which they probably had. As the clock struck twelve, and couples kissed in the new year, Henny opened the doors to the balcony and in rushed two real piglets, to the delight of the boys and the squealing of many of the gathered starlets. It was the home of a highly assimilated, successful and self-confident German family.

The Alexander children were also regularly exposed to Berlin's cultural riches. Hanns' father took him to see plays at the acclaimed Deutsches Theater, and his mother to the Tiergarten park, where they listened to classical music at open-air concerts. He was dragged to the latest Bauhaus exhibit, as well as to one of the first performances of Bertolt Brecht's *Threepenny Opera*. But he had no interest in high art. What Hanns loved were movies. Not the avant-garde – such as Fritz Lang's *Metropolis*, which had received its world premiere in Berlin in 1927 – but the lowbrow films at his local cinema: the early detective movies of Charlie Chan and the Thin Man pictures, both of which were dubbed into German, or films starring Paul Wegener, another of his father's patients. These movies often shared a common storyline: an amateur detective is faced with great odds but at the last minute, and after a few false starts, manages to catch the crafty-but-not-quite-as-intelligent villain.

Hanns and Paul also frequented the Sportpalast, an enormous indoor sporting arena that could hold more than 14,000 people, and which stood only a short walk from their apartment. There they attended weekly ice-hockey matches, often unaccompanied, cheering on their local team. It was also here that the National Socialists held many of their large rallies, plastering their posters over the stadium's walls. On those days thousands of Jew-hating Nazis would be waving their fists in the same venue where the brothers had watched their ice-hockey games.

As a child moving into his teenage years, Hanns was aware of the political struggles that were wracking the country. He read the stories in his father's newspapers and listened in as his parents talked about current events. Each day the headlines were full of the latest political turbulence: millions made unemployed by the American stock-market crash; a failed referendum on renouncing the war reparations that had been agreed in the Treaty of Versailles; the collapse of the 'Grand Coalition'; the new government sidestepping the Reichstag and forcing through economic reforms by presidential decree. He saw the weekly protests in the streets, not only in the city's centre, but also near his home in west Berlin. But the political maelstrom that swirled around the Alexander home registered little with him. It wasn't just that he was only thirteen years old; it was 1930 and he didn't yet feel a threat to his freedom: he could still go to the movies, attend school, and live in the comfort of his home.

In late May 1930, after a painful year of studying their allotted section of the Torah with an elderly Hebrew teacher, Hanns and Paul celebrated their bar mitzvahs. The family was driven by their chauffeur to the Neue Synagogue on Oranienburger Strasse, the city's largest synagogue, with a seating capacity of more than three thousand people. The synagogue's massive golden dome stood two full storeys taller than the buildings on either side; it was located at the centre of the city's commercial district and was the heart of Jewish life in Berlin.

The guests included their grandparents, Lucien and Amalie Picard, as well as their great-aunt, Cäcilie Bing, a short but wide lady with a thick lisp and a fondness for mink coats, all of whom had travelled from Frankfurt for the big occasion. What was unique about the twins' service, at least to the family, was that they would read from the Alexander Torah, which Dr Alexander had brought for the occasion.

Hanns and Paul walked up onto the stage at the front of the massive hall and began reciting the blessings. They were both dressed in white shirts, polished black shoes and dark double-breasted suits, custom-made at the city's most renowned tailors, Peek and Cloppenburg. The boys had become rather chubby, so Henny hadn't been able to purchase anything off the rack. When Hanns read the final verse, and in the tradition of the *Liberale* German synagogue to which he belonged, the congregation called out approvingly: '*Skoiach, skoiach*', congratulations, congratulations. As on all such occasions, Dr Alexander cried with joy, and was handed a handkerchief by his wife.

Their bar mitzvahs now complete, Hanns and Paul Alexander passed into manhood.

5

RUDOLF
BERLIN, GERMANY
1928

Four years after being handed down his prison sentence, Rudolf Höss stood staring at the crowds on the vast open space of Berlin's Potsdamer Platz.

Trams headed north and south, east and west; men on bicycles carrying groceries purchased in local markets wove in and out of the tram tracks; a line of cars sped past the clock tower stationed on the oval patch of grass at the centre of the square; pedestrians gathered on the pavements waiting to cross the crowded streets, while others took a break at one of the many street cafes; and open-topped buses, packed with shoppers and sightseers, careened around the square's tight curves towards the Reichstag and the Brandenburg Gate. It was July 1928, and Potsdamer Platz was the busiest traffic centre in Europe.

Rudolf stood at the busy square for a long time, overwhelmed by a sense of unreality: 'I felt as if I were watching a film in a movie theatre. My release had been sudden and unexpected, and everything still looked too strange and improbable.'

Unsure of what to do with himself, he spent the next few days wandering around the city, meeting up with friends and going on trips to the theatre, to the cinema and to parties. They couldn't have chosen a better city or time to excite their friend: Berlin was the cultural capital of the world, attracting the most famous stars to its stages, the most celebrated singers to its nightclubs.

He also visited the seedier side of Berlin, which he euphemistically called 'the places of entertainment'. With its dancing girls and burlesque theatre – so aptly captured in Christopher Isherwood's novel *Goodbye to Berlin*, and later made into the film *Cabaret* – the city would have been thrilling to many men, let alone one recently released from prison. The National Socialists had castigated Berlin as a city of vice, but Rudolf was not a prude and for a short while he enjoyed the amusements. But he soon grew tired of city life: 'I longed for peace and quiet. I wanted to get away from the noise and all the comings and goings of the big city as soon as I could, and be out in the country.'

In those first few days of liberty, friends suggested that he travel abroad, perhaps to Mexico or the United States, while others urged Rudolf to re-enter politics. He had been a member of the Nazi Party since 1922, after all. But while he agreed with the party's policies and aims, in the end Rudolf concluded that he had had enough of it all – of the politics, of the military, of speeches, and of street violence – and now resolved to follow his passion. He wanted to work on a farm and raise a large family. And so, ten days after arriving in Berlin, he boarded a train and headed north-east, having secured a place on a farm through the Artamanen League, one of the many back-to-the-land groups that were popular in Germany at this time.

The Artamanen League, also known as the Artam League, was set up in 1924 as a means to send young people, most of whom were unemployed and from the cities, to help out on large agricultural estates. Some of these lands were located in eastern Germany – large farms that had become heavily indebted through the economic crisis — while others were in West Prussia, which had been taken from Germany at the end of the First World War, but were still inhabited by ethnic Germans. The focus of the league was *Blut und Boden* — blood (of your family) and soil (of the motherland). Its members believed in the virtues of a greater German state and, above all else, the importance of family. They did not drink or smoke, and eschewed activities that they considered unhealthy. The league was loosely connected with the Nazi Party; it shared many of the same values, most particularly hyper-nationalism, Slavophobia and anti-Semitism.

Rudolf Höss' Artamanen League identity book

Rudolf was a proponent of the anti-Semitism that had been gradually increasing throughout Germany. These sentiments had been fanned by the flames of economic and social breakdown, as well as by orators such as Adolf Hitler, who blamed the Jews for everything from the defeat in the First World War to the collapse in the value of the Reichsmark. Yet Rudolf rejected the outlandish anti-Semitic stories put out by *Der Stürmer* — a weekly Nazi magazine circulating since 1923, which published caricature sketches of Jews with hook noses and bags of gold — which he described as 'foul and unpleasant' and 'designed to play on its readers' worst instincts'.

Instead he favoured a more 'scientific' and 'serious' version of anti-Semitism, one that saw the Jews as a threat to the German way of life. As a 'fanatical National Socialist', he was 'firmly convinced that our ideas would find a welcome in all countries, would be adapted to the nature of their peoples, and that would be the end of Jewish supremacy'. He summed up his position as follows: 'I never personally hated the Jews, but I did see them as the enemies of our nation.'

So it was that, by the summer of 1929, Rudolf found himself working on one of the Artamanen farms in Pomerania, on the southern shore of the Baltic Sea. There, Rudolf's natural instinct for management was recognised. He was quickly appointed as an agricultural inspector, and sent across the region to check on the various estates run by the league.

It was at this farm that he first met Hedwig Hensel, a twenty-one-year-old who had grown up in Neukirch, a small town in south-east Germany. Hedwig had arrived a few months earlier with her brother Fritz. Like Rudolf, she was captivated by the league's ideals and committed to living a rural lifestyle. Hedwig was a stocky woman with an oval face and a body built for hard work and, at the time that Rudolf arrived, was working as a household assistant for the estate owner.

Rudolf knew immediately that they 'were made for each other'. They shared the same views, were inspired by the same ideals, and 'found ourselves harmoniously united in confidence and understanding, as if we had lived together all our lives'.

Rudolf and Hedwig married on 17 August 1929, after only three months of courtship, in a small ceremony on the farm. After the ceremony the newly-weds posed for a photograph: they looked handsome standing next to each other in front of a dishevelled tree, their bodies separated by a slice of sky, he posing rather formally, with his hands behind his back, she with one arm dangling and the other through his. Closed-mouthed and determined, Hedwig was dressed in a plain white frock, her braided hair falling in loops upon her shoulders in the style of a German country maid; he, smiling widely, wore a wide-collared white shirt under a dark jacket and trousers. They appeared young, happy, carefree and calm; a tranquil moment captured in rich sepia.

What is not evident in the photograph is that Hedwig was already pregnant at the time of the wedding. She had conceived three months before, almost immediately after she had met Rudolf.

Did Rudolf marry Hedwig out of duty, to do the right thing by her? Or perhaps to cover up having had sex out of wedlock, a transgression forbidden by the Artamanen League's strict puritanical creed? Or perhaps he indeed honoured the vow he had made back in Palestine, and now found in Hedwig the woman with whom he wished to spend the rest of his life? Or maybe, above all things, Rudolf valued loyalty, and it was to Hedwig that he now pledged himself.

Despite his decision to marry Hedwig, Rudolf felt unable to share his feelings with his wife: 'one thing has always grieved her: I had to deal with all that moved me most deeply on my own, and could not reveal it even to her'.

With a child on the way, and a demanding yet rewarding job, Rudolf set about building a life for his new family, as model members of the Artamanen League. But while he cherished the tranquillity of farm life, he missed the discipline and rigour of the army: the structure, the hierarchy, the sense of purpose. Nor, since his time with General Rossbach, had he found a man he could look up to, to whom he could swear allegiance, to whom he could offer fealty.

Such a person would soon arrive.

In January 1929, Hitler appointed a new leader to run his personal bodyguard, the *Schutzstaffel*, also known as the SS. The new *Reichsführer-SS*, or leader of the SS, was Heinrich Himmler, a twenty-nine-year-old from Munich who had been a member of the party since 1923 and had previously served in the Freikorps. At this time the SS was made up of only a few hundred men, and its job was to provide protection to Hitler and the other Nazi leaders as they travelled around the country. Hitler asked Himmler to build the SS into an elite, racially pure, fighting force that could assist in the rise of the party. This seemed like an ambitious plan, given Germany's calm political landscape.

This all changed when, on 29 October 1929, the American stock market crashed. The effect on the German economy was both immediate and catastrophic. The American loans that Germany had relied on to rebuild its economy, still fragile after the First World War reparations, came to an immediate stop. International trade fell to 50 per cent of its level the year before, crop prices fell 60 per cent, unemployment rose to 14 per cent of the working age population, which amounted to some 3.2 million people.

Suddenly, the National Socialists had a powerful issue to rally around: they campaigned for an end to reparations and for a stronger Germany. The impact could be seen in the next local elections. The Nazis quadrupled their vote in Berlin to 5.8 per cent; in Baden they won 7 per cent; and in the state of Thuringia, they won 11.35 per cent – the first time that they had broken the 10 per cent barrier in any election.

As unemployment levels continued to rise in early 1930, Hitler saw his opportunity. The Social Democratic-led government coalition of Hermann Müller collapsed in March 1930 and, after the minority government of centrist Heinrich Brüning fell in July, President Hindenburg called for elections in September.

Seizing his chance, Hitler travelled the country, tirelessly promoting his party and his ideas. He gave twenty speeches in the final six weeks of the election, including one at the Berlin Sportpalast to more than 16,000 people. He blamed the Jews for the economic collapse; he accused the Weimar Republic of failing to solve the unemployment problems; and he called for the expansion of Germany to solve the population's need for more living space.

In the midst of that summer's election campaign, Rudolf travelled south to a league convention being held in an east German school. The league had grown over the previous few years, and hundreds of young people from across the country attended the meeting. It was at this conference that Rudolf spent considerable time with Heinrich Himmler, who participated as the leader of the Bavarian region's Artamanen League.

Almost exactly the same age as Rudolf, and a mere two inches taller, Himmler was a trim-looking man with a triangular moustache, pursed lips and round wire-rimmed glasses. The two men had first met back in 1921, at the home of General Ludendorff, one of the

Freikorps' leaders. Like Rudolf, Himmler had been actively involved in the right-wing paramilitary groups' campaigns after the First World War, and like Rudolf, Himmler was also passionate about farming, having studied agriculture at university.

Standing in the school's main hall, Rudolf told Himmler that he supported the policy of breaking up Germany's large feudal estates in order to create smaller parcels of land which young people could farm, in the process solving their country's chronic unemployment. Himmler agreed, but countered saying that, given the limited amount of space in Germany, they would have to conquer new territory, using force if necessary, seizing the fertile lands then held by the Slavs. The discussion ranged back and forth, with the two thirty-year-olds spending hours talking about the economy and the radical policies needed to fix it.

While Rudolf did not agree with Himmler's goals – they were 'new to us all', they were 'aiming too high', and 'we did not see how it could be put into practice in the foreseeable future' – he was impressed by the man: his confident analysis, his passion for farming, his unwillingness to compromise, and his unshakeable vision. Most of all he was attracted to his devotion, for Himmler was 'Adolf Hitler's most faithful and by far his most unselfish follower'.

A few days after Rudolf's return to the Pomeranian estate, the national elections were held. On 14 September 1930, the National Socialists' share of the vote increased dramatically from 2.6 per cent and twelve seats to 18.3 per cent and 107 seats, making it the Reichstag's second biggest party after the Social Democrats. Hitler and the Nazis suddenly had everyone's attention.

Unaffected by the happenings on the national stage, Rudolf refocused his energies on developing the estate and building a family with Hedwig. Their first child, Klaus, had been born a few months earlier, on 6 February 1930. They quickly had two more children, a daughter whom they named Heidetraut, born on 9 April 1932, and another daughter, Inge-Brigitt, also known as Brigitte, who was born on 18 August 1933.

This calm life, away from the power struggles in the German cities, suited the couple and their family. To Rudolf it was a 'hard life, that we had chosen voluntarily, and out of our most fervent convictions'. He realised that by living off the land it would be a 'long, difficult, laborious way ahead', but vowed *nothing* was to make us swerve from it'. Despite the hardships, the extended hours, the physical toil, the lack of luxury, they were 'happy and content', no more so than when they 'won over new believers to our way of thinking'. They were even promised that, sometime in the future, a parcel of land would be given to them. Rudolf would then be able to fulfil his dream of owning a farmstead and bringing up his family in the countryside, surrounded by animals and nature.

This, then, was a joyful time for the growing Höss family, and in future years, Rudolf would look back on this period as a golden age.

As Rudolf dedicated himself to his new family and to farming, Germany continued to undergo profound political changes. During the national elections in July 1932, no single German party had won a majority of seats, nor during the November election that followed, in which the National Socialist Party won 33 per cent of the votes. In the absence of any alternative, Germany's president, Paul von Hindenburg, reluctantly appointed Adolf Hitler as Chancellor on 30 January 1933.

With Hitler's rise to power Heinrich Himmler was appointed commander of the Bavarian political police. Almost immediately Himmler began brutally suppressing his opponents. In March 1933, only fifty-five days after Hitler's election as Chancellor, Himmler rounded up hundreds of Communists, Social Democrats and Catholic priests, housing them in an old munitions factory on the outskirts of Munich in the small town of Dachau. He called this facility for political prisoners a 'concentration camp'.

Despite holding only a regional political position, Himmler had retained his title of head of the national SS, and while it was still inferior in size and power compared to the original Nazi paramilitary force, the *Sturmabteilung*, or the SA, with Hitler now Chancellor the SS had been made into a state organisation. More crucial to its growth, the SS was controlled by Hitler, through the loyal Himmler, whereas the SA was controlled by one of his rivals; as such the SS quickly morphed from Hitler's personal bodyguard into a sizeable paramilitary organisation and bureaucracy. At the end of 1932 the SS had over 52,000 members; by the end of 1933 it had over 200,000 members. Applications were intensively screened according to race and lineage, particularly for Nordic and Aryan qualities. In Himmler's own words: 'We took our lead from the principles of plant selection. Like a nursery gardener trying to reproduce a strain which had been corrupted; we proceeded to weed out all the men whom we did not think we would need for building up the SS.'

As a growing government-sponsored military force the SS now had a need for thousands of horses and the means to pay for them. Realising the commercial and political opportunity that this presented, and fully aware of Rudolf's cavalry experience, Rudolf's supervisor suggested that they should establish an SS stable on the Pomeranian farm. Rudolf readily accepted.

Yet, to manage an SS stable one had to belong to the SS. On 20 September 1933, Rudolf applied to join. To do this, he had to complete a lengthy application form, and supply a passport photograph as well as references. The SS officer reviewing this application studied his photograph, looking for any trace of Slav or non-Aryan features, and checked Rudolf's family background to make sure that he was from the correct milieu. Finally he had to meet the criteria of an SS soldier: he had to be over twenty-three years old and at least sixty-six and a half inches tall. Rudolf was thirty-two, and a good half an inch taller than the requirement.

Seven months after submission, Rudolf's application was accepted; he was allotted SS number 193616. As part of his induction, he had to swear allegiance to the SS and the Reichsführer SS, Heinrich Himmler. Most critically, he had to swear an oath of silence.

On 11 June 1934, the new SS recruits were gathered for a general inspection by the Reichsführer in Stettin, the largest seaport on the Baltic Sea in Pomerania. Rudolf wore the standard uniform of the SS: brown shirt, black trousers, black hat with a death's-head emblem, SS armband, black shoes and a black belt. As with all members of the SS, his arm bore a tattoo marking his blood type, information that might become important in case of an injury.

Himmler was surprised to see Rudolf standing in line with the other new recruits, and asked what he was doing there. Rudolf explained that he had only just been accepted, and was now in charge of an SS stable in Pomerania. Himmler said that he understood and indeed shared Rudolf's passion for farming, and was excited that he and Hedwig wanted to build a family, but made clear that this was not the time to pursue the utopian dream. Instead, Himmler told Rudolf that it was time to become a soldier again, suggesting that he train as a supervisor in the political prisoner camp that Himmler had established in Dachau.

Back at the estate, Rudolf struggled with the decision. Should he remain on the farm that he and his wife loved so much, or answer the patriotic call that moved him so deeply? Hedwig at first argued against a return to military life, but eventually she came round to the idea. After all, they didn't have the funds to purchase a small-holding of their own, and the military would provide the means to help them on their way. Yet it was a hard decision. There was no guarantee how quickly they could resume their idyllic rural lifestyle or how this new life would affect their close-knit family:

The prospect of making swift progress, that is to say promotion, with the financial advantages that it entailed, familiarised me

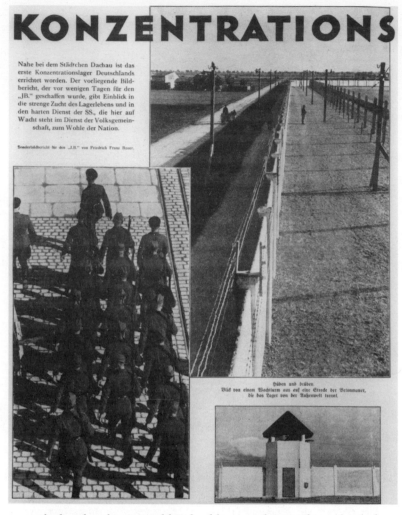

KONZENTRATIONS

Nahe bei dem Städtchen Dachau ist das
erste Konzentrationslager Deutschlands
errichtet worden. Der vorliegende Bild-
bericht, der vor wenigen Tagen für den
„J.B." geschaffen wurde, gibt Einblick in
die strenge Zucht des Lagerlebens und in
den harten Dienst der SS., die hier auf
Wacht steht im Dienst der Volksgemein-
schaft, zum Wohle der Nation.

Sonderbildbericht für den „J.B." von Friedrich Franz Bauer.

Hüben und drüben.
Blick von einem Wachtturm aus auf eine Strecke der Betonmauer,
die das Lager von der Außenwelt trennt.

with the idea that I would indeed have to deviate from the path
I had so far trodden, but I could still cling to the aim of our
lives. That aim, the farm as our home, a place for us and our
children, was irrevocably fixed in our minds, even in later years.
We never deviated from that. I was planning to leave active
service after the war, and work on the farm. After long consideration and much doubt, weighing up the pros and cons, I
decided to join the active SS.

= LAGER DACHAU

SS.-Posten am Maschinengewehr.
Hinter ihm sind Häftlinge bei der Arbeit zu sehen.

Die Essenholer unterwegs.
Je zwei Häftlinge tragen einen Kessel zur Essen-Ausgabestelle.

On 1 December 1934, Rudolf arrived in Munich, from where he boarded a train heading north-west, to Dachau station. From there it was a twenty-minute walk, through a quiet residential neighbourhood of narrow streets and one-level houses, to the camp's entrance.

Dachau was the first purpose built concentration camp established by the Nazis, and its purpose was to house political prisoners. The prisoners were accommodated in the existing buildings of the

Dachau Royal Gunpowder and Munitions Factory, which occupied only one of the five acres that made up the site. The camp held 4,800 prisoners, almost all opponents of the Nazi regime. Dachau was praised for its order and efficiency, with photographic reports featured in German propaganda publications such as *Illustrierter Beobachter*.

Hedwig and the children arrived at Dachau shortly after Rudolf. Klaus, their eldest child, was then four, Heidetraut was two, and Brigitte only one year old. The family was assigned an officer's house just outside the camp's walls.

Dachau's Kommandant, or commanding officer of the entire prison, was Theodor Eicke, a school dropout, failed policeman and professional informant. He had fought in the First World War and

Robert Ley and Theodor Eicke, Dachau

earned the Iron Cross in the process. After the war's end he had led a group of resistance fighters against the French occupiers of the Rhine. Having been sentenced by the French *in absentia*, he had fled to Italy, where he had remained until 1928, when he had returned to Germany and joined the Nazi Party. In 1933, Himmler had appointed him as the Kommandant of the camp.

According to Rudolf, Theodor Eicke was a man from the old streetfighting days of the 1920s, who considered every prisoner an 'enemy of the state' who must be killed if he resisted. Eicke taught his officers to develop an antipathy towards the prisoners. 'Attitude of hatred' was the term that Rudolf used to describe this philosophy. Eicke instructed that prisoners must be whipped for even the slightest infraction, and that such beatings should take place in front of all the guards to toughen up the men, particularly those who had recently joined the SS.

It was Eicke's view that 'there was no room for weaklings in his ranks' and that 'he could do only with hard, determined men who obeyed all orders regardless of personal feelings'. Furthermore, 'any sympathy with "enemies of the state" was unworthy of an SS man'. Eicke was also unforgiving to his own guards' mistakes. The worst wrongdoers were demoted, made to wear prisoner uniforms and whipped in front of their fellow guards. Eicke even ordered that his own cousin suffer this fate. And anyone who showed compassion to enemies of the state must disappear from the ranks.

Rudolf disapproved of Eicke's approach, viewing it as simplistic. Yet there was another side to Eicke that Rudolf admired. For the Kommandant spent many evenings with the guards, talking with them, asking about their lives, showing interest in their problems. In this way, the guards came to call him 'Papa Eicke' and they would do anything he asked.

★

After a year at Dachau, Rudolf was promoted to company commander, or 'block leader'. This was a relatively junior position, with no participation in camp policy or administration, and little interaction with the Kommandant. Yet he was now responsible for the day-to-day lives of 270 prisoners. In his new role, Rudolf checked the names during roll call each evening, assessed whether any prisoners were suitable for release, and ensured that discipline was maintained at all times. His prisoners slept in a block containing fifty-two double-tiered rough wooden bunks with five men billeted to each bunk. Each prisoner was allocated a stool and a small cupboard. The building also contained a day room with four tables, and a large stove located in the centre of the barracks.

With his promotion, Rudolf's doubts about leaving the Pomeranian farm began to grow. For the first time he became exposed to the disciplining of prisoners. On one occasion, a political prisoner was called for punishment for having stolen cigarettes from the canteen. This burly man was told to lie down on a flogging table in front of the guards, who surrounded him in a U-shaped formation. Then, as his arms and legs were held, two guards struck him twenty-five times with the cane. Rudolf was appalled by this treatment.

> I stood in the front rank, so that I was forced to watch the whole procedure at close quarters. I say forced because if I had been standing further back I would have looked away. I felt hot and cold by turn when the screams began. The whole process, indeed, from the moment when the very first blows fell, made me shudder. I was not so agitated later, witnessing the first execution at the beginning of the war, as I was watching this corporal punishment, although I can find no explanation for this.

In his mind, Rudolf distanced himself from the other officers who were eager to watch the prisoner beaten. He thought such men to be 'of a malicious, malignant, thoroughly unpleasant, brutal, base and vile nature', who 'see the prisoner only as an object on which to vent their often perverse urges'. He resolved that next time he would find a way to stand in the back row so that he could avoid having to view the punishment.

As company commander, however, Rudolf increasingly found himself caught up with the camp's brutality. He was forced to witness the harsh punishment of prisoners, and saw inmates commit suicide by running into the camp's electrified fences, or being shot while trying to escape.

Despite his unease, Rudolf refused to abandon his post.

> I could not summon up the courage to do that because I did
> not want to expose myself and admit to being soft-hearted. I
> was too stubborn to confess that I had made the wrong choice
> in giving up my plans to be a farmer.

In mid-June 1936, Heinrich Himmler and Martin Bormann — his old colleague in the Freikorps — as well as *Reichsminister* Rudolf Hess and other dignitaries, paid a visit to Dachau. With the Kommandant absent, Rudolf was asked to show the visitors around. He was only too pleased and warmly greeted his old acquaintances. Himmler was in high spirits, Rudolf felt, and the inspection went without any problems. The prisoners were in good health; they were well fed and lived in reasonable housing. As they toured the camp, Himmler asked the inmates about their backgrounds. When two Communists told him that they had been incarcerated because of their political views, which they asserted they still maintained, Himmler simply listened and then moved on. A little later, he was introduced to two hardened criminals who minimised their offences. When Rudolf reminded them of why they were in prison, Himmler ordered that they be punished for several Sundays.

Shortly after the visit, Rudolf was promoted to second lieutenant, and given charge of the camp's stores and the prisoners' property. For the first time, he would participate in the camp administration. This promotion was recorded in a memo dated 24 June 1936:

To: The Inspector of Concentration Camps

Subject: Recommendation to promote SS-Master Sergeant Höss, SS No 193616, to the rank of SS-Lieutenant.

Following the inspection of the concentration camp Dachau by Reichsminister HESS, and after discussion with Reichsleiter BORMANN, Reichsführer (HIMMLER) called me and told me that SS-Master Sergeant HOSS should, because of his former merits, be recommended at the earliest opportunity to the rank of SS-Lieutenant.

I beg to submit this report to the inspector of concentration camps together with my recommendation.

Shortly after the tour of Dachau, Himmler ordered that the old buildings be torn down and replaced by rows of new barracks. He wanted Dachau to become a model camp, a template for the new facilities that were to be built at Buchenwald and Sachsenhausen. It would also, he said, act as a training centre for guards going on to work in other camps.

The new camp was designed in a rectangular shape, approximately seven hundred yards long and four hundred yards wide, surrounded by an electrified barbed-wire gate, a ditch and a wall with seven guard towers. The facilities included an administrative office and kitchens, as well as thirty-four barracks. At the end of each building, following Himmler's instructions, a flower bed was dug and new roads were laid, with the gravel regularly raked by the prisoners. Roll call took place each evening in a courtyard between the prison and the central kitchen. The space was also the site of executions. All the work was done by the inmates, with few tools and little respite given for weather, hunger or thirst.

Although it was no longer the romantic idyll that they had enjoyed in Pomerania, Rudolf and Hedwig continued to build their family in Dachau. On 1 May 1937, a second boy was born, named Hans-Jürgen. While the newborn was looked after at home by a nanny, the three older siblings attended school in town along with the other officers' children. When Rudolf returned home each night, he played music for the children on his gramophone and recited German folk stories when they were tucked up in bed. At weekends the family took trips into Dachau to shop, or gathered with one or more of the other officer families for lunch, games and group songs.

In this way, Rudolf developed two existences. First, there was ordinary family life: his time with his four children, evenings out with his wife, socialising after work. Then there was the world of the camp guard: a cruel and hard existence during which he became increasingly inured to the pain of those he governed. Somehow, Rudolf was able to reconcile these two apparently opposing aspects of his life. He had mastered a new skill: he could exercise profound cruelty, and then come home to kids and dinner, as if nothing significant or disturbing had happened. The brutality that his loyalty demanded was by now second nature, if not yet fully expressed.

By 1938, the reconstruction of the concentration camp at Dachau was complete, and it was now able to take on almost 20,000 prisoners. Rudolf had proved to be an efficient and hard worker, an officer who was able strategically and mechanically to implement the vision of his superiors. He was ready for his next promotion.

So it was that on 1 August 1938, four years after his arrival at Dachau, Rudolf was told that he was being transferred to the Sachsenhausen Camp, some twenty miles north of Berlin, where he would become adjutant to the camp's Kommandant, Hermann Baranowski.

A mercurial man and a bully, Baranowski was capable of both kindness and ruthlessness. Yet what appealed to Rudolf was that Baranowski's harshness derived not from some irrational, sadistic or psychopathic tendency – traits which Rudolf had found so 'vile' in other guards – but from a seemingly rational framework. What made Baranowski special was that he could transcend the natural empathy that he felt towards others in order to implement a command, thereby furthering the National Socialist doctrine. This was a duality to which Rudolf aspired, and one which echoed the divisions of his own life.

Sachsenhausen was also the headquarters of the administration offices that coordinated Germany's burgeoning internment facilities. The Inspectorate for Concentration Camps was housed in a T-shaped building just outside the camp's walls. The inspectorate was managed by Theodor Eicke, who had by now left Dachau to become supervisor for all the new camps. While Rudolf did not work in the inspectorate directly, as adjutant he had frequent contact with the staff who, among other things, oversaw the supplies to the network of camps.

For Rudolf, Sachsenhausen was an improvement on Dachau. It was a good place to be noticed by his superiors and to scale the political ladder. Working in Sachsenhausen enabled him to travel frequently to Berlin, where he could meet up with old Freikorps comrades, catch up on the latest news and learn more about the inner workings of the Nazi Party. Additionally, as the camp's new adjutant, he came into contact with the Gestapo and the SS administration in charge of the concentration camps.

Another great advantage was that Rudolf's relationship with the prisoners was now changed.

> My personal difficulty in staying in the concentration camp service, despite my unsuitability for it, retreated into the background because I was no longer so close to the prisoners as at Dachau.

Though Rudolf no longer had day-to-day contact with the prisoners, he was now responsible for camp discipline and executions. And despite any misgivings, he was determined to carry out his duties. One man who would test Rudolf's new-found resolve was an SS officer who had arrested a Communist organiser and then made the grave mistake of allowing the prisoner a few moments to say goodbye to his family. As the SS officer was talking to the prisoner's wife, the prisoner had escaped through an open window. This lapse in protocol was punishable by death under SS rules. Rudolf knew the officer well as he had frequently brought prisoners to Sachsenhausen, and just the week before, the two of them had sat down together in the mess hall talking about the increasing number of executions taking place in the camp. Rudolf considered him a friend. Now this same officer, still dressed in his grey SS uniform, was pulled out of a car, handcuffed and blindfolded, and handed over to Rudolf, who led him to the pole in the middle of the main courtyard, tied his arms, stepped back and gave the order to fire.

When his friend collapsed on the ground, Rudolf walked up and shot him in the head. Rudolf was so upset that he 'could barely hold the pistol steady when I had to give the *coup de grâce*'.

> I did adjust to all those aspects of concentration camp life that could not be changed, but my feelings were never dulled to human wretchedness. I always saw and felt it. However, I had to get over that if I was not to appear soft. I wanted to be thought a hard man in order to avoid being considered weak.

Rudolf had demonstrated to his superiors that he was capable of implementing their harshest orders. He was a most trustworthy officer of the SS. He had become a hardened instrument of blind loyalty. His next move would be career-defining.

6

HANNS
BERLIN, GERMANY
1933

On 1 April 1933, storm troopers from the National Socialist Party's SA marched from the Zoo train station in Berlin, across the Kurfürstendamm, and down the Kaiserallee. The anxious Alexander family gathered together. The boycott of Jewish businesses had been announced on the radio and in the newspapers, and they were terrified the apartment would now be targeted. Looking out of the window, Hanns could see a group of brown-shirted thugs gathering in front of their building.

These events had come as a surprise to the highly assimilated and party-loving family. Like so many of their friends, the Alexanders had been optimistic about their future in Germany. And while they were concerned about the rise of the National Socialists, they had not been overwrought by the stories they had read in the newspapers: Hitler being appointed Chancellor of Germany in January 1933; the fire in the Reichstag; the suspension of the basic legal right of habeas corpus – now anybody could be arrested without the opportunity of challenging their imprisonment in court; the so-called 'Enabling Act' of 1933, which granted Hitler the power to pass legislation without parliamentary approval.

It was easy enough for the mob to find the Alexander home. Dr Alexander was the current president of the Berlin Chamber of Physicians, and his name and address were listed in the readily available blue-bound 1931–1932 Jewish Directory.

A volatile crowd now stood in front of the Alexander building, shouting the slogans of the day: 'Don't buy from Jews', 'Boycott the Jews' and 'The Jews are our misfortune'. Increasing numbers of local residents and passers-by joined them, eager to see what was going on, and perhaps thrilled to watch people finally challenge those who, many believed, were to blame for Germany's economic misfortunes.

The storm troopers appeared willing to spend the entire day blockading the Alexanders' door. Then a tall man dressed in the First World War uniform of a colonel strode up and addressed the crowd. He told them that his name was Colonel Otto Meyer, and that the occupant of the apartment was his good friend Dr Alfred Alexander, who had served under him during the war. He said that this man was a war hero who had received the Iron Cross First Class, and ordered the crowd to move away from the property. After a quick discussion, the group complied, perhaps deciding that there were easier targets elsewhere. Otto Meyer remained outside the door for the remainder of the day to protect the building from any further attacks. Before Meyer left, late into the evening, Alfred Alexander thanked his friend profusely for his brave and generous support.

That night the Alexanders discussed the day's events. Would there be other boycotts? Should they leave, perhaps for Switzerland? After all, Henny's father was the Swiss consul in Frankfurt, and he could certainly help them rebuild their lives in Basel or Geneva. Henny urged her husband to consider an alternative future, but he refused. Dr Alexander was convinced that the violence would soon pass and that the German people would come to their senses. During the Great War he had seen the courage and honour his countrymen were capable of, and he was confident that the vast majority of good, virtuous

Germans would stand up, just as Colonel Meyer had, and turn away from this Nazi madness.

Six days after the Jewish boycott, the National Socialists passed the Law for the Restoration of the Professional Civil Service, banning non-Aryans from working for the government. This included not only bureaucrats and office workers, but also teachers, singers, dancers, writers and musicians. Jewish artists were now restricted to performing to Jewish-only audiences through a programme known as *Kulturbund Deutscher Juden* or the Cultural Association of German Jews. The Alexanders joined the organisation, along with 20,000 other people, regularly attending concerts at the Deutsches Theater. Dr Alexander continued to treat many of the performers.

On 10 May, three weeks after the Jewish boycott, over 40,000 students, along with members of the SA, SS and other Nazi Party supporters, gathered in the Opernplatz – a few hundred yards south of the Neue Synagogue on Oranienburger Strasse – to listen to a speech by the propaganda minister, Joseph Goebbels. 'The age of a disproportionate Jewish intellectualism has come to an end,' he said. 'So you do well to consign the pernicious spirit of the past to the flames at this midnight hour. Here the intellectual basis of the Weimar Republic sinks to the ground. But the phoenix of a new spirit will rise from the ashes.' After he had finished speaking, the mob set fire to 20,000 books.

Alfred's optimism did not reassure all of the Alexanders. The Reichstag fire, the boycott and the street violence had taken their toll. Bella announced that she would now be moving to London with her fiancé, Harold Sussmann, an Englishman whom she had met two summers before. A few days later, Bella packed her belongings and headed for London. For the first time, the Alexander family found themselves no longer living all together under the same roof.

While Hanns was not especially close to his sister at this time, her decision raised difficult questions. What would this mean for him? Would things get worse for the Jews in Germany? Would the rest of the family have to follow Bella and start a new life in a foreign country?

He didn't have to wait long to find out. In June 1933, Dr Alexander was summoned to a meeting by the Waldschule's head teacher. He was told that the recent passage of the Law Against the Overcrowding of German Schools and Universities imposed strict limits on the number of Jewish students at any given institution; therefore, the twins were no longer welcome. Either the doctor could remove the boys, or they would be 'slung out'.

Alfred returned home and told Hanns and Paul, who were by then sixteen, that they would now be sent to a private Jewish school. Hanns had liked the Waldschule, and even though he had never applied himself to his studies, he had intended to graduate and perhaps even go on to university, as both his sisters had done. Even worse than the rejection by the school, and the strangeness of the law behind it, was the uncertainty: if he could be thrown out of school because of his culture and race, what else could happen?

But the twins were not the only family members to be affected by the new rules. Following the passage of further anti-Jewish laws over the next few months, it became increasingly difficult for a Jew to run a medical practice, even a doctor as prominent as Alfred Alexander. Furthermore, the government outlawed the reimbursement of Jewish doctors through public health insurance funds, which had previously made up a good part of Dr Alexander's income. And with the Munich mayor having recently forbidden Jewish doctors from treating non-Jewish patients, it was only a matter of time before Berlin would follow suit. If so, he would be forced out of business.

Conversation at the Alexander table became increasingly tense. Henny argued that eventually they would have to leave the country, and if they didn't sell the practice it would soon be worth nothing.

Meanwhile, Dr Alexander remained in denial, counselling patience and a low profile until life returned to normal, as he felt sure it would.

On 13 July 1934, on the twentieth anniversary of the start of the First World War, and within the general context of Germany's swelling national pride, President Paul von Hindenburg announced the creation of a new commemorative medal, the Cross of Honour. Deciding that it would be useful to have a second proof of national service, in addition to his Iron Cross, Dr Alexander filled out the paperwork for the new award. A few weeks later, he attended a ceremony at a local government office where, along with other veterans, he was given a bronze cross, with the numbers 1914 and 1918 embossed at its centre. Attached to the cross was a red, black and white ribbon: the colours of Imperial Germany and the Nazi Party.

Bella, meanwhile, was rapidly adjusting to her new life in England. In December 1934 she gave birth to a son, named Peter, to the delight of Alfred and Henny. Alfred travelled to London to see his first grandchild. While there, a family friend, Otto Schiff, who had moved to London from Hamburg, suggested that he register with a British medical institution – just in case he had to leave Germany. Although Alfred still believed that their problems would blow over, he realised that the time had come to hedge his bets and, before returning to Berlin, took a bus into central London, where he put his name down as a student at Edinburgh University. If he wanted to set up a medical practice in Great Britain, he would have to requalify as a doctor.

Back in Berlin, despite Henny's attempts to persuade them otherwise, the twins decided to drop out of their Jewish private school, believing they could learn more in the real world. Through a family connection, Hanns obtained a job with Leo Perl, a small German bank that was run by a family friend, Franz Perl. This was Hanns' first job and, although his responsibilities there were not onerous, he relished the opportunity to prove himself and was glad to be done with the daily drudgery of school life. Each day he dressed in a dark suit and hat, and joined the other workers heading into central Berlin on the trams. At the end of each month, Hanns handed his meagre earnings to his mother, who thanked him with pride.

Paul was also busy. Despite a new law forbidding Jews from apprenticeships, he had secured a job with a Berlin cabinet-maker. His employer, Johan Geider, refused to acknowledge laws telling him whom he could and could not employ. But as was the custom, Dr Alexander had to pay for Paul's apprenticeship.

A few weeks into his placement, Paul was sent across town to a large hall to work on the preparations for a Nazi Party exhibition called 'German Work, German Labour'. The much feted event was due to be opened by Adolf Hitler himself, and when Paul arrived he found a group of men already hard at work. A few hours later a large truck full of plywood pulled up. When the driver asked Paul where he should unload the supplies, Paul told him to drive in and onto the hall's wooden floor. 'Is it safe?' the driver asked him. 'Of course,' Paul replied, knowing full well that the sprung floor could not support such a weight. The driver slowly backed into the hall until a loud crack was heard and the rear end of the truck broke through the floorboards. The driver jumped out of the cab and ran away, quickly followed by Paul. The next day, Paul learned that the exhibition's opening had been cancelled and that Hitler's schedule had been ruined.

As each twin tried to build an adult life for himself, the familiar elements of their lives began to unravel. Hanns could no longer go to the films he so enjoyed. Signs reading 'Jews Unwelcome' were increasingly common and the family's lavish parties had come to end, with many of their friends too frightened to cross the city at night. Fewer patients visited their father's consulting rooms on the Kaiserallee or the clinic on Achenbachstrasse, for fear of being associated with a Jewish doctor. Hanns too suffered from discrimination and had been called names on the street. Although better than most at concealing his identity, appearing like any other young German professional, it would have been obvious that he was Jewish when he walked in and out of his local synagogue on Fasanenstrasse.

So as the Nazi Party gained influence, Hanns was drawn, like so many others, into the Jewish world, not for religious reasons so much as for an explanation of the anti-Semitism he was experiencing in his life. One Friday evening, late in 1934, Hanns left work and travelled to the Friedenstempel Synagogue to hear the sermon of Rabbi Prinz, a twenty-four-year-old who was fast making a name for himself, especially among the younger members of the Jewish community. That night the rabbi arrived late and for a while the enormous crowd worried that he had been arrested. When at last he did appear, Prinz warned that Nazi anti-Semitism was not a momentary problem, but a long-term threat that should be taken very seriously. He also acknowledged that most rabbis were saying something different: that life would return to normal, that the German people could be trusted to take care of the anti-Semites, who, though virulent, were few, and that he, Prinz, was swimming against the tide of this popular Jewish opinion. The rabbi finished his sermon with one simple message: all Jews should leave Germany as soon as they possibly could. As he was walking home, Hanns was concerned that perhaps his father had it wrong and they really should be thinking about leaving.

To protect themselves, Hanns and Paul joined a progressive Jewish youth group, who met each week to inform and educate each other on the rise of Nazi anti-Semitism, and to share ideas on how to deal with abuse. Here they were told never to go anywhere alone, to walk away from trouble, and that daytime travel was better than night. Such advice was ignored by the twins, as they often moved around when it was dark. But Hanns kept going to the meetings to gather information on the latest attack against the Berlin Jews and to find out about the Jewish elders' efforts to negotiate with the government, all at a time when mainstream newspapers and state-owned radio were controlled by the Nazis. These gatherings also provided a chance to take the temperature of the wider Jewish community, and to gauge whether there were alternative opinions to those voiced by his father.

Regardless of the new laws restricting Jewish activities, nothing was going to stop Hanns and his brother from attending the Monday-night ice-hockey games held at the Sportpalast. It had been decreed that only Nazi supporters could buy tickets for this sporting event – indeed there was a notice plastered on the door saying *'Juden raus!'* ('Jews Out!') – but Hanns and Paul had a different idea. They dressed in normal street clothes and, paying for a ticket at the door like everybody else, were able to watch their heroes knock the puck across the glistening ice each and every week.

The rest of the family also attempted to live as normal a life as possible. In early 1935, Elsie attended one of the Jews-only performances at the Deutsches Theater. There she met Erich Hirschowitz, a short, affable Berliner. Erich's father was a leather merchant, and with one eye on business growth and another on the mounting anti-Semitism in Berlin, he had sent Erich to London to establish a leather import/export business. In July 1935 Elsie and Erich were married. Because the families didn't want to attract attention to themselves, it was a smaller affair than Bella's wedding two years earlier. A few guests were invited back to the apartment on Kaiserallee; no notices were placed in the papers. For their honeymoon they drove to Switzerland. At one point they had to take a detour around one of the towns because a sign had been posted on its outskirts: *'Juden sind hier unerwünscht'* ('Jews are not wanted here'). A few weeks after the wedding Erich returned to London. Elsie would join him once things had settled down in Berlin.

Around the same time, an enraged Nazi Party official banged on the door of Dr Alexander's clinic on Achenbachstrasse, claiming that Alfred had performed an illegal abortion on his sister. Outraged by the accusation, and with a clear conscience, Dr Alexander threw the man down the stairs. Then, realising the danger that he was now in, he immediately set off to the nearest police station, hoping to head off any complaint. He was told that if he wasn't a member of the Nazi Party, he couldn't be helped. It was at this point that he finally reconciled himself to the reality that time was running out. But even now, he hesitated.

At the end of 1935, Henny's parents departed for their native Switzerland – the clean air was recommended for her father's failing health – and it was agreed that Paul should travel with them. Once in Basel, he started an apprenticeship at the city's technical school. It was the first time that the brothers had ever been apart.

In January 1936, Dr Alexander travelled to London, in order to spend some time with Bella and his young grandson. While he was away, Henny received a phone call from Colonel Otto Meyer, the man who had so bravely driven away the Nazi mob from the Alexanders' home during the 1933 boycott of Jewish businesses.

'They will be coming for him,' Meyer told Henny. 'You must see to it that he goes into hiding at once.' He explained that he had seen the doctor's name high on the list of Jews whom the Gestapo intended to round up in the next few days. When Henny replied that her husband was in England, Otto recommended that Alfred should stay there. Henny sent a note to her husband, telling him not to come back.

At last Dr Alexander came to the awful realisation that he had no choice. He made a call to Edmund Dreyfus, an old family friend and an English banker and protégé of Lucien Picard, Alfred's father-in-law. Dreyfus quickly agreed to stake the guarantee that the British required of any refugee seeking temporary asylum. It appeared that, for now, the doctor could remain in London, although he was deeply distressed at having to leave the country he so loved and depressed at the thought of having to requalify as a doctor. Most of all, he worried that if his name had been on the Gestapo's list, then so could those of his loved ones. He sent word back that he would stay in London, and told the rest of the family in Berlin to make plans to join him.

Hanns' life in Germany had come to an end, and while he was anxious about beginning again, he was also excited about the adventure ahead of him. He quickly focused on the practical matters of how to arrange for his departure to England. The first step was to secure an exit certificate from the Berlin *Polizeipräsident*, the chief of police, without which he could not obtain an entry visa. It was not too difficult a task: the authorities were still keen to see Jews leave the country. He took a tram to the police station in central Berlin and, after paying 10 Reichsmark, was granted a certificate valid for six months.

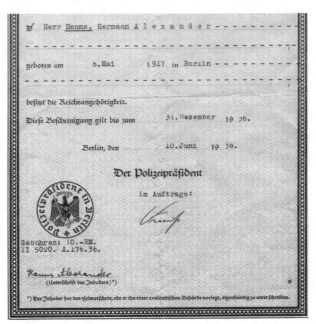

Throughout the spring of 1936, Hanns tried and failed to obtain a British entry visa. The British government had become fearful of how its citizens would react to a wave of Jewish refugees from Germany, and had clamped down on immigration. Moreover, as Hanns was now of working age and no longer a dependant, he could not rely on the fact that his father and sister were already in London. He would have to find his own way to leave, and soon.

Over the previous six months, conditions for Jews had worsened in Berlin. Hanns' friends at university had been expelled and sent back home. Many of his father's friends had lost their jobs – as lawyers, accountants and civil servants – following the enactment of a law forbidding Jews from holding professional or governmental positions. Hanns could no longer read his synagogue's newsletter – one of the last ways to glean uncensored news – following yet another law muzzling the religious press. And then following an announcement by Hitler during one of his Nuremberg rallies, the Reich Citizenship Law was passed, stripping Hanns and his family of their national citizenship: from this point on Germany considered them to be mere 'subjects', separate from the rest of the German nation.

But as spring approached summer, Hanns noticed a change in the Nazi regime's rhetoric. There were fewer boycotts and rallies, no new anti-Jewish laws, and a few 'Jews Unwelcome' signs were even removed from shop windows. Hanns realised that Hitler was attempting to present a positive impression to the world's media, who had already started to arrive in Berlin for the Olympics, scheduled to commence on 1 August 1936.

Knowing that this might be his only opportunity to obtain a visa, before the anti-Semitism resumed with a vengeance, Hanns redoubled his efforts. Sometime that May, he went to see Franz Perl, his boss at the bank, and told him that he had to leave the country as soon as possible. Perl agreed to recommend him to a London bank. The next day, Hanns woke early and walked to the British Passport Office at 17 Tiergartenstrasse, a fifteen-minute walk from the family's apartment. By the time he arrived, scores of people were lined up in front of him, some of whom had been waiting there since four that morning. Many of the men and women stood quietly, papers in hand, facing forward, while others wept openly, terrified at being turned down by the bureaucrats. That one of his father's patients was the British Embassy's First Secretary gave him some cause for hope, but given the numbers queuing outside, there was no guarantee that he would be granted a visa. The doors opened at nine o'clock, and when it was his turn, Hanns entered the small office and filled in an application form. With less fuss than he had anticipated, and after only a few minutes' wait, Hanns walked way with a visa stamped into his passport.

Hanns next went to the French Embassy to ask permission to cross France on his way to England, but was refused. With time running out, Hanns wrote to Paul in Switzerland for help. A few days later, Paul replied that Hanns should join him in Switzerland and then, after a good meal, catch a plane directly to London. With Elsie having managed to obtain a ticket to Amsterdam and soon to depart – she had found it relatively easy to secure a permit with her husband already in London and running a business – only Henny was left with the task of finding a way out of Berlin.

But it would not be so easy for their mother. Individuals with significant assets or incomes were forced to pay the extremely expensive *Reichsfluchtsteuer*, the Reich Escape Tax, to secure an exit visa. So Henny would have to remain in Berlin until she had sold her husband's clinic. Nobody wanted to leave Henny by herself, but there was little choice. They all knew that speed was now essential, given that the world's gaze would leave Germany once the Olympics came to an end in mid-August.

On the morning of 29 May 1936, Hanns said goodbye to his mother and walked out of the giant wooden front door onto the Kaiserallee for the last time. He was filled with conflicting emotions: worried about Henny, eager to be finally on his way, nervous about what lay ahead. He took the S-Bahn to Potsdam station and purchased a train ticket for Switzerland. It was a 500-mile journey taking him past the family's country home at Glienicke, through Munich, where his father had studied medicine, and on to the small rural town of Geislingen, in south-western Germany, where he stopped off for a few hours to say goodbye to his much-loved former nanny, Anna. The next day he continued his journey, via Baden-Baden, to the border crossing with Switzerland.

Late on 30 May 1936, Hanns arrived at the railway station in Basel. He had yet to escape, however. Although on Swiss soil, the station was actually run by the German railway network and controlled by the German government. Hanns pulled his bag from the luggage rack, stepped onto the platform and walked towards the customs office, joining a long line of men, women and children. Most were Jews, exhausted from long hours on trains and the anxiety of uprooting their families.

When it was his turn Hanns handed over his passport with the words '*Deutscher Reich Reisepass*' typed boldly across its olive-green front cover. The German customs officer looked at Hanns' travel document, comparing the man in front of him to the picture of the fifteen-year-old inside, glanced at the British visa, stamped the passport and waved him through. When Paul saw Hanns walking through passport control, he rushed up to his brother and, with a loud laugh, gave him a tremendous hug.

Hanns had now left the country of his birth. He was nineteen years old, with only a train ticket and ten marks in his pocket – all the money the German government had allowed him to take.

On 2 June 1936 Hanns arrived at Croydon airport, south of London. He handed his German passport to the officer at control, who stamped it with the following words:

> Permitted to land at Croydon on 2 June 1936 on condition that the holder registers at once with the Police and that he does not remain in the United Kingdom longer than six months.

Bella was waiting for him and immediately took him out for lunch at the Aerodrome Hotel in Croydon. After the meal they took a taxi back to her apartment in Olympia, where Hanns was greeted by his father, his brother-in-law and, for the first time, his three-year-old nephew, Peter. While he was acutely aware that his family was now split — Henny in Berlin, Elsie in Amsterdam, Paul and his grandparents in Basel — it felt good to be reunited with at least some family members in London.

Over the next few weeks Hanns set about building a life. He took a room at the Regent Palace Hotel off Piccadilly Circus while looking for suitable long-term accommodation. He also registered with the Aliens Registration Office in Bow Street, where he was assigned Alien Number: 594942. Being a registered alien meant that he could not hold a paying job; he could not vote or receive government benefits; as a German foreign national his movements would be monitored by the security services; and in six months' time he would have to apply for the renewal of his visa.

A few days later, Hanns took a bus into the City and walked into Japhet & Co., the small bank owned by Bella's husband's family, where he would carry out his apprenticeship. He was greeted by one of the bank's managers who spoke quickly about the bank's mission, its employees and the tasks that Hanns was expected to perform. With only schoolboy English Hanns was unable to catch any of the details. He realised that if he was to navigate this new environment, then he was going to need help with his language skills.

In a letter to his mother, sent four weeks after his arrival in England, Hanns provided details of his new life. He thanked her for the gifts she had sent: money, which 'I shall diligently attempt to stretch out', and two cans of cherry compote from the family garden in Glienicke, which he had not yet opened, 'as it is so precious'. He had been keeping busy, he wrote, by seeing many of their old friends and acquaintances from Berlin, including Löwenstein, the boy whom Hanns had 'bound to the tree' during the birthday party at the lake house, and whom he 'didn't like any better'. The previous Saturday Hanns had taken a day trip with his father to the Isle of Wight, which he described as 'heavenly'. And while he wished that his weekends were longer, the work at the bank was 'still fun'. In general, then, he was doing fine, particularly because he had found a new restaurant for dinner: Lyons Corner House in the centre of London, which had cheap food, tablecloths and free iced water. Reassuring his mother, he added, 'I for my part am happier than ever.'

In early July 1936, Hanns received a reply. The sale of the clinic would not be as easy as Henny had hoped. According to the Nazi laws, she could not sell to a Jew, nor was she likely to be able to sell to a supporter of the party, who would be less than keen to take over the clinic with its Jewish staff and patients. His mother had found one buyer, but the deal had collapsed at the last minute.

Henny spent the rest of that summer trying to locate a buyer, but when another deal came and went, her situation became precarious. Eventually, in early August, Henny was able to find a couple – she Jewish, he Christian – willing to purchase the clinic, albeit at a fire-sale price. With no other choice, Henny agreed, and with what funds she then had, paid the Reich Escape Tax. A few days later, she boarded a train to London.

★

By the Jewish New Year, in September 1936, the rest of the Alexander family had made it to London. First Elsie, via Amsterdam, and finally Paul from Switzerland. The only family member who remained in Germany was Hanns' great-aunt, Cäcilie Bing, who had refused to leave. Auntie Bing was a believer in the 'old ways' and had a reputation of being hard on the children. She was one of the few people whom the young Hanns and Paul never played tricks on, though they laughed at her strong lisp behind her back. She stayed on in her well-appointed suite at the Excelsior Hotel in Frankfurt.

Now that the family was reunited, the doctor and his wife moved to a two-bedroom apartment in Kensington, west London. While they considered it more than sufficient, it was a far cry from the rabbit warren of rooms that had been their Kaiserallee home. Henny sent word to Hilde, their cook back in Berlin, and asked that all their furniture and possessions be boxed and shipped to England, a feat still possible in 1936 as the Nazis were still keen that as many Jews as possible leave Germany.

Hilde took Henny at her word and packed literally everything into crates – every book, every piece of linen, every item of furniture. Even the waste-paper baskets were sent over still filled with garbage. In one box, buried under clothes, and wrapped up in towels and blankets, the family found the Alexander Torah. Apparently, Hilde had discovered it tucked away in the cupboard in the doctor's library. She had also included the Torah's red velvet covering, the two silver bells and the silver breastplate embossed with the name of Moses Alexander, all of which were as old as the scroll itself.

Unable to bring any of their money into England, every member of the family now had to start from scratch. Later that autumn, the fifty-eight-year-old Dr Alexander took a train to Edinburgh to begin his studies to requalify as a doctor. While Bella and Elsie had the advantage of husbands with significant business interests and associated wealth, Hanns and Paul began their London lives close to the poverty line.

Paul enrolled at Kensington Secretarial College to study English, but he was more interested in chatting to the girls who comprised the vast majority of the students. He then obtained an apprenticeship with Laszlo Hoenig, a fashionable interior decorator who had a gallery at 54 South Audley Street in Mayfair. Bella, who had been living in London since 1933 and therefore knew the city best, acted as guide and counsellor to the others, and took care of her young son, while her husband Harold grew his stockbroker business. Elsie found a small flat with her husband, Erich, in north London. She was resentful of her change in circumstances, her inability to study at university and, to cap it all, of neighbours who sneered at her thick German accent. Her solution was to wear her expensive furs whenever she could.

Meanwhile, Hanns was quickly adapting. Having turned his back on the past he was uninterested in dwelling on all that had been lost – the house, the prestige, the servants. Perhaps it was because he was younger than Elsie, and had not yet established an independent life in Berlin, or perhaps it was simply that he was more optimistic, better able to deal with change and displacement. Whatever the reason, Hanns assimilated more easily.

Hanns and Paul were by now fully grown, handsome men. They stood six feet tall, with their thick dark brown wavy hair cut short and brushed back off their high foreheads. To most people they were impossible to tell apart. But to those who knew them, there were differences. Paul leaned forward slightly when he stood, as if anticipating the future. His chin was more pointed and when he laughed his cheeks dimpled. He appeared the more relaxed of the pair, more easy-going, more happy-go-lucky. Hanns, by contrast, stood tall, pensive and tense. He was square-jawed, serious, and could easily have been mistaken for one of the matinee idols of the day.

Once a week Hanns left his work in the City and travelled by bus to a building in Victoria. There, he climbed a long staircase to the fourth floor and knocked on the door of a flat belonging to a sixty-five-year-old German spinster named Mrs Frank. After a few moments, Frankie, as Hanns called her, would let him into her cramped living room that overlooked St James's Park and which smelled a little too much of pickled onions. She taught Hanns the basics of the English language over warm tea and stale biscuits. In a German accent that was hard even for Hanns to understand, she also explained the basics of the English way of life: what to carry to work (bowler hat, umbrella, briefcase); what to serve your guests for dinner (roast beef and Yorkshire puddings, not chopped liver and ox tongue); and how to behave with strangers (stiffly and somewhat detached).

His English improved rapidly, and while he had retained a slight German accent, he was now able to tackle any situation – from swapping work banter to negotiating rent with his landlady – without feeling self-conscious.

Frankie was a tough and demanding teacher, but Hanns kept coming back. Another young German had started taking lessons with her – a leggy seventeen-year-old brunette called Anneliese Graetz. Ann, as she liked to be known, had also recently fled Nazi Germany, arriving in London with her fourteen-year-old brother, Wolfgang. Her parents, Paul and Käte Graetz, had remained in Berlin. Her father believed that he had a responsibility to continue managing one of Germany's largest grain mills. Ann was deeply worried about them, but as she waited for news, like Hanns, she was learning how to navigate British society.

It was not long before Hanns and Ann attended afternoon tea dances together and went for walks through one of London's many parks. He took her to dinner at his favourite restaurant, the Lyons Corner House, where Hanns excitedly pointed out the tablecloths and iced water. Ann introduced Hanns to Wolfgang, a pupil at St Paul's School. On Friday nights, they went over to Hanns' mother's for Shabbat – Dr Alexander was still in Edinburgh – where they were often joined by Paul, Bella, Elsie and Erich. In addition to the usual family matters, they caught up on the latest news from Berlin.

As the Alexander family made the best of their strange new life, the situation in Germany was getting worse. On 9 November 1938, over 250 synagogues and 7,000 stores and businesses were attacked in what became known as Kristallnacht, the night of the broken glass. One was the Fasanenstrasse Synagogue, where Hanns and the rest of the family had enjoyed celebrating Simchat Torah. Nazi supporters smashed their way into the synagogue and, upon the orders of Joseph Goebbels, set fire to the building. Firemen and local residents gathered at the scene, watching as the flames grew higher. These were the same men and women whom the Alexanders had counted as friends and neighbours, whose children had attended the same community school. Many had even been Dr Alexander's patients. The massive gold-domed Neue Synagogue on Oranienburger Strasse – where Hanns had been bar mitzvahed – was also attacked, its furniture smashed, its Torahs set ablaze. This synagogue would also have burned to the ground if it hadn't been for the actions of Otto Bellgardt, a local policeman, who pulled out his gun and instructed the mob to leave. That the Neue Synagogue in Berlin had refused to accept the Alexander Torah as a loan back in 1906 turned out to be its salvation.

The Kristallnacht attacks were not limited to buildings that the Alexanders knew and loved. Hanns' girlfriend's family had also been caught up in the night's terror. Early on 10 November 1938, on the morning after the burning of the synagogues, armed thugs had come to Ann's parents' house in Berlin and arrested her father. He was then taken to the street where he joined a group of over a thousand Jewish men, who were marched to a train station and transported to the Sachsenhausen camp just outside the city. Upon arrival, her father had been commanded to remove his clothes, his head had been shaved, and he was given a black-and-white-striped prison uniform on which was stamped his prison number: 010065. At the camp he witnessed and experienced the horror and violence of the concentration camps, which were still not known to the outside world. However, Paul Graetz was lucky. Eighteen days after his arrival he, along with hundreds of other Jews, were told that they were free to go, but on one condition: that as soon as they returned to their homes, they must pack their bags and leave the country. As he walked out of the camp he was handed an exit document, bearing his photograph, date of birth, address and the signature of one of the camp's senior guards: Rudolf Höss.

As soon as Ann's father made it home, he transferred his remaining funds to the German government to pay the escape tax, secured a visa from the British consulate, and bought a train ticket to London.

Over the course of that winter, Ann and Hanns continued to see each other, but as winter turned to spring, they drifted apart and eventually agreed to stop seeing each other. While Ann tried to move on, accompanying other men to dances and concerts, Hanns was preoccupied by the continued persecution of the Jews, which was now spreading throughout continental Europe.

Between 1934 and 1939, more than 70,000 Jews fled Nazi-controlled countries — Germany, Austria, Czechoslovakia and Poland — for Britain. These figures included the thousands of unaccompanied children who arrived in Britain on the *Kindertransport*, or children's transport — a last-minute rescue mission of nearly 10,000 Jewish children. In Britain, these Jewish refugees were greeted with a mixture of grudging acceptance by some and open hostility by others. In an attempt to improve their assimilation, the refugees — Hanns among them — were handed flyers made by the indigenous English Jewish community with advice on how to behave. They were told not to 'criticise any government regulations' because that is 'not the way things are done here'. Furthermore, they were advised that they should 'not speak of how much better this or that is done in Germany', because while 'it may be true in some matters, it weighs nothing against the sympathy and freedom and liberty in England which are now given to you'.

As more and more German Jews arrived in London, it became obvious that they needed a new synagogue of their own. It wasn't just that they spoke German, or that they felt uncomfortable attending the services put on by the English Jews. It was more that they missed the style and mannerisms of their own ceremonies. The Berlin synagogues were based upon a *Liberale* tradition which, unlike those in London, relied almost entirely on singing the ancient Hebrew text, rather than reading it aloud, as the English Orthodox and Liberal Jews did.

But the new synagogue had two problems: they had no space in which to pray, and they had no Torah. The first was solved by one of the founding members, a Mrs Gluckman, who offered the use of her dining room in Belsize Park. The second was solved by Dr Alexander, who loaned the Alexander Torah to the nascent synagogue. Soon there was not enough room to accommodate all those wishing to attend. So, starting in March 1939, a regular Friday evening service was held for the German refugees at a synagogue in St John's Wood. In June 1939, this group then formed the New Liberal Jewish Association (later becoming known as the Belsize Square Synagogue). Hanns' father was one of its founding board members, and the family Torah was handed over to the synagogue as a semi-permanent loan.

Then, one month later, on 24 July 1939, the Alexanders learned that there was no going back home. The names of Hanns, Paul, Bella, Elsie, Henny and Alfred Alexander were published in the *Reichgesetzblatt* as part of the *Ausbürgerungslisten*, lists of those (mostly Jews) whose German naturalisation had been officially revoked. Further-more, the Nazis had declared that the state now owned all possessions previously belonging to the Alexanders. The German government now considered the family stateless.

Bekanntmachung

Auf Grund des § 2 des Gesetzes über den Widerruf von Einbürgerungen und die Aberkennung der deutschen Staatsangehörigkeit vom 14. Juli 1933 (RGBl. I S. 480) **erkläre ich** im Einvernehmen mit dem Herrn Reichsminister des Auswärtigen folgende Personen **der deutschen Staatsangehörigkeit für verlustig:**

1. **Alexander**, Alfred John, geb. am 7. 3. 1880 in Bamberg,
2. **Alexander**, Henriette, geb. Picard, geb. am 11. 12. 1888 in Frankfurt a. M.,
3. **Alexander**, Paul Alfred, geb. am 6. 5. 1917 in Berlin-Wilmersdorf,
4. **Alexander**, Hans, geb. am 6. 5. 1917 in Berlin-Wilmersdorf,

Official announcement showing that the Alexanders had been stripped of German nationality

Although there was a disturbing finality to this announcement, Hanns was neither surprised nor disappointed. For with every appalling story that arrived from Germany, his affection for its people had diminished, in tandem with his growing resolve to build a new life in England.

Five weeks later, on 1 September 1939, Hitler's tanks rumbled into Poland, provoking outrage around the world. Britain's prime minister, Neville Chamberlain, sat in front of a large microphone in the Cabinet Room at 10 Downing Street and – wearing a starched white collar, tails and a bow tie – explained that diplomacy had failed. Britain was now at war with Germany.

When he heard that his adopted country was at war with the country of his birth, Hanns felt an immediate urge to act. Perhaps it was a desire for adventure, or for revenge. Or perhaps it was out of loyalty to England for taking him in and his duty to fight, as his brother-in-law Harold had told him a few weeks before. Whatever the cause, Hanns only knew that to do nothing was impossible.

The next day he left his apartment, determined to enlist.

7

RUDOLF
OŚWIĘCIM, UPPER SILESIA
1939

Rudolf was working in Sachsenhausen when war broke out. He followed the dramatic events fervently – the invasion of Poland, the bellicose rhetoric broadcast each evening on the radio, the orchestrated nationalistic marches in Berlin – but the war made little difference to his life. As adjutant at a camp for political prisoners, his daily tasks and responsibilities went unchanged: supplies were still readily available, transportation lines ran smoothly to and from Berlin, and there were no wartime drills to interrupt his routine.

The one difference he witnessed was a shift in the camp's population. In the first few weeks of September 1939, more than five thousand Berlin Communists had been rounded up by the Gestapo, the secret police force, and sent to Sachsenhausen as a wartime national security measure. Soon after that, nine hundred Jews arrived. These were business owners and professionals who had refused or been unable to leave the country. Then, in November 1939, in the aftermath of anti-German demonstrations in Prague, 1,200 Czech university students were delivered to the camp. By the end of the year Sachsenhausen's population had increased to 11,000 prisoners.

Despite the sudden influx, life in the camp proceeded as it had done in the months before. Of more consequence to Rudolf was a rapid change in leadership. At the end of 1939, Himmler had replaced Kommandant Baranowski with Walter Eisfeld, a thirty-five-year-old former member of the Artamanen League. Eisfeld would not last long. Following Himmler's official visit in January 1940 – in which he found the guards to be ill-disciplined – Eisfeld was dismissed and replaced with Hans Loritz, an experienced officer who had been Rudolf's supervisor in Dachau. Rudolf benefited from this revolving leadership, being made second in command of the camp.

Yet Rudolf bridled under the new administration. For Loritz immediately set about imposing the same brutal regime that he had overseen in Dachau. Worse, Loritz carried a grudge against Rudolf for leaving him to work under Baranowski. As a result, Rudolf was sidelined and quickly became frustrated.

Then, in April 1940, Rudolf received a telephone call from Richard Glücks, the recently appointed Chief Inspector of Concentration Camps. A heavyset man with a head that appeared too small for his

Richard Glücks

body and a brain that moved as languidly as his oversized feet, Glücks was a man employed for his loyalty. He was considered somebody who would do what he was told. Glücks said that Himmler wanted Rudolf to set up a new camp in Upper Silesia (the part of southern Poland that had been annexed by Germany in September 1939) near the small town of Oświęcim — or 'Auschwitz' as the Germans called it — and that he needed someone to survey the site, build the facility and then run the camp. They were looking for an energetic and effective Kommandant.

Rudolf was wary. He knew that Glücks viewed him with mistrust, partly for his zealous commitment to completing whatever task was handed to him, and partly because of his relationship with Himmler. Nevertheless, Rudolf accepted the offer. Here at last was his opportunity to manage things on his own terms, to work hard and to prove himself.

It was a cold and damp evening when the newly appointed Kommandant stepped off the train in Oświęcim. A town of 15,000 inhabitants, over half of whom were Jewish, Oświęcim stood forty miles west of Kraków, and was close enough to the pre-1939 German border to fall firmly within the Reich's military control. Carrying his suitcase, Rudolf stepped across the tram tracks to his new head-quarters, a small hotel opposite the station.

The next day, 1 May 1940, Rudolf left the hotel and inspected the grounds that Himmler had chosen for the camp. Situated on rocky land a hundred yards from the narrow Sola River, the site was surrounded by marshy and poorly cultivated fields dotted with a few run-down peasant cottages. All that existed were a few dilapidated brick barracks built for seasonal workers. The buildings were crumbling: the red-tiled roofs leaked in the rain; almost all the windows were broken; the floorboards had been torn up; what was left of the plumbing didn't work; and the few remaining doors hung askew on their hinges. This would be a huge task. Rudolf's workforce consisted of only thirty professional criminals and a handful of guards who had been brought in from Sachsenhausen and Dachau.

One of these guards was Josef Kramer. With no more than a primary school education, Kramer had joined the Nazi Party in 1931 and, after being accepted into the SS, trained as a camp guard alongside Rudolf in Dachau. At six foot four, he was a powerfully built man who projected intimidating physicality. His dark brown hair was swept back from his high forehead and the thick vertical crease that divided his bushy black eyebrows. He also had a three-inch crescent scar that hovered just above his thin-lipped mouth. Kramer had been sent to Auschwitz to work as Rudolf's adjutant.

Another guard was Franz Hössler, a thirty-four-year-old former photographer and warehouse worker who, like Rudolf, grew up in the conservative south-west region of Germany. Like Rudolf and Kramer, Hössler had worked in Dachau before being transferred to Auschwitz. He was put in charge of the camp's kitchens.

The camp at Auschwitz had first been planned as a quarantine facility for Polish prisoners suffering from typhus. Now, however, Berlin wanted to use the camp to house Polish political prisoners arrested by the General Government of Poland, the occupational body that the Germans had put in place to run the country. In June, the first prisoners arrived, 728 inmates from a prison in Tarnow. The first order of business was to rebuild the old barracks to lodge the 10,000 inmates that were anticipated to arrive by the year's end. Accommodation would have to be prepared, the water supply secured, security fences installed, roads laid, and offices and cooking facilities built.

The primary obstacle facing Rudolf was that no building materials had been supplied. The prisoners were marched out to the country-side to dismantle local buildings for their wood, bricks and stone. They stole barbed wire from engineering depots and stripped armoured plate from old bunkers. With few vehicles or tools available, the prisoners then had to carry everything back to the camp.

Rudolf was not only dismayed by the camp's condition and the lack of support from Berlin but, with the exception of a few good men such as Josef Kramer, disappointed by the quantity and quality of his staff. He viewed them as stubborn, malicious and lazy. Despite repeated requests to Richard Glücks for additional men, he was ignored. After a while, Rudolf resolved that he would do everything by himself. So while he could have been meeting policymakers or planning the camp's development, he was actually driving hundreds of miles to the Polish border to purchase kettles for the kitchens, or travelling to western Czechoslovakia to buy bed frames and straw sacks. Determined, as he had never been before, Rudolf recognised that he had become a different person.

> Until then I had seen only the good side of my fellow men, particularly my comrades, until I was convinced of the opposite. My innocent trust has often served me badly. But in Auschwitz, where I found that my supposed fellow-workers were always deceiving me, I suffered new disappointments every day, and I changed. I turned suspicious, I saw nothing but deception everywhere, and thought the worst of others. I instantly looked for what was bad in every newcomer to the camp. As a result I injured the feelings of many good, decent men, and rejected their friendship. I could no longer trust or feel confidence in anyone.

By the autumn of 1940 the construction of the camp was complete. There were now twenty-two brick blocks standing in neat rows, intersected by a cross of cobbled lanes. The majority served as barracks for the thousands of prisoners who had arrived over the summer; the rest were given specific uses: Block 9 was assigned as the infirmary, Block 11 was for detention and punishment, Block 20 was set aside to quarantine prisoners with contagious infections. Rudolf had commandeered a large stone-faced building next to Block 4, in which he had established his offices. The camp was encircled by two layers of twenty-foot-high fencing, topped with razor wire. Guard posts were positioned every few hundred feet. There was only one entrance to the camp, protected by two large iron gates, a barricade and a guardhouse. On Eicke's orders, Rudolf had hung the wrought-iron sign above the gates: '*Arbeit Macht Frei*' ('work sets you free').

Soon after, Hedwig and the children joined Rudolf. The family moved into a modest grey stucco, two-storey, box-shaped house, just on the edge of the camp, a hundred feet from the Sola River and across a dusty path from the Kommandant's newly built offices.

In November 1940, Rudolf travelled to Berlin to provide Himmler with an update on the camp's progress. Using maps and diagrams, he presented a summary of the camp's failings, 'and plainly described the serious shortcomings in the camp at the time'. Himmler remarked that it was up to Rudolf, as Kommandant, to fix things, 'and how I did it was my business'. When Rudolf raised the problem of epidemics due to the lack of hygiene facilities, Himmler cut him off and said, 'You are too pessimistic!' and reminded Rudolf that they were at war, telling him to 'improvise'. Only when Rudolf started describing the wider terrain beyond the original camp did Himmler begin to 'show a lively interest, he began making plans, issuing order after order'. Himmler said it was time to expand the facility and transform it into an experimental station to research agricultural techniques and processes: they should drain the marshes, construct a dam, build plant laboratories and breed new types of cattle. Rudolf found Himmler's excitement contagious. The conversation that had begun with a list of grievances concluded with Rudolf committing to a massive and unrealistic expansion of the camp. Such was his receptiveness to Himmler's persuasive powers.

Before leaving, Himmler asked about Rudolf's family. The enquiry moved Rudolf, who felt that he was almost being treated as a favourite child. He thought it unlikely that Himmler asked many people such intimate questions.

A few days later, Rudolf sent word to the residents who lived in the rural areas near the Auschwitz camp that he was taking control of their property. This land grab would amount to an area three miles long and four miles wide.

The next few months were frenetic, with Rudolf working long hours to fulfil the orders from Berlin, in particular from Himmler whom, above all others, he didn't want to disappoint.

> From the first I was utterly absorbed in my work, indeed obsessed
> by it. All new difficulties only spurred me on to greater efforts.
> I did not want to let the problems get me down; my ambition
> would not allow it. I concentrated entirely on my work.

As Rudolf threw himself into the new scheme, he began to spend less and less time with Hedwig and the children. By this time Klaus was ten years old, tall for his age, and had the jutting jaw of his father; the two girls — Heidetraut, who was eight, and Brigitte, who was seven (Rudolf affectionately called them 'Kindi' and 'Püppi') — were both already beauties, with long blonde hair, big smiles and slender figures; and Hans-Jürgen, the youngest, known as 'Burling', at three, was a pudgy little boy with a penchant for sweets.

The Höss 'villa', as it was now known, had a large garden with flower beds, vegetable patches, a greenhouse and a shed full of pots and tools, which the children raced around on their bicycles. This garden was itself surrounded by a high concrete wall, capped with red tiles, which gave the family privacy and protection. From Rudolf and Hedwig's bedroom window on the second floor it was possible to see far into the camp: to the barracks where the prisoners were housed; to the covered guard posts that had been built on wooden platforms at intervals around the camp's perimeter; and on to the courtyard in which stood the old crematorium, built in the days when the site had been occupied by a Polish garrison.

The family liked to take photographs during their time at the villa. One picture shows Hans-Jürgen, smiling widely as he sits inside a giant toy plane that had been made by the prisoners. Another shows the girls flirting with two handsome young soldiers, on duty next to their garden's gate. There is a photograph of the family at a picnic table in the garden, appearing cheerful and relaxed as they eat their lunch. In another the children sit on a slide at the edge of a small pool, looking happily at the camera. Another shows them playing in a sand pit, while two men walk behind, dressed in their black-and-white-striped prison uniforms.

The children transformed the villa into a small animal sanctuary: Klaus played with and groomed the family's two Dalmatians and hunting dog; Heidetraut liked to watch her two tortoises, 'Jumbo' and 'Dilla', crawl around the garden patio; while Brigitte carried her white mice to the Sola River behind the house, allowing them to explore the high grass alongside the riverbanks until her mother called her home. There was also a beehive towards the back of the garden, where Rudolf would show the children how to extract the honeycomb without upsetting the swarm. Brigitte also liked to pick the raspberries that ripened on trellised vines. She would sneak into the garden to steal some of the fruit, hoping that her mother would not catch her from the upstairs window.

At first, Hedwig employed two political prisoners to help around the house, but she decided that they did not work hard enough, and replaced them with two elderly Jehovah's Witnesses. Hedwig was delighted with these two female prisoners, telling Rudolf that they took care of the house better than she ever could. They also looked after the children, taking them for walks, feeding and playing with them in the garden, as well as out along the banks of the Sola River. Hedwig also employed a gardener, a cook, a governess, a tailor, a painter, a seamstress, a barber and a chauffeur, who was available for errands, picking up goods from town or taking her shopping. Hedwig's servants called her the 'Angel of Auschwitz'.

One day, the children approached the family's seamstress, Janina Szczurek, and asked her to make them armbands with badges like the prisoners on the other side of the garden wall. Klaus, the eldest, put on the badge of a Kapo, while the rest attached shapes of different colours – yellow stars, green triangles, pink triangles – worn by the other prisoners. The children created a game where they pretended to be inmates, with Klaus ordering them about. Their play was brought to a sudden end when their father arrived. He told them he did not approve of the game, tore off their badges and took them inside. The seamstress was not punished, but Rudolf gave her a severe warning.

Hedwig expected her staff to 'organise' the food that she wanted for the house, relying particularly on Stanisław Dubiel, a Polish political prisoner who worked as their gardener. When Hedwig would quietly mention that they were short of a few things, Dubiel would pick up the signal and locate the required items somewhere in the camp. Her wish list ranged from the mundane – sugar, cream, bread, flour and leather – which Dubiel picked up from the camp kitchens and tannery, to the more exotic – women's underwear, artwork, furniture – which he filched from the possessions that had been plundered from the arriving inmates. The gardener was also asked to track down exotic seeds, for Hedwig's greenhouses. Stanisław Dubiel was blunt about the family's wealth: 'They lacked for nothing in their household and nothing could be lacking, considering the immense quantities of all kinds of possessions accumulated in the camp.'

Hedwig needed her staff, for Rudolf had told her that she must be ready to entertain the important guests who would arrive, often unannounced, from Berlin, Munich and Warsaw. She could expect, he said, their guest book to fill with the names of visitors such as Richard Glücks, the head of the Concentration Camp Inspectorate; Dr Enno Lolling, the chief physician at the Concentration Camp Inspectorate; Adolf Eichmann, who was in charge of transporting the Jews to the camps; and, the most honoured guest of all, for whom Hedwig would have to work the hardest and create his favourite dishes – he had recurrent stomach aches and was very particular about what he ate – Heinrich Himmler, or 'Uncle Heiner', as the children called him. On a more frequent basis, they could expect to host the senior officers from the camp, including Josef Mengele, the camp doctor, and Josef Kramer, Rudolf's adjutant. If she was to entertain such luminaries, Hedwig said, the house would need improvements. Rudolf promised to do his best.

Their most frequent guest was Hedwig's brother, Fritz Hensel, who would sometimes stay for weeks at a time. Rudolf walked him around the camp, showing off all that had been achieved. Fritz was also allowed to wander around by himself, to stop and paint pictures, of the buildings, of the inmates. During one of these visits Fritz was sitting with Rudolf in the villa drinking wine, and he asked why Rudolf used the term *Untermensch*, or subhuman, to describe the prisoners. Rudolf replied: 'Look, you can see for yourself. They are not like you and me. They are different. They look different. They do not behave like human beings. They have numbers on their arms. They are here in order to die.'

The work was unrelenting. Rudolf's days were filled with meeting his senior officers, inspecting progress on the camp, hosting visits from party dignitaries, fielding telephone enquiries from Berlin – often late into the night – and drawing up plans for further expansion. He found that it was more efficient to do the work himself, rather than delegate to his staff, something for which Glücks often criticised him. To impress his subordinates he woke up before them and went to bed after them. In the little free time he had, Rudolf would walk over to the stables next to the family's house, tack up his favourite horse and ride away from the camp into the flat countryside that surrounded Auschwitz.

As the pressure from Berlin mounted, Rudolf began to change.

I withdrew more and more into myself. I became unapproach-
able and visibly harder. My family suffered, particularly my
wife, for I was often unbearable company.

A few times, he and Hedwig managed to drive into town to see
a film or play. Such entertainments were rare, however, and Rudolf
often wondered what life would have been like if he had remained
on the farm in Pomerania. He now found that he didn't like company
and he had become increasingly taciturn. Aware of this new tendency,
Rudolf began deliberately to drink more − never by himself, nor
enough to become drunk − which he hoped would help make him
more talkative, more outgoing, and perhaps even funny. Deep down,
Rudolf felt increasingly alone.

My wife was always trying to extract me from the cocoon into
which I had retreated. She invited friends from outside to come
and see us, hoping that in the company of comrades I would open
up to them again, and she organised social occasions outside the
camp with the same end in view, although she liked that kind of
social life as little as I did. Sometimes I was induced, for a time,
to force myself out of my deliberate introversion, but new disap-
pointments always made me retreat quickly behind a wall of glass.

Each week Rudolf had his hair cut by Jozef Paczynski, a diminu-
tive twenty-year-old Polish political prisoner, branded on his forearm
with one of the first tattoos: number 121. At the appointed time, an
SS officer escorted Jozef from his red-brick prison block to the villa,
where he was greeted by Hedwig. She then walked him through the
well-furnished living room, up the narrow stairs and into a small
bathroom on the first floor. Soon the Kommandant would arrive, sit
down, light a cigar and start reading his paper. He would never say
a word to the barber.

Another prisoner, Lee Abraham Biderman, who worked in the villa polishing furniture, making beds and cleaning floors, said that the Kommandant was 'very soft spoken', and that unlike the guards he 'did not bark', nor did he 'use vulgarities'. He also observed that, whenever the Kommandant passed by, other officers would click their heels and salute him. Felix Samelson, who worked as a tailor in the SS barracks, received a permit to visit the SS kitchen in return for his labour. There he could pick up milk and rice, both of which were unavailable to the other prisoners. One day, a Kapo caught him just as he was sharing the illicit supplies with his sister. The Kapo began beating him so viciously that Samelson feared for his life. Just then Rudolf walked over and the Kapo halted his attack. Rudolf asked the prisoner, 'What did you do?' When Samelson explained that he was giving food away that he had earned as a tailor, Rudolf said, '*Ach, verschwinde!*', or 'get lost'. And so his life was saved.

Yet other prisoners had less favourable memories of Rudolf. Sara Juskowitz viewed the Kommandant as 'ruthless', and during roll call 'always screaming that "work makes life sweet"'. Sidney Bloom was also present during these roll calls, in which Rudolf would give such lengthy sermons that he became known as the 'Preacher'. One time, Bloom recalled, they were forced to stand outside in the courtyard in the freezing cold for three hours, while fifteen Polish and Russian prisoners were marched out and hanged for possessing a radio. Another prisoner, Michael Vogel, was present for many of the hangings that took place in the camp, describing the Kommandant as the 'most cold-blooded animal we ever met', and that 'killing meant nothing to him'. George Klein, also an inmate, remembered a day in 1941 when he saw Rudolf sitting on his horse in a field. Beside him was a machine gun mounted on a horse-drawn cart. Moments later, a man climbed into the cart and began firing at a crowd of over five hundred female prisoners standing in the field with blankets over their heads. Klein does not provide an explanation for why they were there. A few minutes later they were all dead. And then Rudolf rode away without a word, the task apparently completed to his satisfaction.

Rudolf Höss (second right) and Heinrich Himmler (second left) in Auschwitz

It was a warm spring day when, on 1 March 1941, a convoy of open-topped blue Mercedes pulled up outside the Kommandant's offices in Auschwitz. From the lead vehicle stepped the imposing figure of Heinrich Himmler. He wore grey woollen trousers that hung wide at the thigh and which were tucked neatly into knee-high black leather boots, and a wide black belt tightly cinching his jacket, and his collar was emblazoned with three silver oak leaves, marking his unique rank of Reichsführer. As always, he wore a peaked hat under which glittered his signature wire-rimmed glasses.

Himmler had arrived for a formal inspection, accompanied by a mob of cronies – governors and high-ranking SS officials from Berlin, political leaders from Silesia, and corporate officers from the IG

Farben company. Also in the party was Richard Glücks, Rudolf's direct boss, who had been trying to remove Rudolf from his post ever since he had been appointed as Auschwitz Kommandant. Glücks had arrived earlier that morning, warning Rudolf not to say anything negative about the camp.

After serving refreshments in his offices, Rudolf gave an overview of the improvements that had been made to the camp since his previous meeting with Himmler. Using maps and diagrams, he pointed out which buildings had been repaired, which had yet to be constructed, and the planned expansion. Having dealt easily with the group's questions, Rudolf then invited them to join him for a tour of the camp.

The Kommandant climbed into the back seat of the car with Himmler and Ernst Schmauser, the head of a local district, whom Rudolf could trust to be discreet. In the privacy of the car, Rudolf launched into a long list of grievances: the lack of resources, the immensity of the task, the threat of disease due to lack of sanitation, the overcrowding, the lack of water and, worse still, the lack of support from Richard Glücks. Himmler had no patience for Rudolf's complaints.

'Gentlemen,' Himmler said, smiling, 'this [extension of Auschwitz] will be built. My reasons are more important than your arguments against it.'

As their car bumped along the camp's rock-studded roads, Himmler reminded Rudolf that in a time of war he too would have to adapt. If the soldiers at the front could cope, so could a Kommandant. He had big plans for Auschwitz: Rudolf was to build a new camp capable of housing over 100,000 prisoners. This would become known as Birkenau, or Auschwitz II, and be based three miles from the original camp. He also said that he wanted to build a synthetic rubber plant near the Birkenau site for the industrial chemical giant IG Farben, which would be staffed by an additional 10,000 prisoners. None of the camps had ever housed such huge numbers, and Rudolf was both honoured and awed by the responsibility.

When Ernst Schmauser pointed out their lack of building materials and supplies, Himmler retorted: 'The expansion of the camp must be accelerated by every available means. You will have to improvise as you go along. Any epidemics of sickness must be kept within bounds and dealt with ruthlessly. I do *not* agree with you about the problems at Auschwitz.'

Later, when the tour was over and the rest of the group had departed, Himmler came to the house to visit Rudolf's family. The children were bathed and dressed in their best clothes, Klaus and Hans-Jürgen in dark suits, the girls in white frocks with their hair tied back in pigtails. They were brought into the living room to meet Uncle Heiner, the boys bowing and the girls curtsying. Photographs were then taken of the children sitting on Himmler's lap; enlargements of these pictures were later hung on the wall in the living room.

Responding to Hedwig's concerns about the villa's condition – she felt it too small and its decor too old-fashioned to host visiting dignitaries – Himmler told Rudolf to remodel and enlarge the house as he saw fit. After a quick drink, Himmler said his goodbyes and got back into the Mercedes for the long trip back to Berlin. As he left, the four children stood in front of their parents, waving goodbye.

Rudolf's complaints were valid. By this time, the conditions in Auschwitz had dramatically declined. As the numbers of prisoners increased, food became scarce, basic living conditions deteriorated and outbreaks of typhus became common. Equally, as the ratio of prisoners to guards increased, so did the frequency of the guards' indiscriminate attacks. To control the prisoners, the guards and their Kapos had returned to the 'attitude of hatred' philosophy that Rudolf had been so disgusted with during his time in Dachau, but which he was now willing to deploy. Many such beatings ended in death; a warning to others not to disobey orders.

Beatings, however, were not the principal cause of death in Auschwitz at this time. In July 1941, Rudolf oversaw the introduction of the so-called adult 'euthanasia' programme. The camp doctors had received an order from Berlin which had been drafted by Enno Lolling, the chief physician at the Concentration Camp Inspectorate: the camp doctors were now to select all the inmates who they believed were incapable of survival and kill them by injection. Following this directive, the doctors walked through the barracks and indicated to the guards which prisoners they wished to be brought to the medical building. These included those with incurable mental diseases, tuberculosis, or those considered too weak to withstand the camp's harsh conditions. The identified prisoners were then escorted to the medical building housed at Block 20, where they were called in one by one to the 'examination room'. Once inside, they were strapped down onto a surgical table. The doctor asked a few questions about their age, background and medical history and then, with two other prisoners holding the victim's hand and a third covering their eyes, an orderly walked over and injected a vial of phenol straight into the inmate's heart, killing them immediately. In this way thousands of prisoners were murdered in the early years of Auschwitz, including hundreds of children. Rudolf would not only have been aware of these murders, he would have been given daily updates on the numbers involved and the quantities of medical resources that had been consumed in the process.

During his visit to the camp, Glücks had reminded Rudolf that Himmler didn't want to hear about any escapes from Auschwitz. Rudolf therefore decided to implement a draconian policy: for every prisoner that attempted to escape, the guards would select ten from their barracks, drag them to the underground cells in Block 11 and leave them there to starve to death. As a result, the number of prisoners who tried to break out of Auschwitz was low: only two prisoners tried to escape in 1940, rising to seventeen in 1941, and 173 in 1942.

In this way, Rudolf had adopted the brutal order that he had earlier renounced in Dachau and Sachsenhausen.

★

Following the outbreak of war in September 1939, Germany had gained swift and significant victories: Hitler's troops had pushed north and east, occupying most of Poland and all of Denmark and Norway, and moved west into France, Belgium, Luxembourg and the Netherlands. By March 1941, Italy, Hungary, Yugoslavia, Bulgaria and Romania had joined forces with Germany, while others – Spain, Portugal, Switzerland – would remain neutral.

Great Britain stood alone as the last European power resisting German colonisation of the Continent. Hitler's plan to invade Britain, code-named Operation Sea Lion, was delayed following Germany's failure to gain air superiority during the Battle of Britain in the summer and autumn of 1940. Soon after this, Luftwaffe planes started bombing major British cities, in what became known as the Blitz; Britain retaliated by bombing German cities, including Berlin. However, despite these setbacks, by the spring of 1941, the global domination of the Axis Powers appeared almost unstoppable.

Then, in June 1941, in one of the most critical decisions of the war, and in clear defiance of the 1939 non-aggression Molotov–Ribbentrop Pact with the Soviet Union, Hitler sent almost four million Axis troops towards Moscow, Leningrad and Ukraine. This was the start of Operation Barbarossa, which would place an enormous drain on both the German and Soviet Union armies, as well as the civilian populations of both countries. It would also prove decisive in the final outcome of the war and the fate of Auschwitz.

According to Rudolf, it was during that same summer that he travelled to Berlin for a historic meeting with Himmler. He arrived at Himmler's offices at 8 Prinz-Albrecht-Strasse, a few hundred yards from the Potsdamer Platz, a white-stone building which occupied an entire city block. This building not only housed the headquarters of the SS but also the Gestapo and the Reich Main Security Office. The building had gained notoriety for the torture that took place in its 'house prison', deep in its basement.

Unlike previous meetings, this encounter with Himmler was short and businesslike. And nobody else was present. Sitting behind his desk Himmler started without preamble: 'The Führer has given orders for the Final Solution of the Jewish question to be implemented, and we – the SS – are to put those orders into practice. The Jews are the eternal enemies of the German people, and must be wiped off the face of the earth. Now, during this war, all the Jews we can lay hands on are to be exterminated, without exception. If we do not succeed in destroying the biological foundations of Jewry now, then some day the Jews will destroy the German people.'

Himmler continued with his instructions: because it was located on a major railway line, yet relatively isolated, thus hiding it from prying eyes, he had selected Auschwitz for this important task. He told Rudolf that he wanted to see copies of construction plans within four weeks, and that while he wasn't sure how many people would be sent to the camp, it would probably run into the millions. Normally, he explained, he would not have spoken with inferiors, but he had felt it necessary to talk directly with Rudolf because the task was so critical. He added that he had originally intended to give the task to a higher-ranking officer, but was concerned that this might cause tension with Rudolf, as Kommandant of Auschwitz. He had chosen Rudolf because he had absolute trust in the junior officer's capabilities, as well as his discretion. Concluding the meeting, the Reichsführer said that this was a *geheime Reichssache*, a secret Reich matter, and as such, it must not be discussed with anybody, not even Hedwig. He would receive further instructions from the man in charge of the Jewish deportations, Adolf Eichmann.

Rudolf remembered this meeting clearly.

> In the summer of 1941, when [Himmler] gave me personally the order to prepare Auschwitz to become a site of mass anni-hilations, and then to have those executions carried out, I could

not form the slightest idea of the extent and effects of the kill-ings. Of course, it was an unusual and monstrous order. But the reasoning behind the extermination process seemed to me right. I thought no more of it at the time – I had been given an order, I had to obey it. I could not allow myself to wonder whether or not this mass killing of Jews was necessary.

Rudolf returned to Upper Silesia with mission in hand, but no clear idea how to achieve its objective. He knew he would not be able to kill enough prisoners using Phenol injections, and shooting them would not work either. Not only were bullets expensive but, from his time overseeing the executions in Sachsenhausen, Rudolf had learned that executions have an emotional impact on firing squads – resulting in excessive drinking and increased suicide rates – and therefore could not be scaled up to any large degree.

Part of the solution was found two months later when Rudolf's thirty-nine-year-old deputy, Karl Fritzsch, told him about an experiment which he had recently completed. Fritzsch had thrown some Zyklon B granules – used at the time to exterminate the camp's vermin – into a small cell in Block 11 holding a group of Russian prisoners. After waiting only a few minutes, he had observed that all the prisoners had died. There were two problems, he said. First, only a few prisoners could be killed at a time; and second, they had to carry the bodies out by wheel-barrow, which caused shock and anxiety among the other prisoners. Rudolf suggested that if they used the old crematorium on the other side of the block buildings, and adjacent to the villa where he lived, they would be able to kill more prisoners. There would also be an on-site solution to the problem of disposing of the bodies.

A few days later a second, larger experiment was arranged, this time with nine hundred Russian political prisoners. Jozef Paczynski, Rudolf Höss' Polish barber, happened to be working in Block 4, which was located next to the crematorium. Hearing some commotion outside, Paczynski raced up to the attic to see what was happening. Once there, he climbed onto a box, lifted a roof tile and looked outside. Down below, on the other side of a high wooden fence that surrounded the crematorium, SS guards were politely instructing about five hundred people to remove their clothes, pile them neatly and move towards the old crematorium. It was eerily calm. Within a few minutes the people were pushed into the building and the doors were locked. An SS guard with a gas mask climbed up the side of the building, dropped powder through a hatch in the roof, and then quickly shut it. Paczynski could hear terrible screaming, even through the thick concrete walls. The guards ran the motors of two small trucks to try and hide the cries, but he could still hear them. Eventually, the screaming died down. An hour later the guards opened the doors and, after ventilating the room, went inside. As he didn't see any bodies being removed from the building, Paczynski assumed that they must have been dragged into the furnaces that roared only a few feet from the killing room. Numb with shock, he stepped down off the box and returned to his work in the room below.

Rudolf also witnessed this second experiment. 'I felt disquiet, a kind of shudder of aversion, although I had imagined that death from gas would be much worse.'

Crematorium II, Auschwitz-Birkenau

Rudolf and his men had found a cheap and quick method to kill hundreds of people at one time and, most importantly, when compared to other forms of execution such as shooting, it would insulate the guards from their victims.

There was, however, one more problem. The old crematorium stood just a few feet from two prison blocks. This meant that the gassings could be too easily monitored by the prisoners in the camp. Again the solution seemed obvious to Rudolf. They would kill prisoners in the new Birkenau camp in one of the two old brick farmhouses, the so-called 'little white house' and 'little red house', which stood away from the main Birkenau barracks. He would have the interior walls removed and the outer walls cemented, rendering them leak-proof and ready for use.

Rudolf had now 'solved' the problem handed to him by Himmler: to find a technique for murdering hundreds of thousands, maybe millions, of people. As he later wrote:

Now my mind was at ease.

8

HANNS
LONDON, ENGLAND
1939

On 4 September 1939, Hanns and Paul Alexander took a number 7 bus to the Royal Air Force recruitment office in Acton, west London. Then twenty-two years old, the twins stood in line with the other volunteers. When called, they proceeded to a brief medical examination, at the end of which they were asked for a urine sample, to check that they were not intoxicated and unfit to sign their enlistment papers. Not realising that there were two Alexanders, the nurse became confused about whose bottle was whose, and asked the twins to return to the toilets. After completing that duty, the twins were called in, separately, to meet the military interviewing officer, who asked about their backgrounds and checked their personal details. At the end of the morning Hanns and Paul were told to go home and await their orders.

In a letter to his sister Elsie, written a few days later on the eve of the Jewish New Year, Hanns explained his decision to take up arms against Germany: 'I am sure we are all glad to see that there is still some justice in the world, although it seems to be a justice of force only.' He felt keenly the significance of the times in which they were living, but held out hope for the future: 'This New Year is probably more important for Jews in general and especially for us, than any other New Year ever since the days of Moses. I wish you the spiritual strength, which the Jews have always shown in difficult times, to see through to the better end of things,' to a time when 'the human beings in this world become human in the true sense of the word'.

Hanns' offer to fight for his adopted country was not immediately accepted. The British government was uncertain about how to deal with applications from newly arrived German refugees. Officially it welcomed all who volunteered and were fit for service, but it was wary of taking in men who it feared might pursue espionage or sabotage. It wasn't until December 1939, three months later, that the twins received word regarding their enlistment: Hanns and Paul were to be part of the Auxiliary Military Pioneer Corps and were ordered to report at once. Hanns was given the army number 264280, Paul 264281.

The Auxiliary Military Pioneer Corps had been created on 17 October 1939 to make use of men who were refugees from Germany and elsewhere who wanted to fight Hitler. For these men the stakes were high. If caught by the Reich, they would be viewed as traitors and shot. Yet, of the more than 70,000 German and Austrian refugees who landed in Britain between 1933 and 1939, approximately one in seven enlisted with the Pioneers.

On the morning of 24 January 1940, having said goodbye to their parents, Hanns and Paul travelled by train to Kitchener Camp, two miles from the south coast near the town of Sandwich. Kitchener Camp had been used as a military base during the First World War and, from the previous year, as a transit point for German Jews awaiting permits to America and Palestine. Housed in dilapidated barracks that let in snow through the holes in the roofs, the Pioneers jokingly called the place 'Anglo-Sachsenhausen', after the Berlin camp in which some of them had recently been held. The toilets were equally basic, housed in a long line of sheds joined together with a gully that ran from one end to the other with water flowing through it. A favourite prank was to light a newspaper at one end and let it float along toasting unwary behinds as it went.

On arriving at the camp, the twins were checked by doctors for lice and typhus and handed stiff khaki uniforms. Hanns, Paul and the fifty other German and Austrian recruits now formed the first enemy alien unit from London: 93 Company.

Later that evening, Hanns sent a quick note to his parents. It was written on Pioneer Corps stationery, with its emblem — a crown, a pickaxe, a shovel and a gun — embossed on the top, underneath which was stamped the Corps' motto: '*Labor Omnia Vincit*' ('work conquers all') — eerily similar to the slogan — '*Arbeit Macht Frei*' ('work sets you free') — that hung above the gates at Auschwitz. He wrote: 'Food very good, much lunch. We will gain pounds and stones easily. Just tried on uniform. Everything fits fairly well. So far, nothing to grumble about.' He added that they would not get weekend leave until they had served a full month but they could leave after their duty was complete around 5.30 p.m. He asked them to send tobacco for his Dunhill pipe, as he preferred to keep his money to purchase drinks in the local pubs, and finished with, 'I have never felt happier anywhere. No worries whatsoever.'

The next day, Company 93 lined up in the dusty courtyard in front of the barracks, where a stocky black-bearded sergeant from Vienna asked them to swear allegiance to the King, in German. This request was in accordance with the British Army's tradition of asking foreign soldiers to swear in their own languages to avoid the potential injustice of enlistment without true consent. But Hanns and his brother were outraged, insisting on swearing in English. Lord Reading, the Pioneers' commander, agreed with them and drove to London where he persuaded his superiors that it would be best to follow the refugees' wishes. So it was that the next day the new recruits swore an oath of allegiance in their adopted language, and signed the following waiver:

> I certify that I understand the risks . . . to which I and my relatives may be exposed by my employment in the British Army outside the United Kingdom. Notwithstanding this, I certify that I am willing to be employed in any theatre of war.

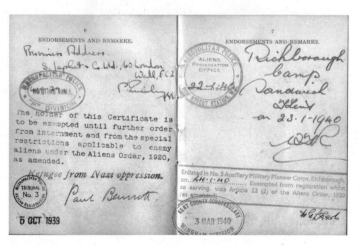

But despite his assurance to his parents, being assigned to a refugee army unit irritated Hanns. By this time he had worked and lived in London for four years and he felt he owed his adopted country his loyalty, even if he had mixed feelings about his new home. In another letter to Elsie, who was missing their old life in Germany, he agreed that England did not yet feel like home: 'Do not think that London is a place of heaven. I don't think it is either.' Yet he felt tied to his new country: 'We are lucky and very fortunate that we are at least living in one and the same country, amongst people that respect us and perhaps even feel a bit with us, in these also for them uneasy times.' Equal to his new allegiance, however, was his anger towards his mother country: 'Although we are told not to hate, I think we are allowed to have some grudge against the people who only want to live, but would not "let live".' He had reason to hate the Germans as much, if not more, than any native Briton, so why could he not be trusted to fight in the regular army? Yet, now that he had enlisted, he would have to do as he was told.

Six companies were raised at Kitchener Camp, numbering around three hundred men. The men were given basic training: taken on runs around the camp, ordered to march in formation – called 'square-bashing' by the men – and taught the basic instructional commands as well as how to polish their boots. There was no gun or rifle practice, for the men of the Pioneer Corps were not to be trusted with weapons. Only the British officers were armed; therefore the entire company's arms amounted to five .303 rifles and five 9mm Smith & Wesson revolvers.

On 11 May 1940, the day after Holland fell to Germany, Hanns and his company arrived in Bruz, France, as part of the British Expeditionary Force. There, they spent the next four weeks performing manual labour – digging ditches, offloading trains and building roads – and, given their lack of arms, hoping to avoid any action.

Then, in June, the German forces pushed into western France, trapping the British around the French port of Dunkirk, and forcing the evacuation of over 300,000 Allied soldiers by a flotilla of public and private water craft. One of the last units to be picked up, Hanns and his company found themselves waiting on the lush grassy racecourse in St Malo, on a hot summer's day. Most of the men had removed their jackets and napped on the ground, while other soldiers played cards in the shade offered by some pollarded willows. Hanns could hear gunfire from the German front line three miles away, and grew increasingly nervous that he would never make it back to England. To make matters worse, his name and place of birth had been written on his identification papers 'Hanns Herman Alexander. Born Berlin, 1917'. If caught, he knew that he would be shot. So Hanns and a few friends lit a bonfire and burnt all their documents. They were now without identity.

When it was finally their turn to go, German troops were already taking possession of the town's suburbs. The Pioneers marched to the boat under a hail of rotten vegetables thrown by St Malo residents, enraged that they were being abandoned to the Germans. 93 Company left the harbour that evening on a sea that was absolutely calm. They were fortunate, for the boat was loaded so high with soldiers that the deck bobbed only inches above the waterline. Sitting cross-legged on the roof of the cockpit, the twins enjoyed a side of roast beef and a bottle of red wine, which they had 'liberated' from a local shop, celebrating their last-minute departure.

Upon arrival in England, the entire 93 Company boarded a train to the site of their new encampment, Alexandra Palace in north London. A few days later, Hanns asked his commanding officer, Lord Reading, if he might change his name to something sounding less German. He did not want to do so officially, by deed poll, he said, in case the Germans were monitoring such changes in the British papers where they were published, but he wanted his army documents to reflect his new identity. Reading thought this a sensible idea and within a few days was able to obtain permission from London. Hanns was then issued a new set of identity papers in the name of Howard Hervey Alexander, the middle name chosen not because of some affinity to unusual English forenames, but because he did not know how to spell 'Harvey'.

Hanns did not view the change as significant. Changing his name was an act of self-preservation. His family continued to call him

'Hanns' and he would forever sign his name 'H. H. Alexander', which worked for both the old and new identities. But the name change would cause some confusion, and from this point on, he would be addressed in a variety of ways, 'Hanns', 'Howard' and 'Alex' being the most common. Paul elected to keep his name, arguing that 'Paul Alexander' sounded sufficiently English.

In early July 1940, Hanns and Paul, who were still serving in the same unit, obtained leave and took a train to the small village of Chalfont St Peter, in Buckinghamshire, to visit their sister Bella. It was a bright summer's day and the family ate lunch outside, sitting at trestle tables that had been set up under a tree. After lunch, Bella's two sons — seven-year-old Peter and four-year-old Tony — showed their uncles a pit in the garden. It was a six-foot-deep hole that had been dug for an Anderson air-raid shelter. The British government had recently advised the nation that air attacks were likely, and Bella had decided it was time to prepare their own family shelter. The men who had been working on it had gone home for the weekend, and seeing an opportunity for a prank, Hanns and Paul grabbed the two young boys, dropped them into the hole and then walked away. At first Peter and Tony thought the lark funny, but when they tried to climb out they found that the hole was just too deep. They called out for help, but nobody came. As the minutes ticked by they became increasingly alarmed and Tony started screaming. Peter, who was extremely fond of both his uncles, did not think the prank funny either. Hanns and Paul did not return to rescue them for twenty minutes.

A few days later, the twins returned to their unit, which was still camped out at Alexandra Palace. From there they were separated. With the British anxious that the Germans were about to invade, Hanns was allotted a series of assignments aimed at bolstering his adopted nation's defences. In Newbury he stocked food supplies for the troops preparing for combat. In Cirencester he cleared a wood that was to be used as a training ground. In Weymouth he fixed the breakwater that protected the nearby naval base in Portland. The work was tedious, frustrating and back-breaking. Yet while it was not what he had imagined when he had enlisted, at least he was doing his duty, and he was able to arrange his leave so that he could return home for the Jewish holidays.

Meanwhile, the other German Jews in England were not so fortunate. In May 1940, the British government, shocked by recent German military victories in France, had introduced a policy of mass internment for refugees who had recently arrived on its shores. Now viewed as potential spies and 'enemy aliens', these refugees were arrested, with the prospect of deportation to the Caribbean, Canada or Australia. Around 27,000 people – all male and mainly Jewish refugees from Nazi oppression – were now rounded up and placed in internment camps, a policy which the prime minister, Winston Churchill, defended by saying that it was necessary to 'collar the lot'.

As privates in the British Army, Hanns and Paul were of course exempt from internment, unlike their poor brother-in-law, Erich Hirschowitz, who had by now adopted the name Harding and was also a refugee from Berlin. On 19 July 1940 Erich was arrested at his place of work and taken to Tottenham Police Station, where, for the first and only time in his life, he spent a night in the cells. The next day he was driven to his small flat in west London, where he gathered a few items and was then loaded onto a coach along with thirty other refugees. Five hours later they arrived at Prees Heath, a hastily erected internment camp near Whitchurch in Shropshire, close to the Welsh border. This 'camp' was, however, no more than a desolate field surrounded by barbed wire. At its centre stood a dozen or so large white canvas tents, open at one end, containing long wooden benches and tables, plus offices, a kitchen and toilets. Conditions at Prees Heath were basic, with no running water and minimal rations.

As soon as they arrived, the internees were told that they could go free if they joined the Pioneer Corps. Erich agonised over whether he should follow his brothers-in-law's lead, and enlist with the British Army. But he wasn't convinced that doing so was the best way to help his adopted country. Elsie agreed, arguing that it was, if anything, Erich's duty to grow his leather business. In one letter Elsie explained how Hanns and Paul were filling their time in the Pioneers:

20 August 1940

Erich,

I hope you are all right and I wish so much to have you back. I saw Hanns this afternoon. He is so busy he can hardly see us. In the morning he played darts, in the afternoon ping-pong. At 5.30 he had a date with a girl, and at 8 with another. Then he is going to Oxford and tomorrow he oversleeps. What a life, they get bored stiff. He telephoned Paul today who is back with the company and waiting for Hanns there, and he too does not know how to fill his days. How very idiotic!

Lots of love, Elsie

Erich was finally released four months later, on 9 November 1940, following the British government's realisation that the German refugees were unlikely to pose any threat. He returned to his family and started working once again in the leather business, sticking to his position that it would be more productive than serving with the Pioneers.

Hanns thought this decision cowardly. But the truth is that no one knew at the time whether it would be Erich or Hanns and Paul who would contribute more to the war effort.

During 1941 and 1942, the Alexanders somehow managed to contact their friends and family in Germany. They received news by letter, which could still be sent through, or by word of mouth, carried by a friend or acquaintance, newly arrived in England.

One person they were all concerned about was the steely Cäcilie Bing. At sixty-nine, Auntie Bing didn't feel she could cope with the adjustment of moving to an English-speaking country. On 11 November 1941, she wrote to her cousin in New York, describing the fate of some she knew, confirming who was alive and asking questions about others she had not heard from. She ended the letter: 'My eyes are growing tired and my hands are shaking so I must finish. I look forward to hearing from you soon. I know that you will provide all the help you can, wishing you all the best . . . Cäcilie Bing.'

The letter made it all the way to America, and then to London, despite being surveyed by the censor. That was the last they had

heard from Auntie Bing. Reports of round-ups, deportations and Nazi concentration camps had started appearing in newspapers in Britain and America earlier that year, indeed Hanns knew that Ann's father had spent some time in Sachsenhausen, and while the details were murky and often contradictory, the idea that Auntie Bing had been taken to one of these places was frightening. Hanns hoped that she was still living in Frankfurt.

Hanns and Paul understood that the only way they were going to be treated with respect by the British Army was to become officers. By the end of 1942 they had spent two years in the army performing little more than manual labour. They had seen as much fighting as their brother-in-law Erich, who continued to sell leather from his workshop in east London. It was then that the twins' applications were finally accepted and they were sent to the Officer Cadet Training Unit in Lincolnshire.

They arrived at OCTU on 3 January 1943. The first four weeks comprised theoretical training. They were taught about field tactics, communications, giving and receiving orders, and, perhaps most importantly, how to discipline those under their command. Then they were faced with 'battle drills and tactics', which meant running through rivers and crawling through mud, sometimes during the night, demonstrating how they might lead while experiencing physical hardship. Hanns told his parents 'we are not looking forward to it but that won't help much. We will try our best but we have both decided that we won't kill ourselves, it is quite strenuous but if the others, who are most of them much older, can do it, why should not we?'

Two months later they graduated and, following the army rule that officer siblings could not serve in the same company, they were again separated, with Paul assigned to the British Army's Northern

Command and Hanns assigned to the Southern. Both now lieutenants, they were delighted to have finally won the respect they felt they deserved, and wore their guns with pride. The newly commissioned officers joined their units, and awaited orders.

It was not until 20 July 1944, that Hanns, now part of 239 Company, finally returned to France as part of the Normandy Landing, the first stage of the Allied ground attack on Germany. Even though he reached French soil six weeks after the first American and British soldiers had fought for control of the Normandy beaches near the small town of Arromanches, the area was still a hub of activity: thousands of soldiers swarmed around the sand on Gold Beach; long lines of men carried supplies from the enormous man-made harbour up the low grassy cliffs a hundred yards from the breaking surf; teams of men, their trousers rolled up above the knee, unloaded tanks and armoured vehicles; troops, who had been living on the beach for some time, ran in formation along the water's edge. By the war's end, this beachhead would act as a gateway for over 2,500,000 soldiers.

Hanns and his company were asked to supervise a small group of German officers who had been captured the day before. They held the POWs in an open field without barbed wire. The only boundaries to this makeshift camp were white anti-mine ribbons that they had strung between some trees. These German Jews, who had been forced out of their homes and were now wearing British uniform, were tasked with controlling their oppressors. It was a strange, awkward situation.

Two weeks after Hanns' arrival in France, Paul's company disembarked onto the beach. Paul immediately started looking for his identical twin. He walked around aimlessly for a few minutes before a private came up to him and saluted.

'Have you seen me recently?' asked Paul.

'Over there,' said the man, pointing down the shore. 'Five minutes ago.'

Paul found Hanns taking part in a parade a few hundred yards down the beach.

'Which one of you is mine?' shouted Hanns' major.

'I am,' said Paul, feeling cheeky.

'You are mine?'

'No, I am,' replied Hanns. The twins hadn't had this much fun since swapping classrooms back in Berlin.

After a few hours together, Hanns and Paul went their separate ways: Paul to Caen, where he was to load and unload railway supplies, Hanns to the medical units that operated out of a sea of enormous cream-coloured canvas tents known as 'Harley Street'. There he was put in charge of the non-medical orderlies, which meant organising the stretcher carriers and scheduling the clean-up crews. His biggest problem was a lack of food and drink. They had packets of dried potatoes, for instance, which were inedible without drinkable water. With so many mouths to feed and an overstretched supply chain, Arromanches was a logistical nightmare. The soldiers on the ground would simply have to make do until the next supply ship arrived.

A few weeks later, Hanns learned that Paul's company was close by and sent word that they should meet in a cafe on the main square of Bayeux, a small town near Arromanches. Hanns was delayed, however, and arrived a little after 7 p.m. He walked past the empty round tables on the street's edge and into the cafe which, though dimly lit, was filled with laughter and smoke; it was Friday night and people were ready to part with the money in their pockets.

With Paul nowhere to be seen, Hanns ordered a beer and asked a British officer standing at the bar if he had seen anybody who looked liked him.

'Yes, I did,' said the officer. 'He left a message. He said he was sorry he had to leave and he'll meet you at seven tomorrow night.'

The officer invited Hanns to drink with his friends at a table in the corner. Hanns sat next to a woman named Jenine, a petite young brunette in a flowery dress that fell to just below her knees.

'*Enchanté*,' he said.

This was one of the four French words he knew. Jenine smiled back and continued her conversation with the person next to her. A few hours later the group staggered back to her house for dinner and Hanns, who had barely exchanged a word with his host all evening, was invited to spend the night.

The next evening Paul was waiting at the agreed time by the bar in the cafe when his twin walked in.

'What happened to you yesterday?' asked Paul.

Hanns apologised for his lateness, and explained what had happened. 'All I had to say was "*enchanté*" to a girl and I slept with her!'

'That's not surprising,' laughed Paul, 'I was chatting her up all afternoon.'

This was September 1944. The Allies now had a foothold on the European continent. Before the war would end they would need to capture the rest of France, Belgium and the Netherlands, and then move into Germany and Berlin. Hanns' war was about to become much more serious.

9

RUDOLF
OŚWIĘCIM, UPPER SILESIA
1942

The first trainload of Jews to be transported to Auschwitz arrived in the spring of 1942. Tired and disorientated by their journey, these men, women and children were taken off the train in Birkenau, where those judged able to work were led away, and the rest were marched six hundred yards to one of the small farmhouses at the back of the camp. Here they were told to undress behind specially erected screens, all the while unaware of the fate that awaited them. On one of the farmhouse doors had been written the words 'Disinfection Room', and towards this the guards directed the prisoners, telling them, with the assistance of interpreters, that they should remember where they had stowed their luggage so that they could locate it after being deloused. Now naked, the prisoners were ushered into the disinfection room, two or three hundred at a time, before the doors were screwed tight. Then guards on the roof dropped two canisters of granulated Zyklon B into the room below. After ten minutes all the prisoners were dead. An hour later, the doors were opened by the *Sonderkommandos* – Jewish prisoners forced to assist with the operations – who pulled gold teeth and rings from the bodies, and piled them high in deep pits next to the farmhouses. With one hundred bodies in each pit, they were set on fire using old bits of cloth doused in petrol. Once the bodies were aflame, additional corpses were added. As they burned, fat from the bodies was collected from the edges of the pit using metal buckets and added to the top of the pile to accelerate the inferno. The fires took seven or eight hours to burn out. Once cooled, any remaining bones were removed by the *Sonderkommandos* and crushed using heavy wooden pestles on flat concrete mortars. The resulting ash was then loaded onto trucks and dumped in the River Vistula a few miles away.

Throughout this process, Rudolf made sure that he was seen as leading by example. He didn't want anyone to believe that he wasn't capable of performing these duties.

> I had to see everything that was being done. Day or night, I had to watch bodies being collected up and burnt, I had to see teeth being broken out, hair cut off, I had to witness all these horrors for hour after hour. I had to stand there myself in the dreadful, sinister stench that arose when mass graves were dug and the bodies burnt. I also, at the request of the doctors, had to look through the peephole into the gas chamber and watch the inmates dying. I had to do all this because everyone looked to me, and it was for me to show them that I not only gave the orders, I was also prepared to be present myself, just as I had to require the men I commanded to be present.

And so, under Rudolf's watchful eye, the mechanism for mass murder was created.

In July 1942, Rudolf drove at Himmler's suggestion four hours northeast of Auschwitz to a camp situated outside the tiny town of Treblinka. Hidden in the remote forests of northern Poland, the camp ran only three hundred yards in one direction and five hundred yards in the other. Here there were no barracks or factories in which prisoners might slave. Treblinka's sole purpose was the extermination of the Jews and other perceived enemies of the state.

When Rudolf arrived, the camp had just received a transport from the Warsaw ghetto. He watched the men, women and children being unloaded from cattle cars and herded through what was known as the 'tunnel': two lines of guards shouting instructions, waving their arms, and beating any disobedient prisoners with the butts of their guns. The prisoners were then forced into a bunker at the other end of the tunnel, where the doors were closed and diesel engine exhaust was piped into the well-sealed space. Once they believed that the prisoners had all died, the guards opened the doors to release the noxious fumes. An hour later, they dragged the bodies outside and dumped them into open pits, where they were later burned.

Rudolf was unimpressed by the crude methods deployed in Treblinka, where 80,000 people had already been killed in the previous six months. The camp's gas chambers were limited to killing two hundred people at a time; there was no easy method for disposing of the bodies; and the camp commander made little effort to deceive the prisoners, resulting in distressing scenes of struggle and resistance. He realised that if he was to handle the numbers soon to arrive at Auschwitz, he must design a more efficient system, which could operate on a grander scale, like a factory, functioning day in and day out, without unduly stressing the guards or the other camp prisoners.

Over the next few months, Rudolf and his team focused on improving their killing methods. Four new crematoria were constructed, purpose-built to handle the larger numbers and situated closer to the railway track. Once these were built, Rudolf ordered Franz Hössler to assemble a team of *Sonderkommandos* and have them dig up the tens of thousands of bodies that had been buried in the mass graves around Auschwitz I camp. They would then transport these corpses to Birkenau, where they were to be burned in one of the new crematoria. Once the task was complete, the *Sonderkommandos* were to be killed and Hössler could help with the next wave of prisoners.

Rudolf and his senior staff now developed a routine of separating the weak from the strong, the young from the old, as they arrived at Birkenau. These 'selections' were to be administered by the camp doctors on the platform as the prisoners came off the trains. As they were unloaded, often exhausted, half starved and terrified after many days of travelling in overcrowded cattle cars, guards carrying machine guns shouted '*Schnell! Schnell!*'; dogs lunged at them baring their teeth and barking menacingly; and a doctor walked up and down the lines, splitting families into groups of men and women, and then into groups of those who would be retained to work as slave labour in the factories, and those who would be sent to the gas chambers. It happened fast. Children were torn from the skirts of their mothers, husbands were pulled away from their wives, brothers from their sisters. If any prisoner disobeyed they were grabbed by the guards, taken a few yards away, and shot.

The 'saved' prisoners were sent to the 'sauna' building, where they were relieved of all their possessions not taken at the platform: the essentials, such as shoes, socks, trousers, shirts, coats, underwear, boots; as well as valuables such as gold, jewellery, watches, luggage, artwork, indeed anything which could later be exchanged for money or freedom. They were then forced to undress, their heads were shaven, and they were pushed into a shower where they were sprayed with delousing chemicals. Still naked, and by now totally degraded, they were funnelled forward to another room, where they were branded on their left upper forearm, using a single needle device that pierced the outline of a serial number onto the skin. The prisoners were then handed ill-fitting prison uniforms – thin black-and-white-striped trousers, a shirt and a hat – and marched in rows of five towards their new barracks, the women to one side and the men to the other.

The 'selected' prisoners were pushed away from the platform and the barracks towards 'bathing houses', where they were told they would take showers and be cleaned of lice. Once inside the cavernous room, they were ordered to undress. The doors were then closed and Zyklon B pellets were thrown into the chambers. In this way more than two thousand prisoners could be murdered at one time. After the killing was over, the *Sonderkommandos* pulled the dead bodies out of the gas chambers and loaded them into the adjacent ovens for burning. All evidence of a struggle was removed before the next group was ushered in. After a given number of such murder and clean-up cycles, the *Sonderkommandos* were themselves rounded up and forced into the gas chambers.

Usually Rudolf would let the junior officers manage the prisoners as they were offloaded from the transports, but sometimes he was required to take an active role. On 23 October 1943, as the latest transport of the sick, the old and the very young from the Belsen concentration camp were being herded into the gas chamber, one of the prisoners, reportedly a beautiful young dancer from Warsaw, began resisting the guards' instructions. She threw her shoe at a guard, grabbed his gun and shot him in the stomach. With two-thirds of prisoners already inside the gas chamber, the final third joined the fight. Suddenly, the *Sonderkommandos* and guards were faced with a few hundred people attacking them with everything that they could lay their hands on. In the ensuing melee, the light fixtures hanging from the ceiling were pulled down and one of the SS guards, who had been sent in to assist the *Sonderkommandos*, was stabbed to death. It was at this point that Rudolf arrived, having been urgently called from his offices in the main camp.

Immediately taking charge, Rudolf ordered that the doors to the chamber be closed and the gas poured in. About ten minutes later, Rudolf and a team of armed guards entered the pitch-black undressing room and, with torches and guns in hand, pushed the remaining prisoners into the corners. Then, one by one, they were taken to an adjacent room in the crematorium and shot.

From time to time some of the guards who were troubled by the gas chambers approached Rudolf, asking if the killings were really necessary. He told them that he had no doubts, as the orders had come directly from Hitler and it was necessary to kill all the Jews in order to keep Germany free from its worst enemy. He later claimed, however, that he did in fact experience significant qualms, which he felt he could not reveal to anyone, least of all to those who worked for him.

> Everyone looked to see what impression scenes such as those described above made on me, how I reacted to them. I was closely watched, everything I said was discussed. I had to exercise great self-control so as not to let any of my personal doubts or my sense of oppression show in my agitation after these experiences. I had to appear cold and heartless while watching things that would go to the heart of anyone with any human feelings. I could not even turn away when emotions that were all too human were aroused in me. I had to watch, unmoved, as mothers went to the gas chambers with their laughing or crying children.

It is impossible to know if Rudolf did indeed feel such doubts. What we do know is that he worked diligently and intelligently to build the means of mass execution and that he eagerly anticipated Himmler's approval.

Until this point, Rudolf had dealt with the horrors of work by compartmentalising his life; no matter how chilling his daytime experiences were, he was able to return to the warmth of his family at night. But any solace that this dual existence afforded evaporated as his work intensified.

At home, I often found my thoughts suddenly occupied with certain procedures, with the killings. I had to go out then. I could no longer bear to sit in my comfortable family circle. And ideas often came to me as I saw our children happily playing, while my wife was overjoyed by the youngest. How much longer, I wondered, will your happiness last? My wife could not explain my gloomy moods to herself, but put them down to my cares at work. On many nights, as I stood where the trains came in, or near the gas chambers or the fires, I could not help thinking of my wife and children.

As had been the case since his childhood, Rudolf found respite with his horses. When he could no longer tolerate his life, he would saddle up and 'ride to banish the terrible images', or creep into the stables at night, finding 'peace there with my beloved horses'.

The killing continued. Between 1940 and 1944 more than 1.3 million prisoners arrived at Auschwitz. Of these some 1.1 million died, of which 1 million were Jews, 75,000 were ethnic Poles, 21,000 were Roma (Gypsies) and 15,000 were Russian prisoners of war.

And his efforts in Auschwitz were recognised by Berlin. On 29 July 1942, a captain in the Reichsführer's office wrote a memo to the SS personnel office, informing them that Rudolf Höss had been promoted to the rank of SS Major. Himmler was pleased with the work of his protégé.

During 1942 the Auschwitz complex was rapidly expanded. The facility now encompassed the two first camps, Auschwitz I and Auschwitz II/Birkenau, along with Auschwitz III/Monowitz, which housed a massive labour camp for the IG Farben rubber plant. In addition more than forty sub-camps sprang up around Auschwitz, most of these satellite sites housing prisoners who worked in local factories. While the gassings dominated the Birkenau camp, there were tens of thousands of prisoners incarcerated in the camps who would never see the crematoria. These men, women and children worked in the nearby factories and, much like any other prison warden, Rudolf found their management challenging.

He developed numerous strategies. He imposed strict discipline throughout the camp, expecting absolute respect for authority, with no tolerance allowed for disobedience. He ordered that all prisoners must work long, arduous hours. This so exhausted the prisoners that it dampened any prospect of rebellion. He even established a brothel, populated by prisoners from the women's camp, which was available to any non-Jewish inmates who deserved a reward.

Perhaps the most intriguing of Rudolf's pacifying strategies was the *Lagerorchester*, or camp orchestra. When he had himself been imprisoned, in the 1920s, Rudolf had learned the value of classical music to calm even the most hardened criminal's mind. He had applied this lesson to Auschwitz, and created an orchestra made up of both professional and amateur musicians. The members of the orchestra were given instruments stolen from other prisoners, and were relocated to a designated Music Block, where both Jews and non-Jews lived together.

The orchestra was split into two, with a symphony orchestra made up of eighty members and a brass band made up of more than 120. Competition for places in these orchestras was fierce, as membership afforded special privileges, such as improved food rations and better sleeping quarters, but most importantly, it usually meant being protected from the gas chambers.

Standing at the front gate of the camp, Rudolf invigilated as the prisoners were marched in neat rows of five to the IG Farben factory, and back again in the evening, as they returned to the camp, heads bowed and barely able to walk. Sitting next to him was the orchestra, whose regular rhythms helped the prisoners march briskly and in step. Despite being poorly dressed and unable to protect their instruments, the musicians played traditional German tunes in all weathers, no matter if it was raining, snowing or blisteringly hot. The orchestra even played during the executions that took place on Sunday evenings.

The other camps under Rudolf's command also had orchestras. One was the Birkenau Women's Orchestra, who not only performed each day at the entrance to their camp, but also gave occasional performances in the SS guardhouse to senior management and visiting dignitaries. It was here that they would play classical pieces, as if nothing was taking place around them: arias from *Rigoletto* and *Madama Butterfly*, 'The Marche Militaire' by Schubert, and 'Tales from the Vienna Woods' by Johann Strauss.

Many of the senior camp officers attended these concerts, including Josef Kramer, who had by now been promoted to lead the Birkenau camp, Josef Mengele, one of the camp doctors, Franz Hössler, the head of the *Sonderkommando* units, Irma Grese, a blonde and blue-eyed twenty-year-old who was the second highest-ranking female guard in the Auschwitz women's camp, and Elisabeth Volkenrath, a twenty-three-year-old who at times ran the women's camp. Rudolf was also present at these concerts.

Remembering all that was on offer within the camp, Rudolf said: 'I really could not complain that life at Auschwitz was boring.'

By this point, Rudolf's family was extremely well cared for. Hedwig described life at the villa as 'paradise' and that 'I want to live here till I die.' With Himmler's approval, she had overseen the villa's renovation: the rooms had been repainted and the kitchen modernised, and artwork and tapestries stolen from the Jewish prisoners upon their arrival at the camp had been hung on the wall. Almost all of the house's furniture was made by camp prisoners. Not stolen were some paintings by Hedwig's brother, Fritz Hensel, showing views of Oświęcim Castle and the Sola River. The parquet floors had been covered with bright carpets and over the windows hung richly coloured curtains embroidered with lace.

Downstairs at the Höss villa, there was a kitchen with a stove and a larder full of provisions. Next to the kitchen was the living room, which contained a sofa, three chairs, two side tables and a standing lamp. Beside that was a dining room, with an elliptical table, which could be extended to seat eight, surrounded by leather chairs. There were also two sideboards with glazed shelves. Rudolf had an office, which could only be accessed from the living room, where he worked at a large desk, the surface of which was covered with family photographs, sealed beneath a transparent plastic cover. The office contained two leather armchairs and a narrow long cupboard, inside which Rudolf stored books, papers and bottles of vodka.

On the first floor, there were three bedrooms and a playroom for the children. In Rudolf and Hedwig's bedroom, there were two beds made of light walnut, a leather armchair big enough to sleep on and a clothes cupboard for each of them. Above their bed hung a large oil painting of a wreath of wild flowers. There were two big dark wooden beds in the guest room, as well as a cupboard and a bookcase. Its walls were covered with wallpaper of light lilac with darker leaves of the same colour. The attic had been converted into three rooms, allowing servants to live in the house and provide prompt service for the family members.

Rudolf and Hedwig tried to maintain some normality in their young children's lives. The four children attended school in the local town of Oświęcim, where Heidetraut became known as the 'Nazi Queen', on account of her father's position and the riches that surrounded them.

Their father would drive them across the fields to the stables, where they visited his horses, feeding them apples and stroking their

coats. He also accompanied them to the kennels, where they petted the dogs. On weekends, Rudolf walked around the house with a sweet-smelling cigar in his mouth, listening to classical music on the family's gramophone. At other times the family would just sit in the living room, with Rudolf quizzing the children about their days and events at school, or reading to them from one of his favourite children's books, such as *Max und Moritz*. On special occasions Rudolf took them rowing on the Sola River. At Christmas, the children put on their coats, scarves and hats, and, wrapped in heavy woollen blankets, were then taken by horse and sledge across the snowy fields to a Christmas show in one of the local villages. There, they revelled in the religious wonder of a nativity play, or sang Christmas carols. On the way home the children, once again bundled up under the blankets, kept warm by drinking from steaming mugs of hot cocoa and snuggling up to their mother and father.

These were happy, lazy moments, snatched from the relentless pressure of Rudolf's hectic work schedule. Yet such moments were rare, and Rudolf regretted not spending more time with his family, always believing that there was more work to be done: 'I have always made life harder for myself than it really was because of this very strong sense of duty.'

While the Höss children may not have noticed the gas chambers, their mother was aware of the mass murder occurring on the other side of her garden wall. Rudolf recalled that she once overheard a local party administrator talking about the extermination programme. Hedwig apparently became very upset at the news and when she asked Rudolf if what she had heard was true, he explained in the same way that Himmler had laid it out for him: that the Jews were a threat to their civilisation, that they must be exterminated, and if the Reichsführer had ordered it, then it must be done.

Hedwig appears to have had a mixed reaction. On the one hand, she felt comfortable enough with her husband's work to continue living next to Auschwitz, a fence away from the horrors of the crematorium. Indeed, to a certain degree, she agreed with Himmler's views, once saying in her garden that the Jews 'must disappear from the face of the earth to the last man'. On the other hand, Rudolf claimed that Hedwig became deeply distressed when she found out about the mass murder taking place within the camp. It was because of this, he said, that Hedwig stopped having sex with him. More likely, it was because Rudolf was turning his attentions elsewhere.

In the spring of 1942, an attractive woman named Eleanor Hodys began working at the Höss villa.

Eleanor was a thirty-nine-year-old non-Jewish-Austrian prisoner who had arrived in Auschwitz two months earlier, having been found guilty of forging a Nazi Party membership card. When Hedwig had needed help mending the carpet in the villa's hall, Eleanor, who was a skilled seamstress, was brought in to fix it.

She spent two days on her hands and knees, working slowly and carefully at the repairs. Every few hours Rudolf walked by. At one point he stopped to ask if her name was Hodys. When she replied 'yes', he retorted that she should not be working in his house as she was a political prisoner, but since Hedwig liked her, she could stay.

Eleanor's next few weeks were busy with a variety of projects at the villa: mending a torn tapestry that hung on the wall, repairing a hole in a silk cushion and darning a wool rug for the Kommandant's car. She still slept in the camp, but was now able to eat in the family kitchen with the other staff, where she was given food which camp prisoners could only dream of: pastries, cakes, meat, soups, fruit salad and coffee. The food, she thought, was as fine as anything that could have been enjoyed in a good hotel before the war.

After her first few visits to the Höss villa, Eleanor became aware of Rudolf's interest in her. His attentions weren't restricted to the family home, for he soon began seeking her out in the camp, cracking jokes and telling her stories to make her laugh. Even though she realised the danger, she found herself oddly attracted to him. When she first met Rudolf she was living with three other women in one of the red-brick prison blocks, but in time she was given her own room in Block 4 and told that she could decorate it as she pleased. She was also allowed cigarettes, which prisoners were strictly forbidden. She was even permitted the extraordinary privilege of spending occasional nights in the nearby town, where she was waited on by her own maid and cook.

In May 1942, Eleanor found herself alone in the house with Rudolf. He had walked up close without her noticing and kissed her on the lips, so frightening Eleanor that she locked herself in the toilet. It was impossible to have a relationship with Rudolf: not only was he married but he was also the Kommandant. She resolved never to return to the Höss villa.

Yet simply keeping her distance was not enough. In September 1942, Eleanor was called back to the villa, where Hedwig formally dispensed with her services. Two weeks after that, Eleanor was arrested and placed in Block 11, the dreaded interrogation block, for an infraction that allegedly had taken place at the house. After writing and pleading her innocence to Hedwig and Rudolf, she was released temporarily only to be detained again, in Block 11. She was put in cell 24, given a bed, a mattress, a table and a stool. She was allowed to read and write as well as to smoke, and was reassured to a degree by these few small luxuries granted her.

Then, nine days before Christmas, at eleven o'clock at night, a man entered her cell. Lying on her mattress in the dark she hadn't heard the door being opened, and assumed it was one of the guards.

'What is going on?' Eleanor said angrily.

'Pst,' came a quiet voice, as the intruder flicked a lighter which illuminated his face. It was Rudolf.

'What's wrong?' she asked, scared.

'You're coming out,' he said.

She thought he had come to let her out of the cell. 'Now? At once?'

'Shh. Be very quiet, we'll talk it over,' he said, sitting down at the end of her bed.

Rudolf edged up the bed and tried to kiss her. She pushed him away and made a threatening noise. Rudolf told her to be quiet for fear of attracting attention. Nobody knew he was there, he said, since he had stolen through a door in the villa's garden wall and let himself in. He tried to kiss her again, this time more gently, but again she pushed him away. Rudolf pulled back saying he would return another day. When she heard this Eleanor seemed to relent, but begged 'please, not during the night'. Taking this as a positive sign, Rudolf said goodnight, walked out and locked the cell door.

Not long after this encounter Rudolf returned to her cell, where they talked for two hours about her life and family. He didn't share his personal story. She again resisted his advances, and he left in a bad mood. Eleanor was then moved to another cell, number 6, which could be unlocked from the inside. Soon after, they had sexual intercourse for the first time.

A few days later Rudolf returned to Eleanor. As they were lying in bed, an alarm went off in the camp. With the lights flickering on in the hall outside, Rudolf hid himself in the corner of the cell behind the door, fearful of discovery by his own staff, as Eleanor stashed his uniform under the bed. One of the guards walked up to the door, opened the cover to the spyhole, looked through, didn't see anything suspicious, and walked away. Once everything was quiet, Rudolf quickly dressed and went outside, only to return a few moments later, worried that he would bump into someone in the camp who might ask awkward questions about his presence at that hour. He stayed with Eleanor until after one in the morning.

These encounters with Eleanor put Rudolf at tremendous risk. Not only were they contravening the official SS rules, but they were also a violation of the oath he had sworn to himself as a teenage soldier in Palestine. Nevertheless, he continued to visit Eleanor in cell 6. In all, Eleanor and Rudolf had sex four or five times.

During one of the visits Rudolf asked what she would do if anyone found out about their affair. Eleanor promised silence. He pushed her and said that if the authorities presented evidence against her, then she should relent and say that she had been visited by a prisoner, not the Kommandant. He went even further, handing her a pen and paper and, under the dim glow of a torch, telling her to write that she'd had an affair with a Kapo. Once she had signed her name, he placed the paper into a leather book and put it in his pocket.

In February 1943, while still in cell 6, Eleanor became violently sick. She was taken to see one of the camp physicians, who examined her and said she was pregnant. He told her she was eight weeks along, and asked her who the father was. Refusing to answer, she pleaded with him to keep the matter quiet. She also asked for help with the pregnancy and the next day a prisoner passed her a couple of pills through the cell window. When she took one she suffered excruciating stomach pains. She threw the other pill away.

A few days later, Eleanor was moved to another cell, deep in the basement of the prison block. This cell was airless, dark and small. Having just enough room to stand, she found it easier to remain on her knees. Here she was kept naked and whenever she cried the guard threw water on her. In the darkness, she could feel a dead body lying on the floor beside her. She was unable to wash and was given meagre rations of bread and coffee. Every fourth day she received a small amount of cooked food. When she asked for clothes the guard called her an 'old cow' and a 'hysterical goat', expressing surprise that she hadn't yet died.

Eleanor was not released until 16 June 1943. She was six months pregnant at the time. On Rudolf's instructions she was taken to the hospital block where a doctor performed an abortion on her. Eleanor was then sent to work in a camp kitchen. She was in and out of hospital for the rest of that year.

Shortly thereafter, Rudolf received an unwelcome guest, Maximilian von Herff, who ran Himmler's personal office. A man with tremendous political power, Herff was in Auschwitz to assess the state of the camp and, in particular, to see what improvements the Kommandant had made since Himmler's last visit. Rudolf need not have worried, for Herff wrote a favourable report to Himmler on 25 July summarising his findings:

> Camp Kommandant SS-Obersturmbannführer Höss:
> Of good soldierly appearance, athletic, horseman, knows how to behave in every situation, quiet and simple, yet sure of himself and objective. He does not push himself forward, but rather his actions speak for him.
>
> H. is not merely a good commander, but also in the field of concentration camp management he has done pioneer work with new ideas and new methods in educational training. He is

a good organiser as well as a good farmer and the model German pioneer for the Eastern territory.

H. is absolutely capable of holding leading positions in the field of concentration camp management. He is particularly efficient when confronted with practical questions.

Five days after Herff sent his report to Himmler, Rudolf received a cable from Richard Glücks authorising the next shipment of Zyklon B. The extermination programme was to continue without hindrance.

As the summer of 1943 came to a close, Rudolf was at the pinnacle of his Kommandant career: he oversaw a network of camps that housed over 80,000 people, manned by over one thousand guards. He had constructed the most effective killing machine in human history, capable of murdering over four thousand people a day. His wife was able to enjoy the benefits of such a position: entertaining the most powerful men in the land in her lavishly appointed home.

Rudolf had begun to fulfil Himmler's most sacred order, the Final Solution of the Jewish Question. For now, his superiors were very pleased.

10

HANNS
NORMANDY, FRANCE
1945

As early as 1942, eyewitness accounts of the atrocities taking place in Germany and Poland were filtering back to the Allied Powers. On 10 August 1942, an unclassified telegram was passed from the consul general in Geneva to the Department of State in the United States – which had joined the war eight months earlier – and the Foreign Office in London:

> Receiving alarming reports stating that, in the Führer's Head-quarters, a plan has been discussed and is under consideration, according to which all Jews in countries occupied or controlled by Germany numbering three and a half to four million should after deportation and concentration in the East be exterminated at one blow in order to resolve once and for all the Jewish Question in Europe. Action reported planned for autumn methods under discussion including prussic acid.

At first, reports of Nazi persecution against civilian populations had been discounted as little more than vague and unsubstantiated rumours. But by the middle of 1943, the reports had grown in both volume and credibility so that they could no longer be ignored: German and French Jews had been rounded up, loaded on trains and sent to the east; the Warsaw Jews had been forced into a ghetto, subjected to beatings and starvation, and then transported to concentration camps; Jews in Belarus, Russia and Ukraine had been marched out of their villages, shot en masse and pushed into giant pits.

In October 1943, Britain, the Soviet Union and the United States, along with the governments in exile, had established the United Nations War Crimes Commission. They agreed that this body would compile a list of war criminals and receive evidence submitted by member states. After hostilities ceased, anyone suspected of committing an atrocity would be arrested and tried. A joint statement signed by Churchill, Stalin and Roosevelt declared: 'Most assuredly the three Allied Powers will pursue them to the uttermost ends of the earth and will deliver them to their accusers in order that justice be done.'

Now that the Allies had delegated the matter to an international organisation, minimal effort was directed to establishing a comprehensive war crimes policy. There was little appetite to explore post-war issues, including the capture or prosecution of war criminals, when victory was not yet assured.

Then, in early 1944, a report landed on government desks in London, Moscow and Washington, stating that thousands of Jews were being gassed in Nazi-run concentration camps in Poland. In response, on 24 March 1944, President Roosevelt issued a statement to the press: 'In one of the blackest crimes of all history — begun by the Nazis in the day of peace and multiplied by them a hundred times in time of war — the wholesale systematic murder of the Jews of Europe goes on unabated every hour.' Adding that 'All who knowingly take part in the deportation of the Jews to their death in Poland, or Norwegians and French to their death in Germany, are equally guilty with the executioner. All who share the guilt shall share the punishment.'

Yet the public pronouncements and extensive media coverage did little to solve the many practical questions facing the Allies: what constituted a 'war crime'? How many people could realistically be brought to justice? And which specific individuals should be targeted? Some argued that only the higher echelons of the Third Reich should be tried; others argued this was not fair. After all, how could the head of the Ministry of Transport be as guilty as the heads of the armed forces? Then there was the question of what was to be done with the criminals once caught: should they be shot or tried according to Western law? And if a trial, where should it be held – in one of the Allies' capital cities or in the country where the crimes were committed?

On 30 August 1944, the United Nations War Crimes Commission held its first press conference. Each day had brought new stories of Nazi terror and abuse, and the public was clamouring to know what action the Allies planned to take. The press conference was an unmitigated disaster. Sir Cecil Hurst, chairman of the commission, was asked by a journalist whether Adolf Hitler was on the list of war criminals. He tried to avoid the question, but when pushed was unable to answer. Another journalist asked how many people were on the list. 'The list of war criminals is not a very long one,' said Hurst. 'It is meagre.'

As the war neared its close, the Allies' efforts to compile lists of war criminals increased. Memos started flying back and forth between the headquarters of Britain – via the various Polish, French and Belgian governments in exile – and the United States. Finally, it was agreed that the list of war criminals should include any person responsible for an act of violence committed since 30 January 1933. This was a huge departure from the narrow definition of crimes committed against Allied forces, which had been the operating assumption the year before, and could, if interpreted literally, result in over a million people being charged in post-war Germany.

In order to narrow the list down, the Allies created a database of alleged war criminals. This tool, known as CROWCASS – the Central Registry of War Criminals and Security Suspects – contained three tiers of suspects: the first was a list of wanted men; the second those detained for specific crimes; and the third a list of POWs. The first list produced more than 100,000 names, but it was out of date and did not include the perpetrators' alleged crimes.

A separate priority list of 165 high-profile war criminals, including Adolf Hitler, Oswald Pohl and Hermann Göring, was also created. And although there were obvious omissions on the list – Richard Glücks' name was absent, as were those of Dr Enno Lolling and Adolf Eichmann – Rudolf Höss had made it onto the list.

> HESS [sic] SS STUBF. 38 [born 1906]; 1m80; 78 kgs; dark
> blond; CO of AUSCHWITZ Concentration Camp. War Crim-
> inal.

Though they had misspelled his name, and got his position, age, height and weight wrong, at least Rudolf had been listed.

By the start of 1945, however, neither the Americans nor the British were fully prepared to run full-scale war crimes investigations. The Americans planned to deploy fewer than two hundred people – including investigators, lawyers, evidence-gatherers and clerical staff – only a small percentage of whom had any investigative experience or spoke German.

The British were even less ambitious. They intended to assemble three investigative teams, totalling no more than forty people, only twelve of whom had any prior investigative experience. But even these paltry plans failed to materialise. In April 1945, less than a month before the war's end, the British pushed eastwards across Germany and began to capture towns and factories; they had no war crimes teams in place to handle the interrogations of captured guards, let alone to track down the Nazi Party leaders who had fled into hiding.

Britain's war crimes strategy radically changed when, on 15 April 1945, their troops entered the Belsen concentration camp. Appalled by what they found, they immediately dispatched reports to headquarters detailing the condition of the prisoners and the need for investigators to interview the captured guards. The British were still in the throes of formulating their war crimes response and did not have a war crimes team in place to send to Belsen. Their solution was to find a team of twelve suitable men – four investigators, four interpreters and four assistants – who would spearhead Britain's war crimes response.

The first task was to select them.

In early 1945, Hanns was working as his commander's adjutant in a newly created Allied headquarters in Normandy. Meanwhile, Paul's company had been put in charge of managing German prisoners of war, picked up during the Allies' push eastwards. In his spare time, Paul dabbled in the black market, purchasing cheap French perfume, blackberry brandy and women's clothing, selling some for profit and sending the rest to his sisters. All parcels mailed home had to be signed off by the company commander and, luckily for Paul, this responsibility fell to his brother.

In a letter to Elsie and Erich, Hanns wrote about the privileges that his new post afforded. He slept on a bed in the barracks rather than outside in a muddy tent. He had to wake at seven and work till late at night, but spent most of his time writing letters home, 'although they don't like to see me in front of all my letters, but they will have to get used to it'. He also thanked the family for the razor blades they had sent, but asked for extra flints so that he could light his pipe.

Hanns then updated his sister and brother-in-law on the situation with Ann. They had kept in touch during his early Pioneer Corps days, and since 1943 had met up when Hanns was back on leave. By 1945, she was looking for a commitment, but he wasn't ready. They had spent less than two weeks together during the past two years and his mind was more focused on getting home than setting up a home. As a compromise, she had suggested that they become engaged without an agreed wedding date, even though he was overseas. 'I think if she keeps on arguing very much longer I'll give way,' he wrote. 'I like her very much indeed, but somehow it all seems very unfair and selfish on my part.'

Paul also thought that Hanns was being unfair to Ann. In a letter to Elsie, he wrote that Ann 'quite rightly in my opinion wants to know where she stands and at least get engaged now. I think personally it is only fair to her, and as she will always be self-sufficient, why not.' He suggested that Elsie 'better talk things over with Ann, and find out carefully what our parents would say, and hint something to Hanns'.

Elsie's reply to Hanns, however, carried only more troubling news from home. Dr Alexander had suffered a mild heart attack. Hanns wrote back immediately: 'I am naturally worried and look forward to every letter. I am in constant contact with Paul as his mail seems to be chasing him around the countryside.' Given that the war effort was coming to a head, Hanns knew that it was unlikely that either of them would be given leave, so they both applied for compassionate leave. Their applications were turned down.

Two weeks later Hanns received another letter from Elsie in which she said that their father was feeling better and that it was no longer necessary for him to return. Hanns replied that he was grateful that she and her sister were in England to take care of their parents, but he wished he were there to help. 'Army life is hard enough as it is but when you can't go home when something goes wrong it is bloody awful. But I am afraid that all the grumbling in the world won't help.'

His father's health scare had shaken Hanns, a reminder that he was far from his family and that he wasn't in control of his life. The only hope was that the war would soon end, but he realised that this was unlikely. 'I suppose it is possible but somehow I can't imagine Jerry asking for an armistice. If we have to fight through and for every town it will take a hell of a time yet.' Most of all he wanted to return to England, find a job and resolve matters with Ann. 'Personally I don't mind if I get sent home tomorrow, I have had enough.'

Another matter troubling Hanns was his long-term future. Still officially stateless, he was eager to find out if Britain would offer him and his brother citizenship. In a letter to his parents, he reported a conversation with the officer responsible for the welfare of Pioneer Corps soldiers. Hanns had asked 'a few questions which every one of our men want answered': would they be offered naturalisation when they returned from active duty? What arrangements were being made for Pioneer Corps members after the war? Could their families remain in Britain? Hanns was not reassured when he was told that no arrangements had been made and 'there is nothing to worry about'. Hanns wrote, 'It is no use to say there is no Jewish problem in England. There damned well is.'

But at the end of April 1945, Hanns' personal problems took a back seat. For he received orders to report to the British headquarters based at the Brussels suburb of Uccle. The British had chosen the members of their first ever war crimes investigation team, and on the list was the name Howard Hervey Alexander.

II

RUDOLF
BERLIN, GERMANY
1943

In the spring of 1943, Heinrich Himmler was anxious about the
corruption endemic in the concentration camps, and particularly
about gold flowing into private hands – something expressly forbidden
by the Reichsführer – which should have been delivered to the country's war coffers. In order to determine the extent of the problem
he appointed SS judge Konrad Morgen to investigate the camps.

Konrad Morgen was an intriguing choice. The thirty-three-year-old
son of an engine driver, who had studied law in his home town of
Frankfurt, Morgen was known as a pacifist and an independent thinker.
At the start of the war he had been appointed as an SS judge, but his
determination to seek out the truth soon earned him some powerful
enemies, and in 1942, following a lengthy investigation into criminal
corruption within the SS, he was demoted and sent to the Eastern Front.
For his tenacity he had earned the nickname the 'Bloodhound Judge'.

Morgen immediately visited the German camps of Dachau, Sachsenhausen and Buchenwald. Within a few weeks he had built sufficient
evidence to instigate criminal proceedings against more than eight
hundred members of the SS, and had arrested the Kommandant of
Buchenwald, Karl Koch. It was clear that Himmler was sincere about

stamping out camp corruption and that his appointee was taking his job seriously.

When he had first received Himmler's orders, Morgen had been unaware of the gassings taking place in Auschwitz or at the other camps. That soon changed after a visit to Treblinka, where he was told by Kommandant Christian Wirth that thousands of Jews were being gassed weekly, and these killings were taking place on Himmler's specific instructions. The vast piles of wristwatches and foreign currency were enough to convince the young judge of the Kommandant's account. At the end of their meeting, Wirth suggested that Morgen should investigate an extermination camp based near the town of Auschwitz which was run by a certain Rudolf Höss, a man whom Wirth described as Himmler's 'untalented disciple'.

For a while, Morgen was unable to find a reason to visit Auschwitz. A few weeks after his return from Treblinka, however, the Berlin Customs Department had intercepted a package containing two kilos of dental gold sent home by an Auschwitz medic. This was evidence enough for Morgen.

In the late summer of 1943, Morgen arrived at Oświęcim station and was driven straight to the camp to see Rudolf. The judge presented his credentials and, unusually given the secrecy surrounding the camp, he was to be granted full access to the entire facility. Rudolf had no choice, since Morgen had Himmler's backing. He offered to help the investigative judge in any way he could and provided him with a junior officer to show him around the camp.

A short while later, Morgen found himself sitting in a car next to the railway platform, close to the camp's entrance, when a transport of prisoners arrived. He watched as a guard ordered the prisoners off the train. Then the camp doctor walked up and down the line, methodically 'selecting' the sick, the old and the children for the gas chamber. The victims were then told to climb aboard some nearby trucks, which Morgen and his driver followed out of the camp and

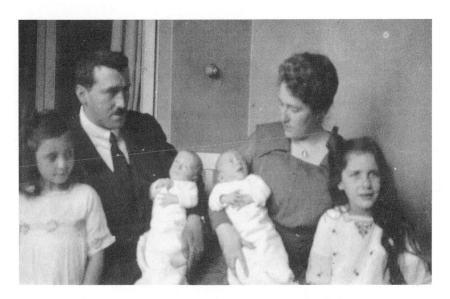

Alfred and Henny Alexander with Bella, Hanns, Paul and Elsie, 1917

Hanns and Paul, *circa* 1920

Fasanenstrasse Synagogue after Kristallnacht, 1938 (Yad Vashem)

Paul and Hanns in British Army Pioneer uniforms
with their mother, Henny, 1940

Rudolf Höss poses for a photograph with his family in the Auschwitz villa, 1943.
Anticlockwise from left: Inge-Brigit, Hedwig and Annagret, Hans-Jürgen,
Heideraud, Rudolf and Klaus
(Institut für Zeitgeschichte, München/Rainer Höss)

The barn in Gottrupel where Rudolf Höss was hiding. Photo taken *circa* 1909
(Geminde Handewitt/Jan Kirschner)

Rudolf Höss under British arrest, March 1946
(Yad Vashem)

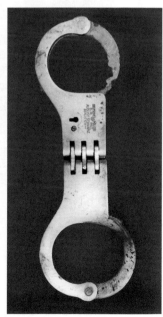

The handcuffs worn by
Rudolf Höss on his arrest
(Intelligence Corps Museum,
Chicksands)

The execution of Rudolf Höss, Auschwitz, April 1947
(Polish Press Agency)

Hanns and Ann's wedding day, London, May 1946
(Paul Graetz and Alfred Alexander stand behind them)

Reading the Alexander Torah in Belsize Square Synagogue, London, 2001
Paul reading (left) and Hanns watching (right)

along a narrow road for a few miles. Eventually, the trucks stopped, and the prisoners were again unloaded and told to enter long buildings that looked like large bathing rooms. Morgen was shocked when the driver explained that these were in fact gas chambers connected to crematoria. The driver went on to explain that after the gassing was complete, *Sonderkommandos* were sent into the chambers and, before dragging the bodies to the crematoria, they pulled the gold teeth from the victims.

Morgen was then driven to the SS guardhouse in Auschwitz-Birkenau. There he was astonished to see guards lazing around on couches, staring blankly as if high on drugs. In one corner of the guardhouse, four or five beautiful young Jewish women cooked potato pancakes on a stove and waited on the guards like slaves. In one of the guardhouse lockers Morgen discovered gold jewellery, pearl rings and stacks of foreign money.

Over the next few days the judge travelled around the camp, talking to the guards, officers and doctors. He learned that in addition to the organised mass execution of prisoners, thousands of others had been routinely and unofficially killed, the vast majority of whom were Polish and Russian inmates who had been shot against the wall between Block 11 and Block 12. He also discovered that Maximilian Grabner, the head of the Auschwitz Political Department which oversaw camp discipline, had been responsible for the unauthorised killing of more than two thousand prisoners.

Morgen returned to the main camp and once again met with Rudolf. He asked about the extermination facilities, and wondered how word of the mass killings hadn't spread back to Berlin or overseas. Rudolf said that secrecy was critical to running the camp and went on to disclose one of their deceptive tricks: Jewish prisoners with good connections abroad were forced to write to their contacts saying that they were alive and that there was nothing wrong with the conditions in Auschwitz. Asked about the corruption and immorality in the camp,

Rudolf said that while he was aware of some problems, they were limited to the junior staff.

Back in Berlin, Morgen presented his findings to two of the highest-ranking members of the SS, both of whom reported directly to Himmler: Ernst Kaltenbrunner, who headed the Reich Security Main Office, and Oswald Pohl, Richard Glücks' boss, who headed the Economic-Administrative Main Office, and was responsible for all the concentration camps. He told them about the shocking stories he had heard from Wirth in Treblinka and the terrible scenes that he himself had witnessed in Auschwitz. His superiors feigned shock and gave him vague promises of further investigations. Realising the futility of any attempt to stop the killings, Morgen instead pursued a legal strategy, writing a report that concentrated on the corruption epidemic among the guards and the unauthorised executions he had uncovered at Auschwitz.

Himmler was displeased with Morgen's findings and instructed the SS judge to arrest those involved with the unauthorised killings and the gold smuggling. Meanwhile, Martin Bormann – who had heard about the report – wrote to Himmler urging that Rudolf be protected. He had not forgotten that Rudolf had taken the fall for his part in the Walter Kadow murder in the mid 1920s. A short while later, Himmler placed a call to Rudolf in Auschwitz. It was a tense conversation.

Referring to Morgen's report, Himmler told Rudolf that his command of Auschwitz was no longer tenable. Rudolf's initial reaction was negative: 'At first I found it painful to tear myself away from Auschwitz, for the very reason that all my problems there, the short-comings of the camp and the many difficult tasks I faced had brought me very close to it.' He also worried about Hedwig, who would be devastated to leave their luxurious villa. She had recently given birth to their fifth child, on 20 September 1943, a daughter whom they named Annegret. Then he realised that the change might actually be good for him, for 'after nine years of working in concentration camps, three and a half of them in Auschwitz, I had really had enough'.

Rudolf asked that he be allowed to fight on the Eastern Front, but Himmler refused. He wanted Rudolf to continue working in the concentration camp system; it would be a waste to send such an experienced officer to the front line. Finally a compromise was struck: Rudolf would take up a desk job at the Concentration Camp Inspectorate, the bureaucracy that managed all the Nazi concentration camps and which was based in Sachsenhausen, while Hedwig and the family would stay in the Auschwitz villa. Though he wasn't keen to work in an office, and he certainly didn't want to be away from Hedwig and the children, Rudolf realised that he had been lucky to escape a far worse fate – prison, torture, possibly even execution.

In the meantime, Konrad Morgen continued his detective work, hoping that, with Rudolf Höss' imminent departure from Auschwitz, the mass murder would slow down. Given time and a little more investigation work, he might even be able to put the soon-to-be former Kommandant on trial. After all, if Himmler had followed the recommendations of Morgen's Auschwitz report, there was no reason to believe that he wouldn't do so again.

On 1 December 1943, Rudolf returned to Sachsenhausen, the camp on the outskirts of Berlin, where he started his new job as chief of *Amtsgruppe D1* (First Division of Department D) of the Concentration Camp Inspectorate.

Rudolf was now responsible for overseeing the stores, security, motor transports, arms and prisoner punishments (including executions) for all the concentration camps, including Auschwitz, Belsen, Dachau and Sachsenhausen. He would work directly under Richard Glücks, who had been so unhelpful during Rudolf's early days in Auschwitz. Glücks had proven resistant to the prospect of having

Rudolf back in Berlin, but his protests had been overruled by Oswald Pohl. Rudolf was now only three steps away from the Reichsführer himself.

Amtsgruppe D's highly secretive offices were housed in the T-building – so named because of its shape – just outside Sachsenhausen's perimeter walls. Then fifty-four years old, Richard Glücks had run the organisation since 1939. He was a man who looked at everything from the bright side of life, cracking jokes about even the worst instance of brutality and, according to Rudolf, was incapable of remembering details or of making decisions. Glücks worked on the second floor of the T-building in an enormous high-ceilinged private office, with a red-tiled marble floor and two balconies that offered extensive views of the town of Oranienburg. From this office, Glücks was tasked with managing the Nazis' extensive network of concentration camps.

In an act of petty office politics, Glücks had assigned Rudolf a small viewless room at the end of the corridor on the ground floor. This was as far as Rudolf could be from Glücks while still working within the same building. His new accommodation was infinitely worse than the rambling administrative complex he had managed back in Auschwitz. Across the corridor worked Rudolf's four immediate staff, men named Wehner, Sug, Pallasch and Unger, who together ran *Amtsgruppe D1*. Two floors above Rudolf was the office of Gerhard Maurer, deputy to Glücks, who ran the second division of *Amtsgruppe D,* overseeing the organisation of prison labour in the camps. Maurer had a great deal of energy and a sharp eye for detail. Whenever Rudolf wanted to sidestep Glücks he would pass a message to Maurer who would then, in turn, relay it to Oswald Pohl. Also on the same floor as Maurer and Glücks, in office number 95, was Enno Lolling who ran the third division of the *Amtsgruppe D*, which was responsible for the organisation's doctors and medical units, including the medical experiments that took place in the camps. It was Lolling who had, in 1941, ordered that the weak prisoners — particularly children and those with incurable mental illness — be 'euthanised' by injecting Phenol directly into the heart. It was also Lolling who, a few days before Rudolf's arrival at the T-building, had delivered a collection of prisoners' tattooed skins to his superiors as a 'thank-you' present for a recent promotion. Lolling was only fifty-five but already looked like an old man after years of morphine and alcohol abuse.

Departmental meetings were held in a large conference room near Glücks' second-floor office. The room had windows on three sides, and its wood-panelled walls were covered with a square motif that mirrored similar designs on the green-and-white tray ceiling. It was here, around tables set out in a U-shaped formation, that the Final Solution was planned in detail; decisions that would determine the fate of millions.

Rudolf's loathing for Glücks increased with proximity. He viewed his superior as a deskbound weakling and as a man who refused to do anything without permission. Glücks was someone who didn't like to visit the camps, and if forced to go, chose to sit in the officer quarters talking about anything except the issues that worried the Kommandants.

> He was at a loss when faced with the most difficult situations in all the camps — and generally left it to the camp kommandants to deal with them. 'Don't ask me so many questions!' was his usual response at meetings of the kommandants. 'You know much more about it than I do!'

Glücks became disorientated when Himmler called him and would try to avoid seeing him. When faced with meeting the head of the SS, he would become withdrawn and uncommunicative in the days before. He was obsessed with prisoner escapes, which had to be reported to Himmler in person. As a result, each morning Glücks asked Rudolf, 'How many have broken out of the camp?' Similarly, Glücks' response to any of Rudolf's requests was, 'Do whatever you like, so long as it doesn't reach Himmler's ears.'

Although there was plenty of paperwork from the various concentration camps stored in his office, Rudolf soon discovered that it was impossible to discern what was actually going on inside each of these facilities. There were long lists of what food was being consumed, how many blankets were shipped, the number of guards on duty and the volume of transports that arrived each day. But as to the day-to-day activities of the guards, the health of the prisoners or the hygiene conditions within the camps, there was little information available.

Oswald Pohl suggested that Rudolf visit the camps – something his predecessors had gone out of their way to avoid – to ascertain their condition. Rudolf spent the first few weeks of 1944 on a grand tour of Germany and Poland, becoming increasingly disturbed at what he found. The camps were overcrowded and lacked basic sanitation. Prisoners were forced to work long hours in extremely harsh conditions with little food or water. More than 10,000 Jewish inmates had died or been killed on a forced march from Auschwitz to labour in a local munitions factory. Rudolf concluded that those running the camps were failing to use prison labour effectively in support of the war effort.

Returning to Berlin, he set about issuing a series of orders to improve the efficiency of the concentration camps.

While Rudolf was toiling away at the Concentration Camp Inspectorate, his superiors remained focused on accelerating the liquidation of European Jewry.

On 20 March 1944, the day after the German Army had rolled into Hungary, Adolf Eichmann arrived in the capital, Budapest. There he met with the Hungarian leaders and discussed the rapid deportation of the country's 800,000 Jews.

The plan was for the Hungarian government and its police force to round up all the Jews over the next three months, starting in the countryside and then moving on to the cities. They would then load the prisoners onto trains: sixty-five people per car, forty-five cattle cars per train, four trains per day, totalling some 12,000 Jews each day. The trains would then travel north three hundred miles through Czechoslovakia, into Poland and on to the camp at Auschwitz.

In order to handle this massive influx, the facilities at Auschwitz would have to be upgraded, the staff trained and the process made even more efficient. They would need someone to run this enormous logistical undertaking – someone with experience, someone they could trust.

On 6 May 1944, Rudolf received a telegram from Heinz Karl Fanslau, the chief of the Concentration Camp Inspectorate's personnel division. The order stated that while he would retain his appointment as head of *Amtsgruppe D1*, he was to travel immediately to Auschwitz to 'proceed with the expected new arrivals', which was a euphemistic code for 'oversee the mass extermination of the Hungarian Jews'.

Rudolf arrived back in Auschwitz on 8 May 1944. His first stop was to visit Hedwig and the children, who were still living at the villa. He had last seen Annegret six months earlier, when she was only two months old. Hedwig was not happy that Rudolf had been absent for so long. She often said, 'Don't think of your duty all the time, think of your family too.' But this visit was no different; Rudolf did not have time to play with his children – there would be no rowing on the Sola River or petting the animals in the garden – for the trains would soon start rumbling out of Budapest towards Poland.

Rudolf set about making the camp ready for the arrival of the Hungarian Jews straight away. He believed that Arthur Liebehenschel, his replacement as Kommandant of Auschwitz, had been too soft and quickly imposed strict rules and regulations on his staff. Liebehenschel himself had already left to take command of an extermination camp in Majdanek. Rudolf conducted an inventory of the Auschwitz camps and ordered that major repairs to the crematoria be undertaken, with additional pits dug nearby in which to burn the corpses. New railway lines that extended to within a few yards of the crematoria had finally been completed, so he also ordered the guards to keep the short walk to the gas chambers free of obstacles. Within a few days the camp was ready for the transports.

On 15 May 1944 the first trains from Hungary arrived in Auschwitz. By 8 July more than 437,000 Hungarian Jews had been deported on 151 transports. Of those trains, 136 were sent to Auschwitz, where

Jewish women and children in Auschwitz-Birkenau, May 1944

90 per cent of the prisoners were exterminated upon arrival. The 'selections' were overseen by Josef Mengele and Fritz Klein, the camp doctors. The crematoria were unable to keep up with the number of prisoners being killed, so the extra bodies were dragged out to the newly dug pits, where they were doused in oil and burned. The black smoke from the pyres could be seen miles away.

This extermination programme was code-named 'Aktion Höss' by the Germans, for it was Rudolf who oversaw the mass murder of more than 400,000 Hungarian Jews in Auschwitz. On 29 July, senior Nazi figures gathered in Solahütte, a retreat a few miles from the camp, to celebrate Rudolf and the successful completion of the operation.

Front row (left to right): Karl Höcker, Otto Moll, Rudolf Höss, Richard Baer, Josef Kramer, Franz Hössler and Josef Mengele, July 1944

At the end of the month, Rudolf was recalled to Berlin to resume his job as chief of *Amtsgruppe D1*. Now that Auschwitz was once again running smoothly, Richard Baer – who had previously worked as Oswald Pohl's assistant – took command of Auschwitz I.

Rudolf spent the latter half of 1944 visiting the camps under his purview, noting how conditions had worsened as the German government tightened its belt during its final push to win the war. One of the camps he visited was Belsen. Until 1943, this camp had acted as a holding facility for prisoners of war. Himmler had then ordered that it be used to process the *Austauschjuden* – a ransom system in which high-profile Jews, mostly from the Netherlands, were released for large quantities of money or exchanged for German citizens held in other countries. Compared to other concentration camps, conditions in Belsen had been fairly reasonable. That was until the spring of 1944, when the camp had become a holding centre for the diseased and dying. At this time the camp housed more than 15,000 Jewish inmates from around Europe, double the number that the camp had been designed to hold.

By the time of his visit in the autumn of 1944, Rudolf saw that the camp had deteriorated rapidly.

> The camp was in a wretched state. The huts for the inmates, the buildings for the staff and even the barracks for the guards were badly dilapidated. Sanitation was far worse than in Auschwitz. In spite of all that I had become accustomed to at Auschwitz, even I must describe the conditions here as terrible.

On his return to Berlin, Rudolf persuaded Glücks that he must remove the Kommandant of Belsen and replace him with his old adjutant from Auschwitz, Josef Kramer. Rudolf hoped that a new leader might improve conditions in the camp.

As he travelled the country, passing through Hamburg, Dresden and Frankfurt, Rudolf found many of Germany's greatest cities in ruins following months of Allied aerial bombardments. Tens of thousands of civilians had now been killed, more had been wounded and millions had been rendered homeless. The attacks were also felt in Berlin, as the city underwent intense fire bombings from the Allies.

Not only was there physical damage — life in the big cities was in great disorder — the psychological effects were also far-reaching. Anyone observing the faces and behaviour of people in the public air-raid shelters, or in the private shelters of apartment buildings, could see their distress and fear of death, whether or not they tried to conceal it, as the carpet-bombing came closer and closer. They clung together, seeking protection from the men when buildings shook and parts of them collapsed.

As life in Germany became increasingly treacherous, Rudolf decided his family should be in Berlin. If things turned out badly, they would be close by in case he had to make a quick exit.

In early January 1945, Rudolf was ordered back to Upper Silesia to instruct those in charge of Auschwitz how best to prepare for the oncoming Red Army. He never made it. By the time he reached the outskirts of Krakow, the Soviet Union forces had cut off access to the camp. Just before their arrival, and under direct instructions from Berlin, the guards had destroyed any evidence of genocide by blowing up the crematoria, dismantling the gas chambers and scattering the doors in a nearby field, and burning all the documents in the administration block. They had then ordered almost the entire population of the camp, many of whom could barely walk, out of Auschwitz, and into the freezing countryside, thereby commencing a forced march away from the approaching Red Army. It was this scene that Rudolf came across, a few miles away from Auschwitz.

I saw columns of prisoners forging a way with difficulty through the deep snow, without any food. Most of the Non Commissioned Officers leading these processions of the walking dead no longer knew which way they were supposed to be going . . . It was easy to follow this trail of human suffering, for every few hundred metres you came upon a prisoner who had collapsed or had been shot . . . The dead at the roadsides were not only prisoners but also refugees, women and children. At the way out of one village I saw a woman sitting on a tree stump, rocking her child and singing. The child had died some time ago, and the woman had lost her mind.

More than 60,000 men, women and children were forced on a 35 mile march to trains waiting for them in Loslau. They wore only thin shirts and trousers. The majority had no shoes or socks. Despite being weakened by years of starvation and hard labour, they were pushed forward at gunpoint, trudging through snowdrifts, across icy roads and in winter storms. More than 15,000 Auschwitz prisoners died during this forced march.

The lucky few who survived were then herded onto cattle trucks on which they spent four days, without food or heat, travelling to what they were told was a 'convalescent camp'. The prisoners had no blankets to fend off the freezing temperatures, so they kept warm by blowing on each other's freezing bodies and sang songs to keep their spirits up. After four wretched days the train was brought to a halt and the prisoners were forced to march for hours across the barren landscape to the camp at Belsen.

In the middle of March 1945, Rudolf returned to Belsen with Pohl. This would be his last visit to the camp. By now its population had risen to 50,000 – seven times the camp's capacity – with as many as five hundred dying every day. Kramer had proven unable, or unwilling, to improve conditions. Food and water supplies, already scarce, were now unavailable for days on end. Raw sewage ran through open gutters into a nearby field. Belsen had reached a point of total horror: typhus and other infectious diseases had spread rapidly, starvation was rife, and thousands of corpses were left unburied. One in ten prisoners had resorted to cannibalism, cutting up the dead bodies that lay around the camp and eating their flesh. 'Kramer was unable to do anything about it,' Rudolf said. 'Even Pohl was shaken when he saw the state the place was in.'

When Rudolf returned to Berlin he was greeted by shocking news: the war had arrived at the doorstep of the German capital. Having swept through Poland and Silesia, capturing Warsaw and Krakow, the Red Army was now gathered along the eastern banks of the Oder River, less than forty miles from Berlin's city limits. The combined Soviet forces included over two million men, 100,000 vehicles and 6,000 tanks. At the same time, Berlin continued to suffer from the British and American air forces' unrelenting aerial campaign, with thousands of bombs striking the city. It was clear to everyone that the war had reached a critical juncture.

When Hedwig saw Rudolf she asked about their future. 'How are we going to win the war?' she said. 'Do we really still have anything in reserve that will decide it in our favour?'

Rudolf realised that the end was near, but even now he found himself unable to answer with honesty. There was still hope, he replied. But he knew better. On his trips he had seen the dysfunctional arms factories, the madness of the camp evacuations and the plummeting morale of the troops.

Time had run out. Rudolf began to make preparations for the family's hurried departure from Berlin.

12

HANNS
BRUSSELS, BELGIUM
1945

Lieutenant Hanns Alexander arrived at the Bruxelles-Nord station on 8 May 1945. Wearing his khaki uniform and peaked hat, and carrying a duffel bag, he crossed the busy street and checked into the Grand Hotel. In his jacket pocket he kept a small photograph of Ann.

Hanns was under orders to report to the British headquarters in Uccle, a Brussels suburb. However, the residents of the Belgian capital were in no mood to allow a dapper young British officer to pass untoasted, for Hanns had arrived on Victory in Europe Day. The city had erupted in national celebration: business owners placed photographs of King Leopold in their windows; the Belgian flag fluttered from balconies; grocers, haberdashers, chocolatiers and tailors had arranged their windows so that the goods displayed the red, yellow and black of the national flag. In the midst of this euphoria, Hanns was pulled into bars, beer was bought for him and girls were kissing him on the lips.

The victory brought Hanns great satisfaction, but it did not bring him relief. For he remained on active duty and he had no idea when he would be returning home.

It took three days for Hanns to make it to Uccle. Upon arrival, he was told that he had been assigned to the Interpreters' Pool, and that he was to help with the interrogation of SS officers who had been captured at a recently liberated concentration camp.

He was in an upbeat mood that morning when he and his driver climbed into their small army truck. As they were leaving, the adjutant told them half jokingly, 'Avoid the military police. Every time you see them, they'll want to give you an injection for typhoid.' Never having heard of Belsen, which the British had liberated only three weeks earlier, Hanns had no idea what he was talking about.

They drove three hundred miles, north through Belgium and the Netherlands and then east towards the German border. Alongside the road lay the detritus of five years of war: burnt-out tanks, overturned trucks, shelled-out buildings. This was the site of some of the heaviest fighting. There were few civilians, as much of the area had been evacuated during the battle for Aachen, which American

Clearing Belsen concentration camp, April–May 1945

troops had won only a few months before. Those still resident had hung white flags outside their houses to indicate compliance. The first major city they came to was Cologne, but after suffering more than two hundred air raids, including one with more than a thousand bombers, there was little left. Its bridges had collapsed, its buildings lay in ruins, its streets were filled with rubble. They skirted the edge of the city and continued on, seeing similar scenes as they passed Düsseldorf and Dortmund. The only vehicles on the roads were military ones, on their way to resupply the forward-positioned forces. This was the first time that Hanns had been in his native country since 1936. The destruction was both disorientating and shocking.

It was early evening on 12 May 1945 when they arrived at the barbed-wire gates of Belsen. Inside the camp, corpses lay piled on top of each other. Bulldozers had begun the work of disposing of the bodies, pushing the dead into mass graves. The living prisoners were so thin that their ribs poked through their skin. Mothers clutched dead children; shaven-headed survivors in black-and-white-striped uniforms stared vacantly by decrepit wooden barracks; painted signs warning of typhus epidemics were everywhere. There was no water, no food, inadequate medical supplies and little shelter.

Hanns' first impressions of Belsen were visceral.

It had only been opened a few days. It had not been cleared yet. It had been closed so that Typhus would not run all over Germany. The SS guards were no longer there, but there were Hungarians who were not much better than the Nazis. Before it came to interpreting it was a question of cleaning the camp out. Everybody did whatever they could. There were dead bodies walking about, dead bodies lying about, people who thought they were alive and they weren't. It was a terrible sight. Whenever one went in and out of the camp we were sprayed with DDT.

Hanns' first task was to help bury the corpses strewn across Belsen's grounds. With the help of other soldiers – one holding the legs, the other grasping the arms – Hanns carried hundreds of bodies to a mass grave. Back and forth he went all day, his arms aching with the strain, the stench awful. Once one grave was full, a British Army rabbi stepped forward and, with Hanns and the other Jewish prisoners and soldiers standing nearby, read the Jewish prayer for the dead. They then moved on to the next mass grave, until that too was full, and so they continued until the grounds had been cleared.

All the British soldiers were deeply disturbed by what they had found in Belsen. But Hanns' reaction was different. The atrocity at Belsen had happened in the country of his birth; its victims were mostly Jews, his people. He could understand the German-speaking prisoners, people with whom he shared a context and background. Their story could so easily have been his. For Hanns, this was his home, and there would be no respite. It was as if Belsen had tripped a switch in him. No longer was he a carefree, selfish young man. He was gripped by a barely controllable rage. And he sensed a purpose.

For the first time in his life he felt compelled to act. During his first week, he was approached by a nurse from the Red Cross, who asked him to help a five-year-old girl who claimed that her mother had been shipped out just before the camp's liberation, and was convinced that she was still alive. Hanns realised that finding the girl's mother among the now millions of displaced people across Europe was a near-impossible task. Nonetheless, he agreed to help and, after asking around, discovered that some Belsen inmates had indeed been evacuated to a camp outside Wolfsburg, near Hanover.

Hanns drove the child and the nurse to Wolfsburg. Once there, he borrowed an armoured car from the British commander and told the nurse to climb up onto the roof. They then drove around the camp with the nurse clutching a megaphone to her mouth and clinging onto the roof as she shouted in German for the girl's mother to come forward. After several minutes they heard a loud shriek from the crowd as a woman came rushing towards the truck. A few seconds later she was reunited with her daughter.

On 16 May, a secret telegram was sent from British Army headquarters to Lieutenant Colonel Leo Genn in Belsen: he was instructed to take command of the teams of investigators and interpreters who had assembled at the camp. This new outfit was to be called Number 1 War Crimes Investigation Team, or '1 WCIT'.

In the three weeks since the camp's liberation a limited number of witness statements had been collected by three investigators: Major Geoffrey Smallwood, Major P. I. Bell and Captain Alfred James 'Freddie' Fox. Two young female former prisoners assisted the team, since the original British Army interpreters hadn't been able to cope with the horrors of Belsen and, according to Smallwood, had 'cracked up and gone sick'. Genn was now instructed to set the investigations on a more formal footing. In particular, he was to begin interrogating the former SS guards and officers, many of whom had originally worked in Auschwitz and who were now being held in a prison in Celle, a small medieval town fifteen miles from the Belsen camp.

Genn sought out Hanns, and told him that he would work as an interpreter for 1 WCIT. This would have been a welcome relief for Hanns after the clearing of the camp. By the end of that day, the team had been assembled: Lt Col. Leo Genn was commander and Major S. E. Champion his assistant. They would be supported by two former detectives — Lieutenant R. E. Robichaud and Captain Fox — who would spearhead the gathering of evidence. These men would in turn be assisted by a small group of interpreters, of whom only one had so far arrived in Belsen, Lieutenant Hanns Alexander. In addition, there were eight non-commissioned officers who would help with driving, administration and provide armed backup when needed. Eight days after Germany's official surrender in Berlin, Genn's team of twelve amounted to Britain's entire in-field war crimes staff.

Genn was told that the team could make use of any resources available in Belsen, including the offices occupied by the former camp administrators. Beyond this, however, they were on their own. There would be no additional help: no typewriters, recording devices, intelligence support, vehicles or communication equipment. They would have to make do, or requisition whatever they could from the local population.

Genn was not happy with the situation. In a memo sent on 21 May 1945 to his boss in London, Brigadier Scott-Barrett of the War Crimes Commission, Genn wrote: 'I will of course do my best but I feel it only right to say that I cannot feel any confidence in producing the right answer, since (apart from the aforesaid inadequacy of the staff) not only have many of the horses gone, but I doubt if I have the necessary strength to shut the stable door on those that remain.'

Nevertheless, Genn set about motivating his team. Their objective was to gather evidence that could be submitted to a British war crimes trial to be held near Belsen at the summer's end. The trials were to follow normal British judiciary procedures: a military court would be established along the lines of a court martial; counsel would represent both prosecutor and accused; and the court was to be manned by British judges and British lawyers. Those found guilty could expect a prison term or to be sentenced to death, either by hanging or by shooting. These rules would be enshrined into British law a month later, on 18 June 1945, via the issuing of a royal warrant.

Hanns was to work alongside Captain Fox, a former police sergeant from Reading, who had been collecting witness statements from concentration camp prisoners for over three weeks. In addition to typing up Fox's reams of handwritten notes, he would have to accompany Fox to retake these affidavits and have them properly witnessed. But first, they were to interrogate the former prison guards and administrators being held in custody.

The British wartime policy on interrogation techniques, particularly when it came to German prisoners, had been developed by Colonel Robin 'Tin Eye' Stephens. During the war, Stephens had supervised the London Cage, where he and his team had been responsible for the interrogation of German spies and prisoners of war. While Stephens maintained that violence had no place in an interrogation room, he encouraged interrogators to be 'breakers', to quickly overwhelm the prisoner and disintegrate all opposition. He believed that the key attributes of a breaker were enthusiasm, common sense, travel and an experience of personal loss. Most important was an 'implacable hatred of the enemy', as 'from that is derived a certain aggressive approach'. Hanns was a natural breaker.

On 17 May, Hanns and Captain Fox drove to Celle, where they were given a small room with a desk and three chairs. After a short wait, Hanns puffing on his Dunhill pipe, Fox studying the questions he had prepared earlier, their first subject was ushered in. Franz Hössler had worked twice in Auschwitz, first running the camp's massive catering operation and then, from January 1944, as head of one of Auschwitz's sub-camps.

Hössler opened by saying that he wanted to help his interrogators in any way that he could. Speaking in German, Hanns asked him for a brief biography and the prisoner replied that he was thirty-nine years old and a photographer by trade. When Hanns asked what he knew about the gas chambers, Hössler responded:

> Everyone in the camp knew about the gas chamber at Auschwitz, but at no time did I take part in the selection of prisoners who were to go to the gas chamber and then be cremated. Whilst I was there selection of prisoners for the gas chamber was done by Dr Klein, Dr Mengele and other young doctors whose names I do not know. I have attended these parades, but my job was merely to keep order. Often women were paraded naked in front of the doctors and persons selected by the doctors were sent to the gas chamber. I learnt this

through conversation with the doctors. I think those selected were mostly those who were not in good health and could not work.

As Hössler spoke, Hanns took notes in German, endeavouring to transcribe the actual words that he used. If his testimony was to be used in court, Hanns had been told, then it would have to be recorded as accurately as possible. Hössler continued:

> When transports of prisoners arrived the prisoners were taken from the train and marched to the camp. Trainloads of 2,000 and 3,000 arrived at the camp and often as many as 800 went to the gas chamber. The doctors were always responsible for these selections.

As the interrogation progressed, Hanns felt a growing sense of hostility and anger towards the prisoner. There had been articles in the papers, rumours circulating in Belsen, but here was one of the participants confirming that murder had taken place in Auschwitz on a colossal, unthinkable scale. This was both new and shocking for Hanns, indeed this may well have been the first time that anybody had heard such unvarnished testimony from such a key figure. Nevertheless, Hanns maintained his composure and continued to convey Fox's questions professionally, and then repeat the answers given by Hössler.

Translating for Fox, Hanns then asked Hössler who was in charge of the camp at the time. Hössler replied:

> Whilst I was at Auschwitz the Kommandant, until June, 1944, was Höss and he was succeeded by Baer. I made many complaints to Höss about the way people were being sent to the gas chamber, but I was told it was not my business.

The next day, Hanns and Captain Fox drove forty minutes west of Belsen to a military hospital in Schwarmstedt. There, they were led to a secure ward and introduced to a fifty-seven-year-old man named Fritz Klein, one of the doctors who had worked in Auschwitz before moving to Belsen. Klein did not look well. Since his arrest he had been working without pause to clear the camp, carrying corpses into the mass graves. Hanns and Captain Fox took a seat next to his hospital bed and the interrogation began. By now Hanns was adjusting to the frenetic pace, and as well as translating Fox's questions, he came up with a few of his own.

Klein was a Romanian, and had qualified as a doctor in Budapest. After joining the SS he had been sent to Yugoslavia as a recruiting doctor and then, in 1943, had been appointed as a camp doctor in Auschwitz, where he had overseen many of the 'selections'. The officer then in charge of the camp, he said, was Rudolf Höss. Explaining that he had worked as one of eight doctors in the camp, Klein then told Hanns how the 'selections' operated:

> When transports arrived at Auschwitz it was the doctor's job to pick out those who were unfit or unable to work. These included children, old people and the sick. I have seen the gas chambers and crematoria at Auschwitz, and I knew that those I selected were to go to the gas chamber. But I only acted on orders given me by Dr Wirths. I cannot say from whom Dr Wirths received his orders and I have never seen any orders in writing relating to the gassing of prisoners. All orders given to me were given verbally. All the doctors whom I have previously mentioned have taken part in these selections, and although SS guards were on parade they took no active part in choosing those who were unfit to work.

Hanns next asked why Klein, as a doctor, did not try and stop the 'selections'.

> I never protested against people being sent to the gas chamber, although I never agreed. One cannot protest when in the Army. It was not a pleasure to take part in these parades, as I knew the persons selected would go to the gas chamber. Persons who became pregnant whilst in the camp and therefore unfit for work were also selected on later parades. I have heard that Himmler had visited Auschwitz camp, although I have never actually seen him. It was certainly known to the higher-ups that these methods were being used at Auschwitz Camp.

The next day, Hanns and Captain Fox returned to Celle to interview Irma Grese, the second highest-ranking female guard at the Auschwitz women's camp before her transfer to Belsen. The press would later call Grese the 'Beautiful Beastess', because of her high cheekbones and long blonde hair. The interrogators developed a rhythm: Fox would quietly ask Hanns a question in English, which Hanns would then put to Grese in German; she would then reply and Hanns would translate back to Fox. Grese, however, refused to cooperate and denied all accusations. Fox and Hanns grew irritated by Grese's evasions and wrapped up the interview.

Having never been coached in police or military techniques, Hanns now studied how Fox ran the interrogations, how he structured the questions to allow the prisoners to give a full answer, and how he made it clear that he was in charge. At one point, Fox had exploded at Grese, telling her in German that she was lying – Fox could actually speak German fairly well, albeit with a bad accent – in a loss of control which had perplexed Hanns. After this interview was over he asked Fox why he had become angry. 'I'm not,' said the ex-policeman, 'it's just the show of the business.'

That afternoon Fox and Hanns interviewed twenty-six-year-old Elisabeth Volkenrath, a senior women's guard in Auschwitz and later the head of the women's camp in Belsen. Volkenrath wore a grey woollen skirt and jacket, white shirt and short black boots. Photographs taken during this time show her as having a pointed chin, wide-set eyes and curly hair, which she wore parted and pinned to the right. During his previous interviews with prisoners, Fox had learned that Volkenrath was cruel and vicious, prone to shooting prisoners for no apparent reason. The woman before them was the most hated woman in Belsen.

With everyone seated, Hanns asked Volkenrath about her background. She said that she had been born in a small town in Poland and that she had worked as a hairdresser before the war. She had then joined the SS and become a guard in Ravensbrück before her transfer to Auschwitz in March 1942. Like Grese, she denied being involved with the gassings, although she admitted being present during the 'selections'.

Throughout the testimony, Hanns continued to translate the guard's words, and then translate Fox's questions back into German. At the end of the interrogation, Hanns asked Volkenrath who was responsible for what took place in Auschwitz.

> It is my opinion that the man most responsible for the conditions at Auschwitz was Höss as he was in charge of all camps in this area. Reichsführer Himmler is, of course, responsible for all concentration camps. At no time did I see any orders in writing relating to concentration camps.

Once they had completed the interviews, Hanns and Fox returned to the small office that the WCIT had established in one of the old army buildings next to Belsen. On the walls were pinned photographs of SS guards and administrators that had been collected by the investigators, underneath which were labels listing their names, ages, titles and any distinguishing characteristics. Also hung up was the list of war criminals that had been published by the UN War Crimes Commission at the end of the war.

Fox next showed Hanns how to prepare the affidavits. With Elisabeth Volkenrath, for example, he selected the salient parts of her statement, typed them up in English, then Hanns translated them into German. Once all the statements were prepared, they returned to Celle and presented the documents to the prisoners. In Volkenrath's case, they asked her to read over her affidavit, and when she had approved its contents, she signed her name, below which Hanns wrote:

Certified that I have accurately translated the above statement from German to English and have read it over to Elisabeth Volkenrath in German, the said Elisabeth Volkenrath having signed it in my presence.

Signed H. H. Alexander

For Hanns, these interviews opened a new door into the reality of the Nazi concentration camps. He had already seen what starvation and appalling conditions had done to the prisoners in Belsen. Now he had confirmation of an even grimmer reality: that the old, the sick, as well as children were selected for execution by the doctors in Auschwitz; that thousands of Jews had been gassed to death – at this point he could not know that the figures would climb to over a million – and that the Kommandant in charge of this horror was Rudolf Höss.

Hanns had by now developed two sides to his personality. On the surface he remained charming and jovial, quick to tell a dirty joke, eager to make those around him laugh. This was the Hanns, or 'Alex', known to the Belsen soldiers and medical staff. Yet his other side, his German-Jewish side, he revealed only to those who shared his suffering, to a few former prisoners in the camp, and to his family back home. To these people, Hanns was serious and determined, fierce to the point of brutality with those he interrogated, and full of hate.

By the end of May 1945, Hanns had spent three weeks in Belsen, translating the words spoken by SS guards. It was important work, but a task that he felt any German linguist could manage. Most of those he had interrogated were low-level guards who could not be blamed for the horrors of the camps. The few senior officers who had been processed had by now given their statements and would sit around in their cells for the next few months waiting for their trials to start. But there were many men missing. For every one guard interrogated, another three or four were implicated.

Realising that he had skills beyond those of a mere interpreter — he understood the German people, he knew the country, he could navigate the streets — he vowed to hunt down these missing war criminals, especially Kommandant Höss.

Hanns walked over to Leo Genn's office and asked permission to start looking. But Genn declined his request, believing that Hanns lacked the necessary experience, and reminding him that there was still plenty of work to be done at Belsen. Appearing to acquiesce, Hanns walked out. But the next day he drove out of the camp. Regardless of protocol, Hanns would become one of the very first, if not the first, men in the British Army to hunt for Nazi war criminals.

Genn was right. Hanns was entirely ill-equipped to carry out his self-appointed task: he had no police experience; he had received no training as a detective; he was without tactical support; he had no intelligence, no leads or clues. He was just an interpreter, barely able to seek, let alone arrest, the wanted men. But his lack of a plan or authority wasn't going to stop him.

Driving around northern Germany he noticed that there were few other vehicles on the roads; if any of the local population still had a working car after six years of war they would have found it virtually impossible to find fuel given the shortages. The towns he passed through were quiet, save for military traffic, and the shelves of the rarely opened shops were mostly empty, stocking only the bare necessities. The residents he attempted to speak to were withdrawn and unwilling to converse with the unofficial detective.

On one of his unsanctioned outings, Hanns paid a visit to his brother, who was at that time in charge of a prisoner-of-war camp north of Hamburg. With Paul by his side, Hanns walked along the line of German soldiers, inspecting their arms for signs of the telltale blood-type tattoo marking all members of the SS. But to Hanns these men were only 'small fry', not worthy of arrest.

Before Hanns left, the brothers discussed their great aunt, Cäcilie Bing. The family had lost contact with her when she was still living in Frankfurt. Paul said that he would be in the city soon and promised to make enquiries. Cäcilie's fate was a source of constant worry for the Alexanders. Since their arrival in England they had pleaded with her to join them, reminding her of the danger she faced in Germany. But in 1941 her responses – bold, resolute, indefatigable – had suddenly stopped.

After their brief meeting, the two brothers went their separate ways. On 15 June, Hanns heard from Paul. His trip to Frankfurt had been fruitless. None of their friends had any news of Auntie Bing. The hotel where she had been staying had no record of her departure. The police were clueless as to her whereabouts. In a letter Paul wrote, 'I don't know whether Lilly [Cäcilie] is still alive, but I doubt she lives in Frankfurt.' Five days later, Henny wrote to both Hanns and Paul with news. The Red Cross had found a partial trace of Cäcilie Bing: she had been forced out of her hotel in Frankfurt on 20 September 1942, loaded onto a train with a thousand other Jews, and sent to Theresienstadt, a concentration camp in Czechoslovakia. They did not know if she had remained at this camp or if she had survived the war. Hanns wrote back immediately, 'Sorry about Lilly Bing but by what I have seen here [in Belsen] she could only have been better off in Theresienstadt. I hope she did not have it too hard and too long.'

Over the next weeks, Hanns made trips out of the camp whenever he was not on duty. On 15 July 1945, he wrote a letter to his sister Elsie, telling her about his new activity and why he had been too busy to write. 'My biggest enjoyment is chasing these SS about, but lately haven't been too lucky catching anything interesting.' He explained that he was conducting this Nazi hunting in his 'spare time' because it was not authorised by his superior officer, Leo Genn. 'Unfortunately my boss has different ideas to mine. He says our job is to deal with those in custody, and I agree with him, but if I can help catch one that is not behind bars, I do it.'

264280 Lt. H.H. Alexander
No.1 War Crimes Investigation Team
c/o 618 Military Government
B.L.A.
Sunday 15th July 1945.

Dear Elsie and Erich,
    Many thanks for letters which I have been unable to answer ever since I arrived in Belsen. We are still very busy, as you will undoubtedly expect after many justified complaints from Ann for my not writing. well all this can't be helped, as there is a job to be done. When other people write letters in their spare time, I do a wee bit of welfare work. It is so very little one can help these people, but every little helps, even if it is only to write a letter for them. My biggest enjoyment still is chasing these SS about, but lately have not been too lucky catching anything interesting. Unfortunately my boss has different ideas ti mine. He says our job is to deal with those in custody, and I agree with them, but if I can help to catch one that is not yet behind bars, I do it, even if it is somebody elses job. But there usually goes my spare time.

Four days later, he wrote to his parents. First, he thanked them for his prized Dunhill pipe, which they had had repaired and returned to him. Then he congratulated his father on having built his doctor's surgery, comparing it to the work he was doing as a Nazi hunter: 'I am very pleased about the practice. It is marvellous what you have done in only a few years, after all under adverse conditions, war after all is war and it has upset almost everybody one way or another. 1800 [patients], jolly good show. I wished I could already say that I have helped to make 1800 SS swing, but I suppose that will never happen. It is amazing, but the least said about it the better. Thank God some die off in the meantime, at last some satisfaction, of those I am certain, but the others, one never knows.'

Throughout the summer of 1945, Hanns made short forays into the countryside, interviewing hundreds of German soldiers and civilians, but few provided any useful information. Despite his lack of success, he was driven to continue.

Meanwhile, back in London, Alfred and Henny Alexander were still trying to rebuild their lives. After the celebrations of VE Day in May 1945, they had struggled like the rest of the population. Food was still rationed – bacon, butter, jam, eggs, chocolate – as was petrol. The doctor could not make journeys out to the countryside as he liked to do, and it was difficult to move around the city, as the streets were full of construction crews and the public transport system had not recovered from the years of bombing. So while he waited for his sons to return home, the doctor focused on his work. He rented rooms at number 62 Wimpole Street and continued to build up his practice.

Elsie and Erich had spent the war living in the countryside outside of London, keeping their children safely away from the Blitz. Each day Erich travelled into the city to run his leather business, which had benefited from the war demand. For Bella, though, the war's end had brought tragedy. A week after VE Day her husband, Harold, had been killed in Wiltshire when his car was hit by an aeroplane that had missed the runway. Bella was now faced with bringing up two little boys alone.

Ann was living with her parents in a small flat in Finchley, north London. She kept herself busy by working at the North London Metal Company, where she helped produce supplies for the post-war effort. She was also a member of the League of Jewish Women, whose aim was to 'intensify in each Jewish woman her Jewish consciousness and to deepen her sense of responsibility to the Jewish community', spending many weekends delivering food and offering company to the sick and elderly.

Hanns and Ann conducted their relationship by mail, written either on thin airmail paper or on tourist postcards. In July 1945, she took a holiday with a couple of friends to Cornwall. The weather was warm that summer and she enjoyed the time away from the noisy streets of London: a quiet lunch by a lake; sunbathing at the beach alongside families enjoying their summer break; shopping at the colourful boutiques in St Ives; walking along the picturesque cliff-lined coast. During teatime she would write a postcard to Hanns,

telling him that 'this is like the end of the world or the part of England nearest to Heaven'.

Since Hanns had begun work with 1 War Crimes Investigation Team, he had been too busy to return home on leave. It had therefore been more than four months since they had last seen each other, and Hanns had spent most of that trip with his family, concerned as he was for his father's health. Ann was becoming anxious about the future, and was placing increasing pressure on Hanns to commit to the relationship. But Hanns was not sure that he wanted to marry Ann, at least not yet, as he confided in a letter to his sister Elsie:

> Talking about problems, there seem to be some more coming up. Ann is very keen on getting married on my next leave, if and when there will be one. Poor me is supposed to get married, have a honeymoon, return to the continent, all this in 10 days, and like it. If I should have 2 minutes to spare in between, I suppose I should also find or at least try to find a job for myself. I feel very sorry for Ann, but she has been warned, one does not start anything with a bloke like me. I had a lovely letter from her a while ago. She asked me what I want, and when I told her, she would have bitten my head off, had I been near enough. Poor thing, trying to get me to solve problems from Belsen. What a hope.
> Hanns

Despite her repeated requests that he apply for leave, Hanns was too preoccupied to visit Ann that summer. Hanns the investigator was taking precedence over Hanns the private citizen.

Throughout August, Hanns and the other members of 1 WCIT were kept busy preparing witness affidavits for the upcoming Belsen Trial. This trial would be the first in which people were to be prosecuted for crimes against their own citizens, and it was viewed by many as a dry run for the Nuremberg Trials of Major War Criminals, which were slated to start later that year. As a result, the authorities were eager to ensure that all documents were perfectly prepared.

Josef Kramer, Belsen, 1945

Hanns' first task was to ensure that the number-one defendant, Josef Kramer, correct his original statement. Back in May, Höss' former adjutant had claimed no knowledge of Auschwitz's gas chambers. Given the overwhelming testimony to the contrary from both guards and prisoners, Kramer had indicated that he was now willing to change his story. On 1 September, Leo Genn asked Hanns to accompany him to Celle to sit down with Kramer.

After brief introductions, Hanns asked the former adjutant about the gas chambers in Auschwitz. His answer, later typed up into an affidavit, would play a key part in the Belsen Trial proceedings.

The first time I saw a gas chamber proper was at Auschwitz. It was attached to the crematorium. The complete building containing the crematorium and gas chamber was situated in Camp No. 2 (Birkenau), of which I was in command. I visited the building on my first inspection of the camp after being there for three days, but for the first eight days I was there it was not working. After eight days the first transport, from which gas chamber victims were selected, arrived, and at the same time I received a written order from Höss, who commanded the whole of Auschwitz Camp, that although the gas chamber and crematorium were situated in my part of the camp, I had no jurisdiction over it whatever.

Hanns then asked Kramer why Rudolf Höss hadn't stopped the killing.

Orders in regard to the gas chamber were, in fact, always given by Höss, and I am firmly convinced that he received such orders from Berlin. I believe that had I been in Höss' position and received such orders, I would have carried them out, because even if I had protested it would only have resulted in my being taken prisoner myself. My feelings about orders in regard to the gas chamber were to be slightly surprised, and wonder to myself whether such action was really right.

Now Hanns and Genn could prove not only that Kramer had been aware of the Auschwitz gas chambers but that he was sufficiently morally alert, if his testimony was to be believed, to have questioned their operation.

They now also realised the centrality of Rudolf Höss' role in Auschwitz. If they could get Höss to testify then they could establish the facts of the Holocaust. But first they needed to catch him.

Over the next few weeks, Hanns accompanied groups of former prisoners to Celle prison, where they signed affidavits identifying Belsen's Kapos, the prisoners who had brutally supervised the other inmates. He took the statement of Miklos Hirsch, for instance, who described a Kapo named Isaak Judalewsky beating a man to death with a wooden plank. Another prisoner, Joszef Silberstein, confirmed that Judalewsky 'went to a sick prisoner on the top bunk. He struck him two violent blows with the buckle part of his belt on the mouth and face and the prisoner leapt down from the bed and collapsed unconscious on the floor.' By the time the doctor arrived, Silberstein said, the prisoner was dead. Hanns also took several female prisoners — women named Blanka Vogel, Margit Spitzer, Ilona Grosz and Helen Jakubovits — to Celle, where they identified Maria Malzyner, a Kapo renowned for her viciousness. Vogel said that Malzyner 'beat me with her fists on the head. She struck me several hard blows and pulled me by the hair tearing whole tufts of hair out.' Another woman, Marian Tatarozuk, identified Anton Polanski, a Kapo who she said viciously beat the other prisoners. And Hanns took Alfred Kurzke to the Neuengamme internment camp in Hamburg, where he identified Oscar George Helbig, an administrator of the Mittelbau-Dora concentration camp, who was later sentenced to twenty years in prison by the Americans.

Finally, in the third week of September, Leo Genn determined that they were ready; it was time to start the trial.

The world's first major war crimes trial, 'The Belsen Trial of Josef Kramer and 44 Others', began on 17 September 1945 in a large courtroom in the German city of Lüneburg. The defendants sat in the centre of the room: twenty-one women and twenty-four men, each wearing their trial number affixed to a white cotton square. The court was presided over by the impressively named Major General Horatio Pettus Mackintosh Berney-Ficklin, who was joined by four other British military judges. Representatives of the world's press and members of the public were also present. Lieutenant Hanns Alexander and Captain Alfred Fox sat at the back of the room, waiting to see how their interrogations would be utilised.

After the forty-five 'not guilty' pleas were heard, the prosecutor, Colonel Thomas Backhouse, stood and gave a summary of the charges: 'At Auschwitz, the prosecution will say there was a deliberate cold-blooded extermination of millions . . . Every member of the gang bore a share in the treatment they knew would cause death and physical suffering. We will produce evidence that they committed deliberate acts of cruelty and wilful murder.' He concluded with the unimaginable assertion that 'a total of at least four million had been gassed' at the camp.

For the next few weeks, the world was transfixed. Witness, defence and counsel statements were all reported by the press in astonishing detail, with almost all the major papers giving front-page coverage to the proceedings. A short film of the Red Army's liberation of Auschwitz was projected, and the witnesses for the prosecution — men and women who had been held prisoner at Belsen and Auschwitz — came forward to give their accounts. The defendants' lawyers had a hard time disputing these testimonies.

When it came to Josef Kramer's turn on the stand, the name Rudolf Höss was uttered for the first time in a war crimes courtroom. Kramer said that he had been adjutant to the Kommandant and that it had been Höss who was responsible overall for the Auschwitz camp. It had been Höss, he said, who had supervised the construction and the operation of the gas chambers that had killed millions of people. The *New York Times* ran the story on Kramer's testimony, describing Rudolf Höss as the 'missing man' at the Belsen Trial, and declared that he was now on the list of most wanted war criminals.

On 17 November 1945, the Belsen Trial came to a close. Of the forty-five defendants, thirty were found guilty of war crimes. Nineteen were sent to prison. For the remaining eleven, including the five that Hanns had interrogated — Kramer, Klein, Hössler, Volkenrath and Grese — the judge pronounced, 'The sentence of this court is that you suffer death by being hanged.'

At 9.34 on the morning of 13 December, the first of these prisoners, Elisabeth Volkenrath, was hanged from a gallows in the courtyard of Hamelin prison. The remainder of the prisoners were executed: Irma Grese was hanged at 10.04 a.m., shouting '*Schnell!*' before the act; Kramer and Klein were hanged side by side at 12.11 p.m.; Hössler was hanged at 3.37 p.m.. It was all over by 4.16 p.m.

With every passing day of testimony, it had become clear to Hanns that the men and women standing trial were but a drop in the ocean of senior Nazis who remained at large in occupied Germany. Towards the end of the Belsen Trials, Hanns again approached his commanding

officer, requesting leave to hunt for the as-yet uncaptured war criminals. This time his commanding officer relented, and suggested that
he begin by exploring the CROWCASS files – the thousands of
names of potential war criminals that had been compiled by the
Allies. Genn provided Hanns with a driver and a car from the War
Crimes Group's vehicle pool, and, most importantly, invested him
with the authority to go anywhere he wanted in pursuit of his
investigations. And for the first time, Hanns was given the power
to arrest.

A few hours later, Hanns headed out of the camp. He had a list
of names in his pocket, a pistol, a pair of handcuffs strapped to
his belt and the travel permit. His modus operandi quickly took
shape: first, he chose a name on the list and headed for the suspect's
last-known address. When he arrived in the locality, Hanns paid
a visit to the police station or town hall to confirm the address
and search for any press clippings or recent photographs. More
often than not, they had vanished. Hanns would then question
whoever was present – a relative, landlady, neighbour – to gather
additional information. And so it went on, from one location to
another, across the country.

Driving from town to town, many of which had seen little of
the occupying forces, Hanns ran into people still committed to the
National Socialist world view. On one such occasion, he was told
by the mayor of Fallingbostel that no Jews had ever lived there.
Hanns let the statement pass. Soon after, he passed a Jewish cemetery
adjacent to the main road. Irritated by the mayor's shameless lies,
he turned back, arrested the man and dropped him off at the local
prison.

By November 1945, a month after he had started his official investigations, Hanns had managed to track down only two people of
significance: a senior policeman in Hamburg and a high-ranking naval
officer who had been hiding near Belsen. But as neither of these men

had been involved with the concentration camps, Hanns did not consider either a major catch.

Nevertheless, Hanns was enjoying his life more than he had in recent months. He relished the freedom of the open road and, even better, he had been promoted to the rank of captain. He was no longer a German refugee who helped out with translations; he was now a fully-fledged British war crimes investigator.

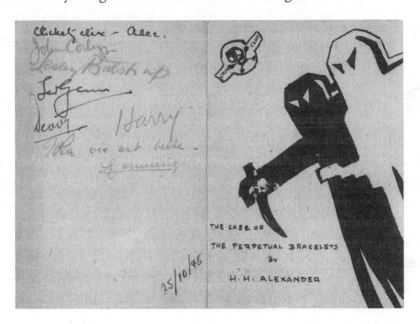

War Crimes Investigation Team dinner menu, 1945

13

RUDOLF
BERLIN, GERMANY
1945

In April 1945, Rudolf and his colleagues prepared their exit from the T-building. With the Red Army closing on Berlin and the American and British tanks creeping through Belgium and into Germany, it was clear to all at *Amtsgruppe D* that the war was coming to an end.

Rudolf now found it hard to reconcile his belief in the Third Reich's thousand-year rule with the reality he saw around him: 'We could not win the war like this. But I could not doubt the final victory, I had to believe in it, even if common sense told me clearly and distinctly that we were bound to lose. My heart was with the Führer and his great idea, which must not be lost to the world.'

On 16 April 1945, after bombs fell close to the T-building in Sachsenhausen, Himmler finally ordered that the entire *Amtsgruppe D* archive – documents, films and any other incriminating evidence – be destroyed. A few days later, Glücks told Rudolf to escort a select group of officers and family members, including the wife and daughter of Theodor Eicke, to the Ravensbrück camp, sixty miles north of Berlin. Hedwig and the children, acting on Rudolf's warning, had already fled Auschwitz for the camp and were awaiting him there.

Rudolf's plan was to head north towards the Baltic Sea and then north-west towards the Danish border. Here they would be far away from the military storm fast enveloping central Germany, and he would be able to drop off his family with his brother-in-law Fritz, who lived near the German city of Flensburg. Six days later they departed. They travelled in a convoy of cars, Rudolf in his Opel Kapitän, moving from one wooded area to the next to avoid low-flying planes. They drove only when it was dark, for fear of capture. 'Our flight was horrible,' Rudolf recalled. 'We travelled on the crowded roads by night, without any lights, and all the time I was anxious for parties to stay together in their cars, because I was responsible for the whole column.'

A few days into their flight, on 30 April 1945, they heard the news that Adolf Hitler had committed suicide in his Berlin bunker, just before Soviet Union forces took the city. Rudolf realised that his work for the Third Reich was finished. 'The Führer's death meant the end of our world.' It was now that he suggested to Hedwig a drastic plan of action.

> Was there any point in living on now? We would be pursued, we would be hunted wherever we went. We thought of taking poison. I had got hold of some for my wife so that, if the Russians unexpectedly advanced, she and the children would not fall into their hands. For the children's sake we did not take poison after all; for them, we would face all that lay ahead of us. However, we ought to have done it, and again and again later I regretted not doing so. We would all, particularly my wife and children, have been spared much. And what will they yet have to face? We were bound and chained to that world of ours — we ought to have perished with it.

In Rostock, a small city on the Baltic coast, the convoy was brought to a halt by tank traps positioned in the road. The group abandoned two trucks, along with the signals equipment and luggage they contained, and crammed into the remaining vehicles. They headed west until they arrived in Rendsburg, a city sixty miles north of Hamburg, where they joined up with Richard Glücks – who was now ill – and his wife and daughter, Dr Enno Lolling and his wife and son, along with Glücks' deputy, Gerhard Maurer, and other former members of *Amtsgruppe D*. Once together, Rudolf attempted to find the group accommodation, but failed to locate anything that was both safe and large enough for them all. The group continued on, late into the night, until they discovered some abandoned billets, twenty miles further north, where they could rest for a few hours. Early the next day, they continued their trek towards the Danish border. Wherever possible they drove on side roads, hoping to avoid the British checkpoints that had been set up on many of the main routes.

As his world fell apart around him, Rudolf was forced to reconsider the cause he had pledged himself to for the past twenty-five years. He still believed in the National Socialist vision, the supremacy of the German people, the need for additional land for its citizens, the threat posed by the 'enemies of the state'. Yet he now thought the Germans had been wrong to start the 'dreadful war' and should never have used its 'regime of terror' and 'highly effective use of propaganda' to make Eastern Europe submissive. Not that he was remorseful for the millions that had been murdered; he merely acknowledged that the means they had deployed had failed to produce their much wished for ends.

On 1 May 1945, Rudolf left the convoy to drop off his wife and children with Fritz in St Michaelisdonn, a small town situated a few miles inland from the North Sea coast. Rudolf had known Fritz for more than twenty years, ever since the days of the Artamanen League, when they had all worked together on the farm in Pomerania. Fritz had found a rudimentary wooden hut, complete with a small pot-bellied stove, an old farmhouse table and a few rickety wooden chairs, in which the family could remain until alternative accommodation could be found. Hedwig and the children would have to sleep on the floor. Having lost their personal belongings during the hurried flight north, the only clothes the Höss family had were the items that they were wearing.

The next day Rudolf and his son Klaus — now fifteen years old — left the rest of the family and set off for Flensburg. Rudolf still hoped that they could challenge the Allies' recent success and was keen for his son to play a part in the resistance. From Flensburg, they drove to a wood a mile north out of town, where they rejoined Richard Glücks and the other members of *Amtsgruppe D* for a previously agreed rendezvous. Also waiting there was Heinrich Himmler, who had made his own way from Berlin. He now told his anxious subordinates that the fight was over: it was time to take on false identities and disappear into the general population. Himmler said that he himself would adopt the identity of a corporal and head into Sweden.

Rudolf was shocked that Himmler was giving up.

> We arrived to report for the last time in Flensburg, where Himmler and the government of the Reich had gone. Continuing to fight was out of the question now. *Sauve qui peut* [every man for himself] was the order of the day. I shall never forget my last report to Himmler and my farewell to him. He was beaming and in high good humour — and yet it was the end of the world, our world.

After the rendezvous, Rudolf said goodbye to Klaus, sending him back to his mother with his driver. Then he and Gerhard Maurer, now on foot, took the sickly Glücks to a nearby navy hospital where they left him under the false name of 'Sommerman'. Rudolf then parted from Maurer, who headed south and set off to find himself a new identity. A few days later Rudolf met a submarine commander in Flensburg who handed him the papers of a certain Franz Lang, a junior seaman who had recently died. He thanked the commander, destroyed any documents that referred to his real identity, and headed north towards the island of Sylt, hoping to remain hidden until he could find his way out of Germany.

Shaped like the head of a hammer, the thirty-mile-long island of Sylt hangs off the north-western edge of Germany, not far from the Danish border. Long favoured as a holiday destination by German summer tourists, who loved the island's thatched cottages, flowering heathland and unspoilt beaches, Sylt was also the home to the Naval Intelligence School. Arriving in early May 1945, Rudolf presented his papers and was accepted into the naval school without question. And it was here, amid the pine forests and the towering sand dunes, that Rudolf spent four weeks, as the surrender was negotiated between Germany and the Allied Forces.

No one knew what the Allies had planned, and there was great anxiety at the school. The only consolation for Rudolf was that during this time he was able to visit his family who were less than 100 miles to the south in St Michaelisdonn. The days went by slowly. The Allied victory had given way to resistance which had given way to defeat and flight. For a man who based his entire life on loyalty and action, this isolation and inactivity made him feel dissatisfied, confused and lost. He was becoming undone.

On 23 May 1945, Himmler's death was announced on the radio. Rudolf was shocked by the news. The Reichsführer had changed his mind after meeting with Rudolf and the others in the woods near Flensburg and had instead headed south, until he was stopped by the British at a checkpoint near Lüneburg. Having assumed the identity of Heinrich Hitzinger, a deceased lower-ranking soldier, Himmler had shaved off his moustache and taken to wearing a black patch over his eye. There was something about the whole get-up which had rung untrue for Major Sidney Excell, the British officer at the checkpoint. He acted upon his suspicions, arrested Himmler and took him to Lüneburg prison. The next day, realising that his charade was pointless, the Reichsführer had identified himself – 'I am Heinrich Himmler' – and had then bitten down hard on a vial of cyanide which he had hidden at the back of his teeth. Despite the desperate efforts of the British medical staff, he died a few minutes later. The news was yet another sign that Rudolf's world was breaking apart and a reminder to keep his own vial of cyanide close by.

A few weeks later the Sylt Navy Intelligence School capitulated without a fight to British forces, and the entire staff was moved to a hastily erected camp near the Kiel Canal, seventy miles north of Hamburg. There, the senior officers were identified and transported to the prison in Heide, a small town located one hundred miles south of Flensburg. A few days after being moved to Heide, Rudolf petitioned for early release, telling his captors that he was a farmer and that he wished to work on one of the local estates. At this time the British high command was desperate to avoid a famine in Germany and had launched a mass mobilisation of former soldiers to help bring in the harvest in an operation code-named Barleycorn. Rudolf was masquerading as a junior seaman so successfully that he was never questioned, and his desire to work on the land chimed well with the British policy. He was discharged and, shortly after applying for a job with the Labour Office, obtained a position on a local farm.

On 5 July 1945, Rudolf arrived in Gottrupel, six miles west of Flensburg's city centre and two miles south of the Danish border. A village of some 280 people, Gottrupel was surrounded by flat open fields on one side and a small wood on the other. Rudolf reported to the Hansen Farm situated at the edge of the village. There he was taken to the barn where he would be sleeping: a long, single-storey Danish-style structure with whitewashed stone walls and a tall, pitched slate roof.

Luckily for Rudolf, the farm's owner, Hans Peter Hansen, was absent, having been interned in an American camp for former members of the SS. Rudolf had the freedom to work the land as he saw fit. Over the course of that summer Rudolf laboured tirelessly. During the days he worked on the farm, and at night he stayed up late reading in the barn. The villagers were reassured by his polite and humble manner, and impressed with his quiet diligence. Introducing himself as a former sailor named Franz Lang, he soon gained the trust of the community, and before long was acting as secretary for the village council. Nobody suspected his true identity.

In September, he travelled twice to St Michaelisdonn to see Hedwig. They met on the sandy flats outside of town. Their meetings were brief, for they feared being seen by the British patrolling the area. They had just enough time for Rudolf to share his plans and for Hedwig to provide an update on the children, and the day-to-day difficulties of their new life.

Rudolf spent the rest of the autumn working on the farm; stowing the harvest in the barn, ploughing the fields, preparing the land for winter. A few days after Christmas 1945, Rudolf met his brother-in-law at a Flensburg bar. There Fritz handed Rudolf a letter and a package of clothes from Hedwig. Before he left that day, Fritz reminded Rudolf that he remained in grave danger and that the British were keeping a close eye on Hedwig and the children in St Michaelisdonn. He should now have no direct contact with them, Fritz warned, and all communication was to be conducted through Fritz himself. If he wanted to avoid arrest and escape Germany, Rudolf must keep hidden and out of sight.

14

HANNS
BELSEN, GERMANY
1945

By the end of 1945, the British War Office had realised that it was time to reinvigorate their war crimes team. True, they had successfully overseen a major trial at Belsen and – along with the Americans, Soviets and French – were now embarking on an even bigger series of trials at Nuremberg. But they also knew that the vast majority of war criminals were still on the run.

The British established a new War Crimes Group based in Bad Oeynhausen, a small market town near Hannover which the British Army had requisitioned in May 1945 – evicting the German residents in the process – as the headquarters for the British Army of the Rhine (BAOR). One of the houses that had been taken over, at 24 Lettow-Vorbeck-Strasse, was allocated to the group. It was from this building that all investigations were now coordinated.

Heading the War Crimes Group was Anthony George Somerhough, a bear-sized man whose keen intellect was masked by a jovial face and who would often stay up late making omelettes for his hard-working investigators. Somerhough was assisted by Colonel Gerald Draper, a short and slim bespectacled London lawyer who had served as an infantryman with the Irish Guards, and now ran the

War Crimes Group's legal section. In another change, Lieutenant Colonel Leo Genn had returned to England, and 1 WCIT was now headed by one Lieutenant Colonel Thomas Humphrey Tilling.

In a memo to Somerhough drafted in early November 1945, Draper summarised the position of the outstanding members of *Amtsgruppe D*: Dr Enno Lolling had committed suicide; Karl Sommer was in American custody in Berlin; Richard Glücks was said to have committed suicide after being discharged from a hospital near Flensburg in north Germany, although Draper was not convinced by this story; and Oswald Pohl, Gerhard Maurer and Rudolf Höss were still at large. There was much work to be done.

Group Captain Somerhough, who was affectionately known as *Gruppenführer* by his men, now received word from London that his team must speed up their investigations, and was given orders that at least five hundred people were to be captured and brought to trial by the end of the following April. By this time Hanns had impressed his superiors with his hard-won local knowledge and investigative skills. As a result, on 15 November 1945, Somerhough sent word to Tilling that Hanns Alexander had been ordered to start looking for one of the most hated figures in the Third Reich, the Gauleiter of Luxembourg, Gustav Simon.

RESTRICTED
BOAR/15226/7/JAG
15 NOV 45
CC NO 1 WCIT
SUBJECT – Gauleiter Gustav SIMON
   A letter has been received from the Ministry of Justice, National Office for War Crimes, WIESBADEN, to the effect that the Luxembourg Government is much concerned that the above named Gauleiter, formerly, 'Chef der Zivilverwaltung in Luxembourg', whom they regard as a major war criminal has so far escaped arrest.

There seems to have been some investigation by the French authorities which seems to establish the fact that SIMON is hidden in the British zone near Cologne (Eifel area).

Although these clues are somewhat meagre, I should like to assist if possible and I am therefore writing to ask if you could detach Captain Alexander to undertake this special consignment co-operating with whatever British security services in the area are disposed to assist.

A. G. SOMERHOUGH

Gustav Simon, Luxembourg, August 1942

Gustav Simon was born in the city of Saarbrücken in 1900 to a railway bureaucrat father and a homemaker mother. He trained as a teacher, and joined the Nazi Party in 1925, rising rapidly through the ranks. Although he never joined the SS, Simon was considered an 'old fighter' because of his early enrolment, and trusted with increasing responsibilities. He was appointed regional leader, or 'Gauleiter', of Koblenz by Hitler in 1931, and, following Germany's invasion, regional leader of Luxembourg in 1940. Simon's instructions were to dismantle the principality's state apparatus, to ban the use of the French language, and to Germanise its people. Sometime in late-1940, Gustav Simon initiated a new programme: the deportation of the entire Jewish population of Luxembourg.

As part of the pre-occupation exodus, over a thousand Jews had fled into France, Portugal and Belgium. The Jewish community that remained in Luxembourg was led by Rabbi Dr Robert Serebrenik, a thirty-eight-year-old Austrian who had been Chief Rabbi of Luxembourg since 1929. In the following months, an additional few hundred Jews managed to escape to neighbouring countries. Some were able to find safety; the less fortunate were rounded up by the Gestapo.

On 16 October 1941, the first group of Luxembourg Jews were loaded onto trains and transported to the Łódz ghetto in Poland (later trains were sent to Theresienstadt and then on to Auschwitz). The next day, on 17 October, Gustav Simon proudly declared that Luxembourg was '*Judenfrei*' – free of Jews. He was the only Nazi Gauleiter to claim that his region had been entirely 'cleansed'. Altogether, of the 3,900 Jews living in pre-occupation Luxembourg, 1,290 died in the Holocaust.

Since the American liberation of Luxembourg in September 1944, little had been heard of Simon, who was presumed to have fled back to Germany. There were rumours that he was hiding somewhere near Cologne.

Up until this point, the British war crimes investigations had been limited to interrogating SS guards and political leaders who were already in custody. This was about to change. Hanns was called in to see Lieutenant Colonel Thomas Tilling. A thin man with short red hair, a narrow moustache and piercing blue eyes, Tilling told Hanns that he was to hunt down and arrest Gustav Simon. If he successfully arrested the Gauleiter, his mission would become the prototype for a new unit-wide programme in which investigators would be sent out into the general population to track down a single war criminal. This new strategy would be called 'Operation Haystack'. Hanns' job was to find the needle.

While Hanns would be working on his own, Tilling said that if he needed assistance, he could contact the American and the Belgian security forces. Both had been made aware of his mission and would provide backup should he ask for it. Most importantly, Gustav Simon should be brought back alive.

On 23 November 1945, the day the American prosecutors concluded their opening statements at the Nuremberg Trials, Hanns drove four hours south to the German city of Wiesbaden to talk to Judge Léon Hammes, the Luxembourg representative of the War Crimes Commission. The judge gave Hanns two photographs of Simon: he had a predatory look, with small eyes and a small mouth, a pointy nose and a cleft chin. His dark hair was parted on the side and shaven two inches above his ears, emphasising their large size.

Hanns returned to Belsen to report what he had learned to Tilling. But just as he arrived at the camp, a terrible storm swept across central Europe, delaying his trip by a week. The delay gave him time to gather supplies: two days' rations, blankets, snow chains, warm clothes, a clipboard for his notes and a first-aid kit, as well as his pistol and handcuffs. Also critical was the waxed road map of north-western Germany, given to him by the War Crimes Group.

At last, the snow stopped. Hanns and his driver left Belsen on 1 December 1945, and having decided that he should start at Gustav Simon's last-known address, they made their way across snow-covered roads to Koblenz, a city three hundred miles south-west of the camp. Upon arrival, Hanns met the chief of police, hoping to pick up clues from the time that Simon had lived in the city in the mid-1930s. The police chief confirmed that Simon had indeed lived at number 15 Rheinallee, but queried the need for Hanns' journey, given that he had read, in a Frankfurt newspaper, that Simon had been arrested shortly after the war's end. This was news to Hanns, so, thanking the police chief, he rushed over to the newspaper's offices, a two-hour drive to the south-east. But when he arrived, he was told that the paper had never run such a story. Hanns learned an important lesson: from now on, he would treat all informants, even those in positions of authority, with greater scepticism.

Hanns returned to Koblenz, this time visiting the district police station. There, he met a policeman who was much more helpful, informing Hanns that Simon's wife's maiden name was Friedel Henning, and that the couple had divorced in 1942. He also said that Friedel's parents lived in Hermeskeil, and that she and the Gauleiter had a son called Gustav Adolf Simon, who was now fourteen years old.

Hanns hurried over to Hermeskeil, where he interrogated Gustav Simon's in-laws. The elderly couple were only too willing to help – Simon had apparently 'left their daughter in the lurch' – but unfortunately they had not seen or heard of him recently, and had no idea as to his current whereabouts. However, they told him that Simon's mother was still alive and could be found at her home in Friedewald, another hour's journey south.

The chase continued. The next day, 4 December, Hanns drove over to see Simon's mother in Friedewald. She remained cold and abrupt throughout the interview, claiming that she had no information on either her son or her grandson. Realising that any German town would likely hold both anti- and pro-Nazi inhabitants, Hanns decided to knock on her neighbours' doors and, after a few false starts, was able to gather some useful information. From one neighbour he learned that the Gauleiter had indeed been in town, leaving for an undisclosed location on 27 March 1945, the day before the Americans took Friedewald. They also told him that a young man carrying a rucksack had been visiting the old lady at night, and that this young man, along with the Gauleiter's two nieces, had headed for the town of Marburg. Hanns presumed that the 'young man with the rucksack' was Gustav Simon's son.

Hanns now backtracked to Marburg, a small town seventy miles north of Frankfurt, where he was able to locate the Gauleiter's two twenty-something nieces. To his relief, they seemed cooperative, telling Hanns that the Gauleiter's son was now living in Dassel, south of Hanover, and that he had taken his mother's maiden name, now going by 'Gustav Henning'.

Hanns next visited the Dassel town hall to pick up any intelligence that they may have gathered on this 'Gustav Henning'. To his delight, the mayor there handed him a bag that had been dug up in a wood just outside of town. Inside were documents belonging to 'Gustav Henning', including his identity cards, a Hitler Youth uniform, an up-to-date photograph and propaganda papers from the Werwolf resistance movement.

Thinking that he was closing in on his quarry, Hanns hastened over to the address given by the two nieces, only to be told by the house's occupants that Gustav Henning had not lived there since August, five months earlier. The nieces had given him old information; once again those trying to protect Gustav Simon had duped Hanns. He was furious. Not only was he desperate to catch the Gauleiter — as could be seen by his single-minded efforts to track him down — but he hated the idea that these young Nazis thought they could deceive him.

Hanns returned to Marburg on 6 December, and arrested the nieces for obstructing justice. At the local prison they were slung into separate cells and Hanns immediately started the interrogations: Where is Gustav Simon? When was the last time you saw Gustav Adolf or 'Gustav Henning'? Why did you lie to me? For hours he pounded them with questions, threatening to send them to trial as war criminals if they refused to cooperate.

At last one of the girls broke. She confessed that they had indeed given Hanns old information, and that Gustav Henning was now living with another relative, named Alvis Scheideler, at 11 Eschenlohe Strasse in Plettenberg, Westphalia, some seventy miles north of the Marburg prison.

Sensing that he was at last getting somewhere, Hanns drove to Plettenberg and, with the support of soldiers from the Belgian 3rd Infantry Brigade, searched Scheideler's home. But the son was not there. Turning to Scheideler, Hanns asked if the boy was living at her house. She told him that he had recently moved. Furious, Hanns asked for Gustav Adolf's current address, little expecting it to be offered. In this he was surprised, for Scheideler told Hanns that she was sure that Gustav Simon's son was now living at number 38 Dingeringhauser Weg, just round the corner.

Still fearful that this was yet another red herring, Hanns hurried over to Dingeringhauser Weg with the Belgian soldiers following close behind. Once at the property – a detached building in a side street, away from the town centre – he met the landlady, who not only confirmed that the boy was registered as a resident of her building, but that he was upstairs in his room.

With Hanns and the soldiers waiting behind her in the corridor, the landlady knocked on the door, swung it open and pointed inside at a surprised and surly-looking young man in travelling clothes. Hanns marched in, announced that he was a British war crimes investigator, and asked for the boy's name and identification documents. The young man reluctantly acknowledged that he was indeed Gustav Adolf Simon, the son of Gustav Simon.

A quick check of the room unearthed a British Ordnance map of Hanover, but no weapons were found. Hanns then asked Gustav Adolf about his activities since the end of the war, to which the boy replied that he had been working and had had nothing to do with politics. Exasperated by the boy's recalcitrance, Hanns said that the police had found a bag that had been dumped in a nearby woods containing literature from the Werwolf resistance movement and that it had included his identity papers. Caught out in the lie, the young man kept silent. Detecting an advantage, Hanns pressed him for his father's location, but, as if repeating a line that he had been taught, the young man said that his father hadn't visited Plettenberg and that he hadn't seen him since Easter Sunday. Furthermore, he had no idea as to his father's current whereabouts or identity. Hanns arrested the boy for possessing the map, and asked the Belgian unit to deposit him in the town's prison.

A short while later, Hanns returned to the house of Alvis Scheideler, the most helpful person he had found thus far. He was in luck. Not only had she seen Gustav Simon, but she had a vague sense of where he was staying, where he worked and what he was wearing. The Gauleiter had recently booked in at both the Harpe and Hoppes hotels in Plettenberg, she told Hanns, and he was now working as a gardener for a nearby kindergarten. She thought that he was using the name 'Volter' or 'Hofler', and he had changed his appearance. The man Hanns was looking for now had grey hair, he had grown a moustache and he was wearing glasses.

It was late evening when Hanns, accompanied by Scheideler, arrived at the Harpe Hotel. Handing the receptionist at the desk a few marks, Hanns asked if he could see the register. The man pulled a leather-bound book from under the counter and passed it to Hanns, who flipped it open, tracing his finger down the recent entries, of which two caught his eye.

> – 14.9.45. Hans Woffler, born 26.9.00, born and domiciled in Frankfurt, left hotel 15.9.45.

> – 13.11.45. Hans Woffler, born 26.9.00, proper address Steinbeck, Schusterstrasse 1, identity card A13882, left hotel 16.11.45.

Here, just maybe, was proof, contrary to the boy's claims, that Gustav Simon had visited Plettenberg four weeks earlier. The name was not exactly the same as the one Alvis Scheideler had given him, but it was close.

After writing the information in his notebook and thanking the man at the desk, Hanns and Scheideler walked round the corner to the Hoppes Hotel, and again asked to see the register. Here too he found useful information:

> – 12.11.45. Heinrich Woffler, born 26.9.00, born at Frankfurt, domiciled in Einbeck, identification number A13882, left hotel 13.11.45.

The next day, Hanns visited Gustav Adolf at the Plettenberg prison. Confronted with Hanns' fury, the fourteen-year-old soon buckled, acknowledging that his father had indeed been working as a gardener in the British Zone, and that he had recently seen him in Plettenberg. Hanns was one step closer.

Now that he had confirmation that Scheideler was telling the truth, Hanns took a closer look at the hotel register. He saw a pattern. Two guests had used the same last name, Woffler, with two separate addresses listed: 'Steinbeck' and 'Einbeck'. Hanns had never heard of a town named Steinbeck, and speculated that the similarity was not a coincidence; perhaps, he thought to himself, 'Woffler' was living in Einbeck.

Leaving before dawn, on 10 December 1945, Hanns made his way to Einbeck, one hundred miles due south of Belsen. Heading straight for the police station, Hanns was informed that they had no record of a 'Hans Woffler' or a 'Heinrich Woffler'. Back outside on the street, Hanns glanced at his notes and on little more than a whim decided to visit the only street address listed in either of the hotels' registers. A few minutes later, he was standing outside 1 Schusterstrasse, looking at the list of residents next to the door. To his delight, there at the top was the name of Hans Woffler.

After pressing the bell, Frau Blumenberg, the elderly homeowner, came to the door. The woman recognised Simon from Hanns' photograph, but said that he hadn't lived at the house for two months. Hanns was not to be deterred. Sensing he had finally caught up with the Gauleiter of Luxembourg, he asked for the man's name. He called himself 'Hans Woffler', she said, and as far as she knew, he was working as a gardener in a nursery just outside of Paderborn, seventy miles west of Einbeck, halfway between Hamburg and Frankfurt.

Hanns made for Paderborn town hall. There, a city official informed him that a 'Hans Woffler' had indeed recently registered with them, and that he was living with a Frau Berhorst, in Upsprunge, a town fifteen miles to the south of Paderborn.

At eleven o'clock that night, Hanns and a few men from the Paderborn police gathered outside a house on a quiet street in Upsprunge. After a quick conversation about tactics – who was to go in first, what would they do if they were met with resistance – one of the men kicked down the door and, on an agreed signal, the group barged in.

The elderly-looking man inside appeared shocked as the soldiers entered the house. He shrank back from the officials, trembling and very nervous. Hanns would not have recognised the Gauleiter if he had walked past him in the street. The man before him bore little similarity to the pictures Hanns had been given by Judge Hammes. Unlike the man in the photographs, whose cheeks had been fat with wealth and power, this man looked gaunt after his six months on the run. His hair was long and grey; his face was weathered by the sun; and he wore spectacles and had grown a moustache. His clothes hung off his body as if they had been purchased for a larger man. But having been forewarned about his physical transformation by Frau Scheideler, Hanns was sure that here, at last, was Gustav Simon.

While the policemen trained their pistols upon Simon, Hanns checked his mouth and ears for suicide pills. Satisfied that there was no immediate threat, he now demanded that Simon hand over his papers, which confirmed his supposed identity as Woffler. When Hanns questioned the authenticity of these documents, Simon maintained that 'Woffler' was his real name. But the Gauleiter had made one mistake. After a brief search of the room, Hanns discovered a coat which bore Simon's name and rank. Confronted with the evidence, Simon reluctantly confirmed his true identity.

Hanns then asked a series of rapid-fire questions: where had he been since the Americans occupied Luxembourg? Who had collaborated with him? When was the last time he had been in touch with the Nazi leaders Himmler, Pohl and Eichmann? The interrogation went nowhere, and beyond a few muttered generalities, the prisoner revealed nothing.

Hanns collected all of Simon's possessions − clothing, books, writing materials − and had them taken to his car outside. He then paid any remaining rent that was due to the landlady, using money found in the prisoner's wallet, and told her that she could keep the large stock of food that Simon had hoarded.

Hanns steered the now handcuffed Simon to his vehicle outside, and drove him to Paderborn prison, where he was handed over to the warden. As he was leaving, he instructed the warden that the prisoner should be put on suicide watch and that he was not to be released to anybody but Hanns. After travelling more than fifteen hundred miles across the country in seventeen days, Hanns finally had his man.

Hanns and his driver travelled through the night, arriving in Belsen early on the morning of 11 December. Still not having slept, Hanns walked into the office of Lieutenant Colonel Tilling and announced that he had arrested Gustav Simon. Tilling was delighted. Given how cold the trail had become, he had thought it unlikely the Gauleiter would be caught, and he congratulated Hanns for his good work. When Hanns requested that he escort Simon to Luxembourg, Tilling said, 'Sure. He's your fish, you can fry him.'

Hanns' transfer orders arrived from Group Captain Somerhough on 18 December, eight days after the arrest: Captain Alexander was to go to Paderborn prison to meet Captain Léone Muller, a female member of the Luxembourg War Crimes Bureau, and pick up Simon; he was also to pick up Richard Hengst, the former mayor of Luxembourg who had run the country alongside the Gauleiter from 1940 to 1943. The two escorts were then to deposit the prisoners in Bonn's jail, while ensuring that the warden follow the standard operational procedures, including mounting a twenty-four-hour suicide watch. The next day they should proceed to Luxembourg and hand over the two prisoners to the authorities. Somerhough ended his order with the warning: 'As the hostility of the local population to Simon is very strong it will be advisable that the prisoners not be seen in the car or in the streets.'

But things did not go as officially planned. Hanns' field report described what happened next:

SECRET
Report of the Disposal of Gustav Simon and Richard Hengst
Capt H. H. Alexander
NO 1 War Crimes Investigation Team
2 Jan 1946
HOHNE (BELSEN) CAMP

1. On 19 Dec 45, on instructions received from Judge Advocate General's branch (War Crimes Section) I proceeded to Headquarters, British Army of the Rhine, accompanied by Richard HENGST, the former Mayor of Luxembourg-city. I was met at Headquarters by Captain (Miss) Muller of the Luxembourg War Crimes Bureau. We proceeded to Paderborn with the intention of collecting Gustav SIMON, but on arrival were informed by the [commanding officer] of Paderborn that SIMON had hung himself on the 18 Dec 45, whilst in the Paderborn Police Prison. This was the second attempt he had made to commit suicide. I was informed that the first attempt took place on 11 December when he attempted to cut one of his veins; however this attempt was discovered before it was successful. Before endeavouring to take his life on the 11 December, SIMON made a voluntary statement to the police officer guarding him admitting that he was in fact Gustav SIMON, Gauleiter of Luxembourg, and that the reason for making such a statement was to save his family from further trouble. This statement together with the police officer's report is attached marked 'A'. The original was handed over to the Luxembourg authorities and Exhibit A, attached, is a certified true copy of the original.

2. I was informed that SIMON hung himself between 1145 hours and 1215 hours on 18 December 1945. A piece of rope made out of canvas covering on his bed was used and SIMON hung himself on the bed post of his double bunk bed. The piece of rope was handed

to Miss Muller and taken back to Luxembourg. It was ascertained that the prison had taken all necessary precautions against any such attempt and his braces and boots, etc, had been removed. In addition, after the first attempt the guard was doubled.

Now with a corpse instead of a prisoner, Hanns decided that he should still deliver the body 'dead or alive'. He wrapped a blanket around the corpse, tied it up with string and then strapped it onto the luggage rack fixed to the back of the car. They then drove with the 'stiff', as Hanns called it, flopping up and down, all the way across Germany. They arrived at the border at two in the morning of 20 December, where they handed the dead Gustav Simon, and the living Richard Hengst, to Victor Bodson, the Luxembourg justice minister, and Judge Hammes. After a brief retelling of the tumultuous day's events, Hengst was dropped off at the city's jail and Hanns was taken to a local hotel. The former Gauleiter spent the night in prison.

De cpt. Alexandre am gespre'ch matt dem hèr minister Bodson a mam hèr J. Thorn.

The next day a press conference was held on the ground floor of the Ministry of Justice in the centre of Luxembourg City. Standing before the cameras were Victor Bodson and Mr Jos Thorn, the President of the Luxembourg War Crimes Commission, along with Captain Alexander and Captain Muller. The press were then invited to go to the prison building where the corpse could be seen and photographed. Gustav Simon was still dressed in his prison clothes, but shorn of both moustache and glasses. His head was tipped back, exposing a stubbled neck that was still red and swollen.

The *Tageblatt* – one of Luxembourg's largest-selling newspapers – described what happened at this press conference.

GAULEITER SIMON COMMITS SUICIDE IN PADERBORN
The wild goose chase for the Gauleiter seemed like a novel or detective story, and attested to the skill of Captain Alexander's group. It is a pity that the virtually tireless efforts of the English captain did not lead to the result hoped for by the people of Luxembourg: the trial and execution of the war criminal in Luxembourg. Captain Alexander gave a report in fluent German, about his 2,500 km odyssey that began on 23 November and ended with the arrest of the Gauleiter on 10 December at 11 o'clock in the evening.

'Please excuse me,' Alexander began, 'that I was unable to bring the Gauleiter to Luxembourg alive, unhappily it didn't happen the way I hoped it would. But Gustav Simon got what he deserved, the rope.' With English phlegm, he added, 'It saved us quite a few expenses.'

That the dead man is the Gauleiter there is no doubt: an examination of the corpse in Luxembourg's main prison, together with the facts we have just given, clearly reveal his true identity.

In spite of our disappointment that Gustav Simon committed suicide the thanks of our entire people go to Captain Alexander who secured the monster.

There were, however, conflicting reports. Some claimed that Gustav Simon had been alive when Hanns picked him up from Paderborn prison, and that he did not hang himself, as Hanns had written in his field report. Instead, Hanns had then been joined by seven Luxembourg partisans, Captain Léone Muller among them, taken Simon to a forest outside of Paderborn and executed him. Having sworn an oath never to reveal what took place, Hanns was alleged to have covered up the murder, presenting the 'official version' at the press conference the next day in Luxembourg.

Whichever story was true, Hanns had successfully tracked down and arrested his first major war criminal. Mission accomplished – just about.

After the press conference in Luxembourg, Hanns received an invitation to a reception at the splendid Salle des Fêtes in the Grand Ducal Castle, hosted by the Grand Duchess Charlotte and her family, who had recently returned from self-imposed exile in London. Standing by the drinks table, his worn khaki uniform neatly pressed, Hanns was approached by the Grand Duchess herself, who thanked him, in perfect English, for tracking down Simon. He, in return, handed her a crisp five-pound note: repayment for bedding her son Jean had bought for a fellow officer when they were both serving in the Irish Guards.

Hanns spent the next week in Luxembourg boozily celebrating the arrest of Gustav Simon with Victor Bodson. The two men were as matched in their loathing of the Nazis – before the war, Bodson had helped over a hundred Jews escape from Germany – as they were in their ability to drink.

Throughout that summer Hanns had written to Ann on a regular basis, but he had fallen silent during the autumn, kept busy in his new role as war crimes investigator. Ann wanted an explanation for Hanns' prolonged silence.

When Hanns returned to Belsen, Tilling handed him two pieces of correspondence: the first was a letter that Tilling had himself received from Ann in London, while Hanns had been scouring the countryside for Gustav Simon, and the second was his reply.

28 November 1945
Dear Lt. Col.,

This is not going to be a proper letter but merely a few lines full of complaints which, the writer sincerely hopes, will produce the necessary effect. The writer was going to ask for help but decided to deal with the matter herself after all it is a very personal matter which is involved and any help might make things worse in this case.

All the writer is really trying to point out is that Cpt. Alexander's writing efforts during the last few weeks, not to mention months, have been absolutely appalling, and have not only been commented on by his 'oh so beloved fiancée' but also by his family. Surely there is no earthly reason why Capt. Alexander can't manage to scribble a few lines every second day. To use the words of a former officer in the artillery, there is always time for a letter and the writer is certainly of the same opinion.

Please see what you can do to satisfy the writer or else the undersigned will have to take drastic steps.

Yours sincerely,
Ann Graetz

A few days after receiving Ann's letter, Tilling wrote back.

10 December 1945

Dear Madam:

As Captain Alexander's Commanding Officer I feel that some explanation is due from me as to his apparent unwillingness to write to you.

Owing to the peculiar qualities of Captain Alexander's character, he is invariably chosen for the most hazardous tasks, and in fact at the moment has been detailed by me to carry out a priority investigation into a German harem. This will, of course, entail working at high pressure by day and night, but in spite of working single handed, it is anticipated that with Captain Alexander's enthusiasm and drive the job should be completed in time for a well earned rest at Christmas in order that he may replenish the lead in his pencil.

In conclusion Madam, may I wish you a very happy Christmas, but I feel I must add a word of sympathy with you in your gallant, but I fear, unavailing task, of piloting Captain Alexander successfully through the troubled waters of married life.

I am, Madam, your obedient servant

T. H. Tilling (Lt Col)

P.S. Actually Alex has no excuse, so if I were you I'd make your next letter even stronger.

Having read the exchange between his girlfriend and his commander, Hanns wrote a letter, which he admitted was 'long overdue', to Ann, or 'Poppit' as he called her. It was three pages, and written on stationery stolen from Gustav Simon. He explained that he had been busy tracking down the Gauleiter, which took more time than he had expected as he had 'put his pride into catching the swine'. He jokingly thanked her for sending her ring finger size, though made it clear that he was not ready to commit, at least for the present. But he did reassure her that he remained loyal to her despite their being so far apart. 'Don't worry about me keeping the Dutch girls warm. I have not got much time to keep anybody warm these days.' He said he would buy her an umbrella from Brussels the next time he visited the city and promised to arrange a leave soon, maybe after

Christmas. 'Otherwise there is little news here. Plenty of work, and no Xmas spirit as we're used to when in the city at this time of year.'

A few days after returning from Luxembourg, Hanns joined his colleagues in the Belsen Officers Club for the 1945 Boxing Day dance. As men and women in uniform crowded together drinking punch, Hanns regaled his colleagues with stories. Above the Yuletide clamour hung a warm veil of excitement, for many would soon be going home, after six years at war.

Belsen had by now been transformed from a German concentration camp into a massive displaced persons' facility. The original barracks had been burned by the British, in an effort to rid the area of disease. The more than 10,000 people that remained in the camp, almost all of whom were Jewish, were housed in a set of old army buildings. Conditions had vastly improved, but most of the survivors were desperate to return home. At the time, it was almost impossible to leave the camp, let alone cross a national border. Belsen was effectively under quarantine.

As Hanns walked around the crowded club that night, he noticed an attractive-looking young woman sitting in the corner. She had shoulder-length brown hair and differed from many in the room in that she hadn't dressed up for the occasion. Apparently impressed by the woman's lack of pretence, he introduced himself and asked her to dance. As they swirled around the dance floor, she told him that her name was Anita Lasker and that, from time to time, she helped the British with translating. She too was a German Jew and had been deported to Auschwitz, only surviving by playing the cello in the Women's Orchestra.

As they danced, Hanns said he could help get Anita and her sister out of the camp. Like the other thousands of former inmates who were still living in Belsen, the two sisters had been unable to secure travel permits to another country. Anita said that if Hanns could get them as far as Brussels, they could then make their own way to London. He agreed and they made plans to meet at the main gate at seven the next morning. Anita then returned to her barracks and stayed up all night forging documents which she hoped would help her out of the country: 'The above mentioned ex-internee of Belsen Concentration Camp is authorized to travell [sic] to Brussels in order to complete repatriation procedure. She is to travel in the custody of Capt. Alexander 12–27–45.'

At seven the next morning, Anita and her sister waited nervously by the camp's main guard post. Next to them stood Anita's cello and an old typewriter case full of their combined belongings. As the minutes went by, she watched the guard raise and lower the red-and-white-striped barrier, allowing trucks to enter and leave the camp. Prisoners wandered along the dusty track in twos and threes to the food tent, where they had breakfast and, an hour or so later, trudged back to the barracks to fill their days playing cards, writing letters or dozing. With every passing minute Anita became more anxious. But Hanns was nowhere to be seen. As the hours went by, Anita began to think that she had imagined the conversation from the night before.

Anita Lasker (left), Belsen

She was just about to give up hope, when Hanns pulled up in a large dark green Mercedes-Benz. 'Sorry,' he said, 'I slept in.'

The two sisters climbed into the back of the vehicle, joining Lucille Eichengreen, another girl whom Hanns had invited along. Hanns and the driver sat in the front. Nobody spoke as they left Belsen and headed towards Holland.

After three hours they arrived at the border where a Dutch guard asked for their papers. What happened next is disputed. By Anita's account, she handed over her obviously suspect document. The guard then pointed out that displaced people were meant to travel in transports, not in private vehicles, and it looked as if he was going to stop them. Hanns, who outranked the guard, stepped out of the car and ordered him to call headquarters. The guard obliged and within a few moments they were through the border post.

Lucille Eichengreen remembers it slightly differently. As they arrived at the border the guards grew suspicious and started yelling. Hanns argued back but was unable to persuade the guards. He turned to the driver and told him to reverse the car and then gun it down an embankment and up another slope. 'Hit the floor,' Hanns shouted. 'The bastards are raising their guns.' Once at a safe distance, Hanns told them they could sit up. They had arrived in Holland.

Whichever story is true, the car made it across the border. A few hours later, the Mercedes arrived in Brussels, and Hanns, his driver and the three young women spent the night with a friend of Hanns' mother. This was the first time in six years that any of the girls had slept in a private house.

The next day, having helped the girls on their journeys, Hanns returned to Belsen.

After months of procrastination, Hanns finally decided it was time to propose to Ann. He had hoped to be demobilised before becoming engaged, and for a long time he had put Ann off by explaining that they should wait until he had a job and a place to call home. But the war was over and her patience had worn thin. Thankfully, Hanns' commanding officer agreed to his extended leave.

In January 1946, Hanns hitched a ride on a series of military trucks and cars, which drove from Belsen, past the ruins and chaos of Holland, Belgium and France. He then caught a boat from Calais to Dover, where he hopped on a train to London. As usual, his twin brother Paul — who was still working in the prisoner-of-war camp in north Germany — was in tune with his plans and was also in town.

Hanns spent a week with Ann, catching up on news and spending a couple of evenings at the pictures. Over a coffee at a small table in the Lyons Corner House, where they had gone on their first date, Hanns asked Ann to marry him. Although she had heard from Hanns' sister Elsie that the proposal was on its way, hearing it from Hanns in person proved to be a great relief to Ann. Of course, she said yes. They agreed to postpone the wedding until he was out of the army and able to support them both.

Back in Germany, Hanns' bosses at the War Crimes Group were drumming their fingers. They needed their investigator back.

15

HANNS AND RUDOLF
GOTTRUPEL AND BELSEN, GERMANY
1946

Rudolf continued to meet his brother-in-law in the early months of 1946. On 3 March, Fritz drove to the farm in Gottrupel to hand over some letters from Hedwig and update Rudolf on the family. They had now moved from the hut to an apartment above an old sugar factory in St Michaelisdonn. Their new home was less exposed to the elements, its roof did not leak and the wind did not penetrate the walls, but Hedwig still struggled to take care of her children.

The one blessing was that Leo Helger, for many years Rudolf's driver at Auschwitz, had managed to track them down (perhaps via one of the other SS officers who had gathered in Flensburg), and passed on money and a few items rescued from Rudolf's accommodation in Berlin: an engraved cigar slicer, a dagger with the SS symbol on its hilt, and a large wooden box carved with ancient rune symbols which had been a gift from Himmler.

Hedwig was grateful for the money, but it did not last long. Food was hard to come by, and the weather was freezing. With few clothes to keep them warm and no money to pay for any kind of assistance, the children had taken to stealing coal from the train cars that stopped for a few hours each week in a siding near the sugar factory. However, these stolen briquettes provided enough heat for only two days, leaving the family without warmth for the remainder of the week. Hedwig had made wooden clogs for the children to wear and while this was an improvement to walking around barefoot in the snow, they were no substitute for real shoes. Brigitte's feet had become frostbitten, and Hedwig dealt with this by placing a piece of liver on each foot and then wrapping them in old rags. They needed better clothes, more heat and more suitable housing. There was no solution in sight. Rudolf was tantalisingly close, but could do nothing to help as his family suffered.

Fritz and Rudolf also talked about the future, particularly the problems that the family would face if they remained in Germany. The resistance movement, such as it was, had failed. There was no hope of the Nazi Party regaining power. The Americans, Soviets and British had total control of the country. Most of the top party leaders and SS officers had been arrested and were standing trial. Many had been hanged.

One option discussed by Rudolf and Fritz was smuggling the family out of the country. Many high-ranking members of the SS and National Socialist Party planned or had already taken this path, typically making their new homes in South America. The list included Adolf Eichmann, with whom Rudolf had worked closely during the liquidation of the Hungarian Jews; Franz Stangl, the former Treblinka Kommandant whom Rudolf had met during one of his many tours; as well as Josef Mengele, the notorious Auschwitz doctor with whom Rudolf had worked and socialised. These Nazis fled along established routes, or 'ratlines'. One ran south, via Italy or Spain. Another route ran north, through Denmark and Sweden. Given his location, this would be the one that Rudolf would take.

But if Rudolf were to flee, he would have to journey ahead alone. Travelling with a wife and five children would be too dangerous for them all. Rudolf struggled with this decision. He did not want to abandon his family, but he knew that if he were caught he would be of no use to them. After much thought, he decided to leave. He would somehow arrange for the family to join him later. Now that the decision was made, there were arrangements to be set in motion, people to be contacted, tickets to be purchased. Fritz would help with the preparations.

In the meantime, one of the most wanted men in Germany would remain hidden, waiting for the right moment to make his move.

In early January 1946, the British War Office in London sent a memo to the War Crimes Group in Germany, criticising their lack of progress in tracking down the war criminals who were still at large and describing the members of the unit as 'static minded'. Group Captain Somerhough wrote back and explained, tersely, that his men could not be faulted for their lack of progress given how severely they were hampered by supply shortages.

> We have found twenty-four wanted men, taken over one thou-
> sand statements. A check on correspondence emanating from
> this team with regard to vehicles, the need for mechanics and
> policemen, will show that for months past we have been
> screaming for facilities to make us less 'static minded'. We cannot
> move if we have no transport.

It was time to shift strategy. Following Hanns' successful arrest of Gustav Simon, Somerhough decided that rather than continuing to interrogate the Nazi officials already in custody, they should attempt to track down the uncaptured war criminals, focusing on a number of high-profile cases which he deemed winnable in court. Somerhough now instructed the War Crimes Group to zero in on the men who ran the concentration camp inspectorate, *Amtsgruppe D.*

In a memo written in the third week of January 1946, Lieutenant

Colonel Tilling outlined his plans: he would send two investigators to *Amtsgruppe D*'s headquarters in Berlin. One would be Major Caola, a barrister from London who had recently joined the team; the other was Captain H. H. Alexander. The only problem was that Hanns was still in Britain with his new fiancée.

18 January 1946

Subject: Availability of Capt HH Alexander PC

DJAG (War Crimes Section)

HQ BOAR

1. Reference your BAOR/ 15228/ 2/ c.1821 dated 12 Jan 46
2. Captain ALEXANDER will be instructed to report to you immediately on his return from leave, which is expected to be 24 Jan 1946.
3. At the moment, Major CAOLA is acquainting himself with the Amtsgruppe D set-up and it had been the intention that he should be responsible for the investigations in this department. In view of this Major CAOLA will be interrogating the members of Amtsgruppe D known by this team to be in custody.
4. It was understood that Captain ALEXANDER would be engaged mainly on the location and arrest of further wanted persons from Amtsgruppe D. It is suggested that it would be preferable if Major CAOLA could be present at any interrogation of such persons located by Captain ALEXANDER.

Commander No 1 War Crimes Investigation Team

Lt Col Tilling

(HOHNE) Belsen Camp

In the last week of January, Hanns arrived back at 1 WCIT's headquarters. He was hastily briefed by Tilling, and then, four days later, on 28 January 1946, Hanns and Major Caola drove out of the camp towards Berlin.

After ten years away, Hanns found the city unrecognisable. The two men slowly navigated the snowy streets, horrified at the scale of the devastation: the People's Court, the Reich Chancellery and the Gestapo headquarters had all been heavily damaged; the shopping district of Unter den Linden, where Hanns had been taken by his nanny to buy his birthday presents, was also damaged. Many of Berlin's finest monuments lay in ruins. The Neue Synagogue on Oranienburger Strasse, where Hanns had been bar mitzvahed, was little more than a blackened carcass, having received a direct hit from a British firebomb.

Hanns then drove to Berlin's west end to see his old neighbourhood. His father's four-storey sanatorium on Achenbachstrasse had been reduced to a pile of rocks and timber. Round the corner the apartment building on Kaiserallee, where Hanns had grown up, was still standing, although it looked as if it would soon have to be torn down. Even the zoo, which he had visited so often as a young boy, had not escaped the destruction; its monkey house and reptile buildings were now shells, although the animals, luckily, had been removed before the bombs had hit.

In a letter to his parents, Hanns described the damage: 'Berlin as a town has had it, for twenty years I reckon at least. What is not destroyed by bombs was done in by street fighting. Kaiserallee 220 finished, Achenbachstr. 15 finished . . . Adlon, Eden, and all the decent hotels have had it. We were in the Savoy in the Fasenenstrasse, first class, with the exception of hot water, which is only available Sunday afternoons. I passed Glienicke. House O.K. Garden very *verwildert* [wild]. And looks tiny, as the trees etc are all so big, that it looks much more closed in and smaller.' He added that he had news on his father's First World War colleague who had defended their home during the 1933 Jewish boycott. While he did not know the cause or the circumstances, sadly he could now confirm that 'Oberst Meyer is dead'.

Hanns next went to the Red Cross offices, where he learned that his great-aunt, Cäcilie Bing, had been put on a transport and sent to Auschwitz in September 1942. From his time in Belsen and having followed the War Crimes Trials, Hanns knew that if she had reached Auschwitz then it was unlikely that she would have survived.

Hanns spent the next few days checking the rest of the names that had been given to him by Ann and his sisters. The story was always the same: 'No, the person is no longer living in Berlin' and 'Yes, they had been sent to the camps in the East.' He walked up and down the streets of Wilmersdorf, the Jewish neighbourhood where his family had lived — Fasanenstrasse, Kurfürstendamm, Rankeplatz — checking the old grocers, shoemakers, tailors and jewellers he had once frequented. Hanns was unable to find a single person who remembered him. It was as if this part of his history had been wiped clean.

Hanns rejoined Major Caola and together they drove out to Oranienburg to investigate the T-building, the offices of the Concentration Camp Inspectorate. Remarkably, the structure had survived the war. Hanns opened the large front doors and, walking into the main hallway, he found an office layout chart hanging on the wall. The map detailed the name of each office's occupant, along with their titles and their telephone numbers. For the next few hours Caola and Hanns worked their way through the now deserted offices, searching the desks and cabinets for any information that would lead them to the wanted men. The exploration was fruitless. The building's archives had been destroyed, just as Himmler had ordered.

With little in the way of physical evidence, Hanns and Caola set off in search of former staff. They first visited an American-run prisoner-of-war camp located just outside the city centre. There they found Karl Sommer, the thirty-one-year-old from Cologne who had been third in command at *Amtsgruppe D*, beneath Richard Glücks and Gerhard Maurer. Sommer told them that the Concentration Camp Inspectorate leaders had headed north in April 1945, just before the war's end. He also provided a clear outline of who had worked for whom in the T-building, and from this they drew a chart.

Organisation Chart of the SS Economic–Administrative Main Office (WVHA)

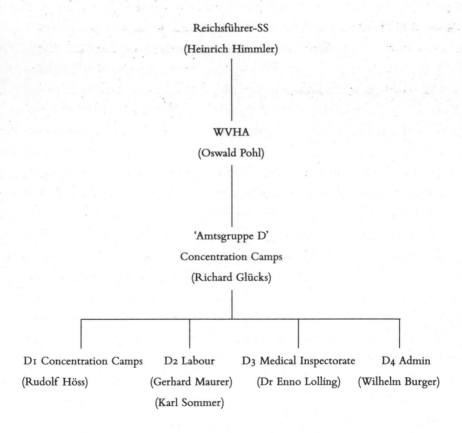

Reichsführer-SS
(Heinrich Himmler)

WVHA
(Oswald Pohl)

'Amtsgruppe D'
Concentration Camps
(Richard Glücks)

D1 Concentration Camps	D2 Labour	D3 Medical Inspectorate	D4 Admin
(Rudolf Höss)	(Gerhard Maurer)	(Dr Enno Lolling)	(Wilhelm Burger)
	(Karl Sommer)		

Given the chaos that dominated Berlin at this time, their efforts to locate senior members of *Amtsgruppe D* proved futile. For instance, they discovered that Oswald Pohl's former secretary, Frau Fauler, had secured a job in the Allies' administrative offices, but when they arrived to question her they were told that she was away on leave. Pohl's driver, Walter Seinfert, had also been working with the US military, but the two men could now find no trace of him in Berlin.

They had more success at a Berlin press agency, where they collected photographs and clippings of the SS leaders, taken before and during the war. Then they tracked down Oswald Pohl's former adjutant, Georg Witt, also in American custody. Witt told them that Pohl and his staff had departed Berlin ten months earlier, on 12 April 1945, intending to establish a Southern Command near Munich. However, following the Americans' swift advance through southern Germany, they had been forced to abandon this plan and, after a short stay in Dachau, the group had split up. Witt said that he and Pohl had only just managed to avoid the oncoming American forces. They reached the home of Pohl's former wife, in the Bavarian town of Brunningsau, sometime later that evening. This was the last that he was to see of his superior; Pohl fled sometime during the night. Punctilious as ever, Hanns wrote down Witt's testimony, along with the name and address of Pohl's former wife, and cabled the information back to the two Haystack investigators who were hunting down the former head of the WVHA.

By 18 February 1946, Hanns and Major Caola had built up a list of more than 130 people who had been employed by the WVHA, over 50 per cent of whom had worked for *Amtsgruppe D*. Each name was carefully written into a small notebook, which they called the 'Black Book'.

Most critically, almost everyone they had spoken to had described the flight of the Concentration Camp Inspectorate's most senior officers north towards the Danish border. The group had included Glücks, Maurer and Höss, along with their family members.

In a report summarising their trip to Berlin, Major Caola wrote:

The main efforts of the Investigating Officers have so far been concentrated on gathering information, which, it is hoped, will lead to the location and arrest of 'wanted' persons and with the exception of any lead which Capt. Alexander may obtain in Flensburg area, which he hopes to visit within the next few days, it is considered unlikely that additional information will be forthcoming until some further arrests are made. It is therefore suggested that the 'Hunt' should commence as soon as Capt. Alexander has collected whatever clues are available at Flensburg. As it is the intention that Capt. Alexander will himself conduct the search for the higher officers, it is suggested that the task of searching for the minor officers and others who may be considered as potential witnesses is one that can be carried out by 'Haystack'.

Back in Belsen, Tilling briefed Hanns on the latest intelligence on the *Amtsgruppe D* leaders: two Haystack operatives were hot on the trail of Oswald Pohl and the Americans were looking for Gerhard Maurer, who was believed to be in their zone. Meanwhile, British intelligence had confirmed that Dr Enno Lolling had committed suicide in May 1945, while Sommer was in American custody and Burger was being held by the Poles. This meant that Hanns' primary targets should now be Richard Glücks, the notorious head of *Amtsgruppe D*, and Rudolf Höss. Both were suspected of being in the Flensburg area, near the Danish border.

Hanns was handed a report on Glücks from a British intelligence unit based near Flensburg. Since May 1945, rumours had swirled around Glücks' fate: some suggested that he had fled to South America; others said that he now ran a secret network of former Nazis called ODESSA; while others believed that he was still hiding in southern Germany. According to interviews with the staff at the Murvik Naval Hospital near Flensburg, the report stated that a man calling himself 'Sonneman', but believed to be Glücks, was admitted in early May 1945 and was pronounced dead only a few days later: 'Poisoning by prussic acid (suicide)', the report declared, going on to state that a body had been buried in the Flensburg cemetery on 18 May, and later exhumed, but with no positive identification made.

There was no specific information on Höss, but Hanns was told to check in with British intelligence operating in the area, who apparently had a lead on members of his family.

Taking a vehicle from the War Crimes Group's car pool, Hanns set off for Flensburg. The roads were congested with the post-war reconstruction traffic. Large trucks and lorries transporting tools and goods from the ports around Hamburg to the cities to the south slowed the journey, and the uncleared snow from the previous week's heavy storms made the roads slick and treacherous.

Hanns' first stop was at the home of Glücks' wife, Aloise, at 25 Friedrichshof. She confirmed that she had left Berlin with her husband at the end of April 1945 — along with the other members of *Amtsgruppe D*, including Höss, Maurer and Lolling — arriving in Flensburg on 1 May 1945. She said that she believed that her husband had committed suicide on 10 May, though she admitted that she was not a witness. When pushed, she confessed that she had heard a rumour from Professor Gebhardt — Himmler's personal physician no less — that her husband was alive. He had said that Glücks was 'well and hidden' and that she should not look for him any further as she would be 'endangering the lives of others'. Yet, she repeated, she still believed that her husband was dead, and produced what she claimed was her husband's bottom jaw, pointing out that the bone and teeth were still filled with glass splinters, apparent evidence that he had bitten down on the poisonous capsule. Hanns remained sceptical. In a field report he wrote:

Frau Glücks is wearing black mourning. I noticed that she wears only one wedding ring, contrary to the custom of widows wearing both,

husbands and wives wedding rings, on one finger. I did not interrogate on that point, so as not to raise any suspicion.

With Glücks' case grown cold, Hanns turned his attention to the
next name on his list: the Kommandant of Auschwitz, Rudolf Höss.

A few days later, on 8 March 1946, Hanns stepped out of his car
and walked towards a modest white-brick building in the centre of
Heide, a small town situated fifty miles south of Flensburg. This was
the headquarters of British Field Security Section 92.

The British had created more than a hundred Field Security
Sections to oversee the massive swathe of land which they controlled
in post-war north Germany. Falling somewhere between a police
organisation and a counter-intelligence force, these Field Security
Sections filled a critical hole created by the collapse of the German
security apparatus, suppressing any acts of armed resistance by the
local population and imposing basic law and order.

Hanns was ushered into a back office and introduced to Captain
William Victor Cross, the commander of FSS 92. At thirty-three,
Cross was just four years older than Hanns. A man with a ruddy face
and a stout build, Cross had served in the Intelligence Corps since
1939 and was well loved by his men.

Hanns explained his mission: that he worked for 1 War Crimes
Investigation Team, had orders to hunt down and arrest Rudolf Höss,
and that he had recent intelligence suggesting that the Kommandant
was hiding somewhere in the Flensburg vicinity. Cross replied that his
unit's prime activity was to maintain the peace, but as Höss' name
appeared high on the list of wanted war criminals, they too had been
keeping an eye out for him. Unfortunately, they didn't know where
he was hiding or if he had adopted a new identity. However, they had
been monitoring his wife and children, who were living in the old
sugar factory in St Michaelisdonn, and his men had recently intercepted
a letter from Rudolf Höss to his wife – they monitored all the local

mail – proving that Hedwig knew the whereabouts of her husband, or at least knew someone who did. As a result, the day before Hanns' arrival, on 7 March, they had pulled Hedwig in for questioning.

Hanns was delighted to hear this good fortune. A few minutes later he and Sergeant Koolish, a member of Field Security Section 92 who also spoke German, were driven to Lunden prison. Inside one of the cells sat a round-faced woman wearing a dirty blouse and a peasant's skirt. Although Hedwig no longer had servants to order about, nor the fine furniture or artwork which filled her house in Auschwitz, she retained an air of arrogance. Hanns told Hedwig in German that he was a captain in the British Army and that he had some questions regarding her husband. He asked her how long she had been living in the sugar factory and how had she made her way from Auschwitz to Flensburg. Had she been in contact with her husband? Where was he living? What identity had he adopted? In almost theatrical fashion, Hedwig refused to reveal anything.

Given their lack of progress, Hanns suggested that they should employ one of 'Tin Eye' Stephens' interrogation tricks: use a child to pressure their parent into talking. The next day Hanns and four members of Field Security Section 92 drove to the sugar factory on the outskirts of St Michaelisdonn. Hanns walked up the stairs and into the apartment. It was dark, unkempt and cold. With the mother in custody, the children had had to fend for themselves. The place had little furniture – a small wooden table, some old chairs. There were no mattresses on the floors or pictures on the wall. It was more temporary accommodation than a home. Hanns was met by the four oldest children. He told them to sit on the table (the youngest was asleep under a blanket in the corner). Hanns began barking questions, demanding that they tell him where their father was living. The children replied meekly that they did not know. Hanns walked up to Klaus, and, putting his face close to the boy's, screamed the question again: 'Where is your father?' Again the same answer. Hanns banged his fists on the table in frustration. 'You must know!' He walked up to the oldest daughter, Heidetraut, and shouted that if she didn't tell him the truth then he would arrest Klaus. The girl whimpered, saying she didn't know any more than the other children. Brigitte was next. When Hanns bellowed that he would kill their mother if she didn't confess, Brigitte ran out of the room and hid under a tree behind the factory with her hands over her ears. A few minutes later she looked up and saw the British soldiers leave. Sitting in the back of their truck was her brother, Klaus.

As soon as they arrived in Lunden, Hanns pulled the boy from the truck and escorted him into the prison, where his mother was being held. She was shocked to see her son. Yet, despite any fears that she might have had over his safety, her answer remained the same as it had been for days: 'I do not know where my husband is living.' But having seen her anguish when the boy was brought in, all Hanns needed was to find the best way to convince her that Klaus's life was in danger.

When Hanns came in to question the boy the next day, the young Höss seemed willing to talk. He said that he hadn't seen his father since the last days of the war, in May 1945, when he'd carried a letter from Rudolf to Hedwig, along with Rudolf's *Totenkopfring*, the silver death's-head ring with the Reichsführer's signature engraved inside which he'd been given personally by Himmler. However, he maintained that he did not know where his father had been staying for the past few months.

Seeing her son being interrogated, Hedwig decided to retaliate by announcing that she and Klaus were now on a hunger strike. In response, Hanns asked the prison warden to move Hedwig to a separate cell. But each time Hanns entered Hedwig's cell and asked one question – 'Where is your husband?' – she replied, 'He is dead.'

With their tactics of isolation and intimidation failing to produce a result, Hanns realised that they must develop an alternative approach. At twilight on 11 March 1946, a noisy old steam train was driven past the rear of the prison. Hanns burst into Hedwig's cell and informed her that the train was about to take her son to Siberia and that she would never see Klaus again. Allowing the message to sink in for a few moments, Hanns then added that she could prevent her son's deportation if she told him where her husband was living and under what alias. Hanns then left Hedwig sitting on her cot with a piece of paper and a pencil. When he returned ten minutes later, he saw that she had written a note with Rudolf's location and his alias: the Kommandant of Auschwitz was living at Hans Peter Hansen's farm in Gottrupel under the name 'Franz Lang'.

16

HANNS AND RUDOLF
GOTTRUPEL, GERMANY
1946

As soon as Hanns had heard Hedwig Höss' confession, he rushed over to Captain Cross, and the two quickly agreed a plan. They should carry out the arrest under the cover of darkness, and as soon as possible. And they would need serious firepower. It was unclear if Rudolf was alone, and there was every chance that he would resist arrest.

Over the next hour the men of Field Security Section 92 were assembled and briefed on the operation. Many of them were German Jews like Hanns, from the Pioneer Corps – men who had been driven out of their country and who had lost family members in Auschwitz. Some had kept their original names, such as Kuditsch and Wiener. Others had taken on British-sounding names, like Roberts, Cresswell and Shiffers. There were also English-born soldiers from Jewish families, similarly enraged, men such as Bernard Clarke, from the south coast, and Karl 'Blitz' Abrahams, from Liverpool.

Rifles were checked and supplies loaded into the trucks: blankets, a field radio, cartons of extra ammunition. A box of axe handles was stashed into the back of one of the vehicles. Hanns, meanwhile, put a call in to the commander of Field Security Section 318, explaining the mission and requesting additional backup. He also arranged for a doctor from the 5th Royal Horse Artillery regiment to join them.

Two hours later, the small convoy of trucks and jeeps hurried along the narrow roads towards Gottrupel. Darkness had descended on the German countryside. Inside the vehicles twenty-five men sat nervously on benches, fidgeting with their gear. Hanns knew that they all wanted to be 'in on the kill'.

It was pitch black and utterly quiet when the convoy rolled into the farmyard in Gottrupel at eleven o'clock on 11 March 1946. Getting out of his jeep, and accompanied by the medical officer and the driver, Hanns ordered the others to hold back. He walked towards the barn and knocked loudly.

Rudolf was 'woken with a start' by the commotion outside. At first, he was unconcerned, assuming 'that it was one of the robberies which were very frequent at this time in the area'. Then he heard a stern voice ordering him to open up. Realising that he had no alternative, Rudolf opened the door. Two men in British uniform stood facing him. Rudolf could tell by their insignia that one was a captain, the other a doctor. Behind them stood at least twenty soldiers, their guns drawn. He was confused by the lights and the presence of all these men.

Without warning the tall, handsome, fierce-looking captain thrust a pistol in his mouth. He was then searched for cyanide pills. 'Go and see that he is clean,' Hanns said to the doctor, holding Rudolf while his mouth was searched for vials of poison. After a few seconds the doctor gave the all-clear.

The captain began talking in perfect German. It was immediately obvious to Rudolf that the man was a native speaker. He introduced himself as Captain Alexander of the British War Crimes Investigation Team, and demanded to see Rudolf's papers. The Kommandant handed over his identity documents — Franz Lang, temporary card number B22595. Hanns had seen this name on the plate next to the barn door, but knew it to be untrue. The man looked too similar to the figure in the photograph that he carried with him. Older, sicker, thinner, to be sure, but similar.

Hanns flashed the photograph and told Rudolf that he believed him to be the Kommandant of Auschwitz. Again Rudolf denied the claim, pointing once more at his identity papers. Perhaps he would be able to wriggle out of this: after all, the British had let him slip through their fingers in the past.

However, Hanns remained convinced. He rolled back the man's shirtsleeves to see if there was a blood group tattooed on his arm, but there was nothing. The conversation went round in circles. Yet Hanns wasn't going to give up. His eyes roved about the barn entrance searching for a way to prove the man's identity.

At last Hanns looked down and noticed his wedding ring.

'Give it to me,' he said.

'I can't, it has been stuck for years,' Rudolf answered.

'No problem,' Hanns said, 'I'll just cut off your finger.'

Hanns asked one of the members of Field Security Section 92 to fetch a kitchen knife from inside the barn. When this man returned, he handed the knife to Hanns, who stepped forward, clearly intent on carrying out his threat. Realising he would lose the ring either way, Rudolf reluctantly removed the wedding band from his finger. Then, staring furiously at Hanns, he handed it over. Hanns held the ring up to the light and looked inside the band, where he saw the names 'Rudolf' and 'Hedwig' inscribed. Hanns thanked him and put the ring in his pocket.

Having identified his man, Hanns was ready to make the arrest. But he sensed that his colleagues wanted to vent their hatred. Indeed, he wanted to join in. He had to make a quick decision: should he allow them free rein, or should he protect Rudolf? Turning to his men, Hanns said, 'In ten minutes I want to have Höss in my car – undamaged' and walked off. He knew that this made him responsible for what was about to happen, but he was prepared to face the consequences.

Rudolf was immediately surrounded by the remaining soldiers, who dragged him to one of the barn's slaughter tables, tore the pyjamas from his body and beat him with axe handles. Rudolf screamed, but the blows kept coming. After a short period, the doctor spoke to Hanns: 'Call them off,' he said, 'unless you want to take back a corpse.'

Just as suddenly as it had started, the beating stopped. A rough woollen blanket was wrapped around Rudolf's shoulders, and he was carried out of the barn.

At around midnight the prisoner was loaded into the truck. Hanns and three sergeants climbed in after. Hanns told the driver to make for Heide where they would deliver Rudolf to the local jail. Hanns sat on one of the benches next to Rudolf in the back of the truck. As the vehicle rumbled along the narrow roads, Hanns asked the prisoner a series of questions: What is your name? What was your rank in the SS? What role did you play during the war? Did you work at Auschwitz? At last, after repeated questioning, Rudolf confirmed to Hanns that he had worked as the Kommandant of Auschwitz, and that he had been 'personally responsible for the deaths of 10,000 people'. Hanns realised with rising excitement that not only had he captured his man, but that he was willing to talk.

When they arrived in Heide two hours later, the trucks pulled up at a bar in the centre of town, where Paul was waiting for them. With Rudolf left in the truck, under guard, Hanns and the other men, around twenty-five in all, piled into the bar. Extraordinarily, Hanns had interrupted the safe delivery of the most wanted war criminal into custody, in order to celebrate.

Paul described this scene to his parents in a letter he penned the next day:

13 March 1946

Hanns had a very successful time here, though very busy. But he is not leaving empty handed. He caught the bastard from Auschwitz. I have never seen such a shit in all my life. After all was over I found the party for celebration while Rudolf's feet got cold in the car under escort. We drank to the success with champagne and whiskey. Just right for the job. But will have to leave the details of the description to Hanns. He is a good bloke but don't tell him otherwise he gets *eingebildet* [smug].

After they were finished celebrating, Hanns walked back to the truck, pulled Rudolf out of the vehicle, removed the blanket from his shoulders, and made him walk naked to the prison on the other side of the snow-covered main square. Once inside the prison Hanns,

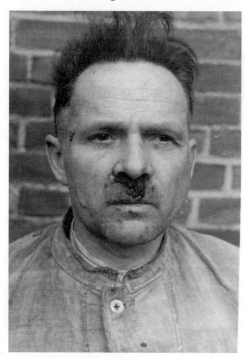

along with a sergeant from the Field Security Section, began Rudolf's first formal interrogation. Alcohol was forced down the prisoner's throat and they beat him with his own whip, confiscated from the barn in Gottrupel. A pair of handcuffs were on his wrists at all times, and with the temperature in the cell well below freezing, Rudolf's uncovered feet quickly developed frostbite.

Three days later, on 15 March 1946, Hanns delivered Rudolf to Camp Tomato, a British-run prison near the town of Minden. There, Colonel Gerald Draper — the War Crimes Group's lawyer — began a further round of intensive questioning. A few hours afterwards, Rudolf's statement was typed up into an eight-page confession and a one-paragraph summary. It was the first time that a concentration camp Kommandant had provided details of the Final Solution. Rudolf had confessed to coordinating the killing of two million people.

17

HANNS AND RUDOLF
BELSEN AND NUREMBERG, GERMANY
1946

After dropping Rudolf off in prison, Hanns drove to Hamburg and checked in at the Atlantic, a luxurious hotel on the banks of Lake Alster. He headed for the bar and began an evening of heavy drinking. Later that night, on the way back to his room on the third floor, he noticed that some guests had left their shoes outside their rooms. Looking around to make sure nobody was watching, he snatched them up and slung them down the stairwell.

The next day he was happily surprised to see his twin brother at breakfast. He had imagined that Paul was still busy supervising a prisoner-of-war camp but, as had so often happened during the war, their schedules coincided.

'What did you do last night?' Paul asked.

'I drank too much and threw officers' shoes down the stairs from the third floor!'

'Funny, I did exactly the same thing, but I took them from the fourth floor!'

At breakfast, they did not speak about their work at any great length; it was not something they talked about, either then or later. Paul was tired of life in the army, furious at all that the Germans had done, and simply wanted to go back to England. Similarly, Hanns, while proud of his war crimes work, had so much that he didn't want to relive: the horrors he had seen in Belsen, the testimony given by the SS officers from Auschwitz, the intensity of tracking down the war criminals. Far better, they both thought, to get drunk. And so, the twins embarked on a grand tour of Hamburg's bars, drinking vast amounts together, continuing their celebration of the arrest of Rudolf Höss.

Five days later, Hanns drove back to Belsen. There he was congratulated again by his commander, Lieutenant Colonel Tilling, and given some big news: it was time to go home.

With the end of the Belsen trials, and with the Nuremberg Trials well under way, Haystack needed to undergo a transformation. They would now focus on different targets: some of the lesser SS guards, industrialists who had collaborated with the Nazis, and a new breed of enemy — the men and women who were undermining the British and American efforts in the burgeoning Cold War. New investigators had arrived in the camp, men with real police and legal experience. Amateurs such as Hanns were no longer required.

Hanns was not disappointed; he was more than ready to return to civilian life. He spent the next few days typing up a report of his time in Berlin and Flensburg and filling out administrative forms. A few days later he said goodbye to his colleagues, and then hitched a ride on an army truck to Brussels. As he crossed the border out of Germany, Hanns swore that he would never return to the country of his birth.

From Belgium he took a ferry across the Channel, and from there, a train to Guildford. Here he was given his demobilisation papers and a brand-new dark blue suit. It was 20 April 1946. Hanns' war had finally ended.

A few days later, he received an envelope in the mail. Inside were his naturalisation papers. After six and a half years in the British Army, Hanns Herman Alexander had finally become a British citizen.

On Sunday, 19 May 1946, Hanns and Ann were married at the recently formed New Liberal Jewish Synagogue in north-west London. Hanns wore his starched khaki British Army uniform and shiny patent leather boots, his cap tilted roguishly to one side. Ann had chosen an ivory bridal gown, accessorised with a matching pillbox hat, a short veil and high-heeled shoes. Paul – who had been demobilised on the same day as his brother – stood next to them, also dressed in his army uniform. Behind them, in a curtained cupboard, lay the Alexander Torah.

The Trial of the Major War Criminals before the International Military Tribunal, more commonly known as the Nuremberg Trials, had opened four months before Rudolf Höss' arrest. The city had been chosen to host the trial partly for its historical significance – it was here that tens of thousands of people had attended Hitler's rallies at the height of Nazi power in the 1930s – but also because it was located in the American Zone. And although the trials were considered an international effort, the Allies had agreed that the US would run the show.

The trials were being held at the Palace of Justice. Built from a blend of white, beige, bronze and almond-coloured stone, the building occupied an entire block. Despite suffering some damage during the war, the palace had survived mostly intact.

The trials began on 20 November 1945. Justice Robert Jackson, the chief prosecutor for the Americans, provided the opening statement.

> The wrongs which we seek to condemn and punish have been so calculated, so malignant, and so devastating, that civilization cannot tolerate their being ignored because it cannot survive their being repeated. That four great nations, flushed with victory and stung with injury, stay the hands of vengeance and voluntarily submit their captive enemies to the judgment of law

is one of the most significant tributes that Power has ever paid
to Reason.

Charges of crimes against humanity were read out against twenty-
four of the highest-ranking Nazis then in captivity, including
Hermann Göring (head of the Luftwaffe and designated successor to
Hitler), Rudolf Hess (Hitler's deputy), Albert Speer (responsible for
armaments), Joachim von Ribbentrop (foreign minister), Hans Frank
(head of the government in occupied Poland), Ernst Kaltenbrunner
(chief of the *Reichssicherheitshauptamt*, or Reich Security Main Office,
and the highest-ranking SS officer after Himmler's death). Martin
Bormann (head of the Nazi Party), who was still missing, would be
tried *in absentia*.

Over the course of the previous four months, the prosecution had
called hundreds of witnesses and submitted reams of affidavits from
concentration camp victims. They had entered stacks of correspondence, from one senior leader to another, into evidence, as well as
purchase orders and receipts which evidenced the supply of Zyklon
B in the camps, and copies of the personnel files that proved the
precise whereabouts and responsibilities of the defendants. The
evidence was undeniable: the Nazis had overseen mass murder and
atrocity on an unprecedented scale. But when the time came for the
accused to take the stand, each in turn denied knowledge of this
genocide.

The Nuremberg Trials were covered extensively by the world's
media. With each passing day, the newspapers published increasingly
alarmed editorials speculating that many of the men on trial might
avoid guilty verdicts, despite their apparent involvement with the
murder of millions of Jews, Communists and Gypsies in the camps.
It looked as though the trials might become an abject failure.

Meanwhile, news of Rudolf's arrest had spread.

★

On 17 March 1946, the *New York Times* reported that, after a nine-month search, British agents had captured Rudolf Höss, 'probably the greatest individual killer in the history of the world'. A few days later, British military newsletters published in Hamburg, Flensburg and other German cities, ran similar stories under the headline 'Two million persons gassed! The Kommandant of Auschwitz confesses'. These articles provided details that Rudolf had given to the British at Camp Tomato, including his description of the selections, the gas chambers and the crematoria.

Yet despite his arrest, confession and new-found publicity, it was not clear where Rudolf himself would stand trial. The Allies had agreed that war criminals should be handed over to the countries where their crimes took place. The problem was that such a trial required considerable organisational skills and resources, not something readily available to the nascent Polish government now struggling to run a war-ravaged country, let alone supervise a major war crimes trial.

Cables zipped back and forth between London and Warsaw, with the British offering to try Rudolf themselves, and the Poles refusing to commit to a hearing.

While the argument raged as to where Höss should stand trial, Whitney Harris, a young American prosecutor at the Nuremberg Trials, came up with an idea. He was coming to the end of the case against Ernst Kaltenbrunner and was desperate to find a high-ranking figure willing to confirm what had taken place in the concentration camps. After reading one of the news reports, Harris realised that if Rudolf Höss appeared as a witness, then his testimony would not only become part of the official record, thus corroborating the evidence given by so many of the victims, but, just perhaps, other defendants might be implicated, or shamed into admitting their own guilt.

Harris sent an urgent cable to Camp Tomato requesting that Rudolf Höss be brought to Nuremberg:

30 March 1946
British War Crimes Executive
European Section Nuremberg
211430A
Restricted

PRESS REPORT THAT RUDOLF HÖSS FORMER KOMMANDANT OF AUSCHWITZ CONCENTRATION CAMPS HAS BEEN CAPTURED (.) CONSIDER HÖSS CAN PROBABLY PROVIDE INFORMATION IMPLICATING KALTENBRUNNER AND OTHERS AND WOULD BE GRATEFUL IF HE CAN BE BROUGHT TO NUREMBERG SOONEST (SOONEST) FOR INTERROGATION (.) ON ARRIVAL HERE HE SHOULD BE TRANSFERRED IN CARE OF 6850 I.S.D. PALACE OF JUSTICE AND ESCORT SHOULD REPORT TO ROOM 216 PALACE OF JUSTICE (.) PLEASE SIGNAL E.T.A.

The next day, two British military policemen transported the manacled Rudolf Höss from Camp Tomato three hundred miles south to Nuremberg. He was processed at the palace by a clerk who filled in a 'Prisoner of War Preliminary Record', which included basic information such as name, date of birth, rank, height and weight. Under 'characteristics', he wrote that the prisoner had gold-filled teeth, brown eyes, fair hair, and 'frozen' left and right feet, and then had Rudolf sign the page.

After being fingerprinted, Rudolf was taken down a spiral staircase to the basement, his footsteps echoing off the corridor's whitewashed walls. Outside each cell stood an American guard, posted there on twenty-four-hour watch ever since the suicide of one defendant, Robert Ley, a few months earlier. Rudolf was placed alone in a bare concrete-walled cell in the basement of the palace's C Wing. The cell

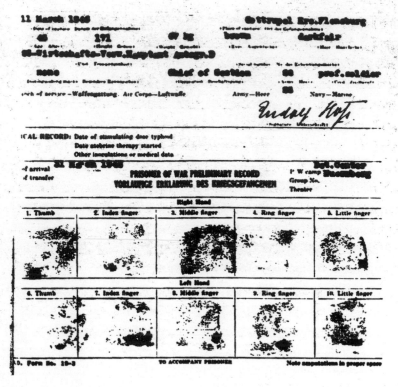

had a tiny window near the ceiling. All it contained was a cot with a thin mattress and a woollen blanket folded neatly at its end, a wooden stool and a bucket in the corner.

The next morning, on 1 April 1946, Rudolf was taken to a small office where Whitney Harris sat behind a wooden table, with a court reporter and a translator beside him. The three weeks in British captivity had taken their toll. Rudolf's eyes were bloodshot, his cheeks were unshaven and gaunt, his frame appeared fragile. He was a shrunken man. Nevertheless, Harris was surprised by Rudolf's appearance. He had expected to meet a larger man, someone who exuded power and brutality, someone with charisma. Instead, Rudolf seemed to Harris like an ordinary-looking fellow, like a 'grocer's assistant', somebody you wouldn't give a second look to if you passed him on the street.

By contrast, Whitney Harris looked dapper, dressed in a dark blue navy uniform with double-breasted jacket and large brass buttons. Harris was excited, for while he had been in Nuremberg since the previous summer and had talked face-to-face with many of the senior Nazis held there, he still hadn't met anybody who could provide details on the inner workings of the concentration camps.

Rudolf sat before him, his eyes fixed on the floor, waiting for Harris to speak. The only sound was that of the prisoner cracking his knuckles. After a few moments the American prosecutor asked for a brief rundown of Rudolf's biography. As the interpreter translated Rudolf's words, Harris wrote the answers on a legal pad lying on the table. Eventually, they came to Auschwitz. How many people had been killed there? Harris asked. Without hesitation, Rudolf told him that three million had died: two and a half million in the gas chambers and another half a million from starvation and disease.

While Harris was deeply disturbed by the emotionless confession, he was also quietly pleased. Such a statement would play a key role in the trial, since all the defendants had refused to confirm what had taken place at the concentration camps up until this point. By now Harris had rested the case for the prosecution, but he had managed to persuade Kaltenbrunner's defence lawyers to call Rudolf as a witness. They were happy to oblige, for their defendant had been charged with the construction and the maintenance of camps, and Rudolf's testimony would prove that Kaltenbrunner had never even visited Auschwitz.

The next day Harris interviewed Rudolf again, and spent the evening typing up his confession. Harris selected only the most pertinent parts of the Kommandant's testimony, which he put into his own words. The thrust and meaning of the affidavit was the Kommandant's, he would later maintain; all he had done was to select words that would have the most impact in court. Returning the next day to Rudolf's cell, he then presented the prisoner with a polished affidavit. With only minor changes, Rudolf agreed – after all, he had learned to speak English while in jail in the 1920s – and signed at the bottom of the last page. Now it was only a question of the defence deciding when to bring Rudolf forward as a witness.

With so many senior Nazis held in one place at the same time, the Americans had instructed a panel of psychologists to conduct extensive interviews and tests with the defendants. While Rudolf waited in his cell to be called as a witness, he was visited by a psychologist and a psychiatrist.

The first was Gustave Gilbert, a New Yorker born to Jewish-Austrian immigrants. Gilbert asked Rudolf to complete a simple intelligence test as well as a Rorschach ink-blot test. He concluded that, like the other Nazis he had interviewed, Rudolf tested above average for intelligence. Gilbert then asked for a brief career summary. As he had done with Harris, Rudolf admitted in an unemotional tone that he had been responsible for the deaths of more than two and a half million Jews. The American then asked how it was possible to kill so many people. 'Technically,' answered Rudolf, 'that wasn't so hard – it would not have been hard to exterminate even greater numbers.' Gilbert then pressed him for an emotional response, but Rudolf continued in a similar tone: 'At the time there were no consequences to consider. It didn't occur to me that I would be held responsible. You see, in Germany it was understood that if something went wrong, then the man who gave the orders was responsible.' Gilbert started to ask, 'But what about the human —' before Rudolf interrupted, 'That just didn't enter into it.' After a few more questions, Rudolf said, 'I suppose you want to know in this way if my thought and habits are normal.' 'Well, what do you think?' Gilbert asked. 'I am entirely normal,' said Rudolf. 'Even while I was doing the extermination work, I led a normal family life.' When Gilbert then asked about his social life, the Kommandant replied that he was a loner by nature, unable to interact on any deep level with friends and colleagues, and that he felt at his best when he was alone. He confessed that he had stopped having sex with his wife after she found out about the gas chambers in the camp, and although he confirmed having affairs during his marriage, claimed that he was not a very sexual man. When Gilbert asked about his feelings towards his Jewish victims, Rudolf explained that it was just assumed that the Jews were to blame for the economic and social hardships in Germany and that this came from the newspapers as well as the military, who declared that they had to protect Germany from the Jews. 'You can be sure that it was not always pleasant to see those mountains of corpses and smell the continual burning,' he continued, 'but Himmler had ordered it and had even explained the necessity and I really never gave much thought to whether it was wrong.' Rudolf added, 'The problem itself, the extermination of Jewry was not new — but only that I was to be the one to carry it out, frightened me at first. But after getting the clear direct order and even an explanation with it — there was nothing left but to carry it out.'

Wrapping up his notes, Gilbert wrote, 'In all of the discussions Höss is quite matter-of-fact and apathetic, shows some belated interest in the enormity of his crime, but gives the impression that it would never occur to him if somebody hadn't asked him. There is too much apathy to leave any suggestion of remorse and even the prospect of hanging does not unduly distress him. One gets the general impression of a man who is intellectually normal but with a schizoid apathy, insensitivity, and lack of empathy that could hardly be more extreme in a frank psychotic.'

Two days later, a US Army psychiatrist, Major Leon Goldensohn, came to visit Rudolf. Thirty-five years old, Goldensohn was, like Gilbert, a Jew who had been born and raised in New York. When he arrived in the cell, sucking at a pipe dangling from his mouth, Goldensohn found Rudolf sitting on the edge of his cot with his trousers rolled up, bathing his feet in a tub of warm water. Through an interpreter, Goldensohn asked what the problem was and Rudolf explained that he had had pains in his feet ever since they had become frostbitten in Camp Tomato.

The psychiatrist asked him how he felt mentally. Rudolf replied: 'I feel less nervous now than I did.' He was then asked if he felt upset over what he had done in Auschwitz. 'I thought I was doing the right thing,' said Rudolf. 'I was obeying orders, and now, of course, I see that it was unnecessary and wrong. But I don't know what you mean by being upset about these things because I didn't personally murder anybody. I was just the director of the extermination programme at Auschwitz. It was Hitler who ordered it through Himmler and it was Eichmann who gave me the orders regarding transports.' When Goldensohn asked if he was haunted by nightmares – by images of the executions, gas chambers or burning corpses – Rudolf replied: 'No, I have no such fantasies.'

In a letter, written on 20 May 1946, Goldensohn gave his assessment: 'His character is that of the amoral psychopath, which in itself, and correlated with his personal development history, indicates a dearth of parental love and unconscious hostility toward the father. Secondly, there is the influence of National Socialism, which enabled this sadistic psychopath to commit unprecedented inhumanities in a framework of apparent social and political respectability.' He concluded by saying, 'In summary, this man has no moral or ethical standards, his reaction to the mass murders of which he is charged, is apathetic.'

On 15 April 1946, it was Rudolf's turn to appear in court. Wearing a newly pressed black suit and a striped tie, with his hair recently cut and combed, Rudolf walked up to the wooden witness stand at the front of the room, placed a pair of black headphones around his head and, with his hand upon the Bible, swore to tell the truth. To either side of him stood burly white-helmeted American military police officers, hands behind their backs. Directly behind him hung a large map of Europe showing the major cities as well as the locations of the various concentration camps.

The defence lawyer, Dr Kurt Kauffmann, introduced Rudolf with the following summary: 'Witness, your statements will have far-reaching significance. You are perhaps the only one who can throw some light upon certain hidden aspects, and who can tell which people gave the orders for the destruction of European Jewry, and can further state how this order was carried out and to what degree the execution was kept a secret.' He then asked him a series of questions, which were mostly intended to prove that Ernst Kaltenbrunner had never visited Auschwitz and which Rudolf quickly affirmed.

The prosecution team was led by Colonel John Amen, a broad-shouldered man who, like all the soldiers present, wore full uniform, his chest patchworked with medals and his shoulders emblazoned with the eagle insignia of his rank. Amen sat at a small desk at the front of the courtroom, on which sat a microphone and two light bulbs, one red and one white. The lights were controlled by the court's clerk, whose job it was to indicate when it was time to start speaking. When the white bulb lit up, he started reading from the affidavit that Rudolf had signed in front of Whitney Harris a few days earlier. This testimony is the only audio-visual record of Rudolf Höss. As he answered the questions put to him by the prosecutor, Rudolf spoke in a high-pitched, nasal voice.

> Colonel Amen: You signed that affidavit voluntarily, Witness?
> Rudolf: *Jawohl.*
> Colonel Amen: And the affidavit is true in all respects?
> Rudolf: *Jawohl.*

The prosecutor then read a section that described Rudolf's career in the SS, working as a camp guard in Dachau, Sachsenhausen, Auschwitz and then *Amtsgruppe D*. He looked up from his papers, paused for effect, and then read out the most shocking part of Rudolf's confession:

> 'I commanded Auschwitz until 1 December 1943, and estimate that at least two and a half million victims were executed and exterminated there by gassing and burning, and at least another half-million succumbed to starvation and disease making a total dead of about three million.'

There was total silence in the court, as Amen briskly read on. Sitting in two rows at the centre of the courtroom, the twenty-three defendants looked gloomily on. The prosecutors knew they had finally found their trump card. The reporters crowded onto the visitors' gallery took notes. The four judges placidly stared down from their elevated benches, grateful that the clarity of this testimony would help them deliver a definitive result at the end of the trial.

Colonel Amen: 'This figure represents about 70 or 80 per cent of all persons sent to Auschwitz as prisoners, the remainder having been selected and used for slave labour in the concentration camp industries; included among the executed and burned were approximately 20,000 Russian prisoners of war (previously screened out of prisoner-of-war cages by the Gestapo) who were delivered at Auschwitz in Wehrmacht transports operated by regular Wehrmacht officers and men. The remainder of the total number of victims included about 100,000 German Jews, and great numbers of citizens, mostly Jewish, from Holland, France, Belgium, Poland, Hungary, Czechoslovakia, Greece, or other countries. We executed about 400,000 Hungarian Jews alone at Auschwitz in the summer of 1944.' That is all true, Witness?

Rudolf: *Jawohl*. It is.

Colonel Amen: 'I personally supervised executions at Auschwitz until 1 December 1943 and know by reason of my continued duties in the Inspectorate of Concentration Camps, WVHA, that these mass executions continued as stated above. All mass executions by gassing took place under the direct order, supervision, and responsibility of RSHA. I received all orders for carrying out these mass executions directly from RSHA.' Are those statements true and correct, Witness?

Rudolf: *Jawohl*. They are.

Once his cross-examination was concluded, Rudolf removed his heavy black headphones, set them on the edge of the witness stand, and stepped back to a row of chairs to the rear of the courtroom. A few minutes later the proceedings were adjourned and Rudolf was escorted back to his prison cell.

Rudolf's testimony was reported around the world. *The New York*

Times described it as the 'crushing climax to the case'. In Britain, *The Times* went further. They said of Höss' signed testimony: 'its dreadful implications must surpass any document ever penned'.

It was also clear to everyone in the courtroom that Rudolf's testimony would have a profound impact on the proceedings, including the defendants themselves. At lunch in the prisoners' canteen, Hans Frank, the former governor general of occupied Poland, told the psychologist Gustave Gilbert, 'That was the low point of the entire trial – to hear a man say out of his own mouth that he exterminated two and a half million people in cold blood. That is something that people will talk about for a thousand years.' Hermann Göring also shared that he had been shocked by Rudolf's confession but then attempted to distance himself saying that it was only because Rudolf was from southern Germany that he had been able to commit such crimes – crimes of which a Prussian, such as himself, would never have been capable.

The next day, Frank took the stand and for the first time confessed his role in the atrocities. To the direct question 'Did you ever participate in the destruction of the Jews?', he replied: 'I say Yes. And the reason I say yes is because I have been burdened by guilt for the five months of this trial, and particularly burdened by the statement made by Rudolf Höss.'

Finally, the major war criminals had begun to admit their guilt.

While Rudolf had been appearing as a witness, the Polish government sent word that they were now prepared to try him themselves for the crimes he had committed in their country.

So it was that on 25 May 1946, almost exactly a year since the end of the war and eleven weeks since his capture by Hanns, Rudolf was driven to the Nuremberg airport, where he was forced to pose for the Pathé news cameras, looking dishevelled and unkempt in his rough woollen prison clothes. He was then flown in an American plane, along with two other German war criminals, to Warsaw, where he was handed over to the Polish authorities. At the city's main

prison, he was processed, checked once again for cyanide pills, and placed in his own cell.

There is little record of his time in the Warsaw prison. The only source is Rudolf himself. He wrote that time passed slowly and that he endured beatings, including the vicious assaults of a twenty-year-old guard, but that he never complained as the other guards treated him well.

On 30 July 1946, two months after his return to Poland, he was transported by train, along with seven other former SS officers, from Warsaw to Krakow in southern Poland. When they arrived there were no cars waiting at the station to pick them up. Rudolf grew nervous, especially when an angry crowd began to gather around the group, having recognised the Kommandant. Just as they began to pose a real danger — some heckling, others threatening to throw stones — the cars arrived and whisked them away.

It was then that he was taken to the old jail at 7 Montelupich Street, on the outskirts of Krakow where, after being processed again, he was escorted to a tiny basement cell. Somehow Montelupich prison had avoided the worst of the aerial bombardments and, by the end of 1946, it housed many of Poland's most notorious war criminals.

Rudolf's cell was six feet by ten, walled in grey concrete with a small grilled window set seven feet off the ground. He had a metal cot with a thin worn mattress, a bucket in the corner, a single light bulb hanging from the ceiling, a small stove in one corner and, in the other, a metal jug from which to drink and wash. The prisoners were allowed to shower once every two weeks, although soap and towels were rarely available. They wore their own clothes and, by rule, underwear had to be changed every six weeks. Food was provided by the prison – coffee, potato soup, a small chunk of bread – and a lucky few received extra provisions from family members. The Poles had been kind enough to give Rudolf warm woollen socks.

He had nothing to occupy him. The other prisoners either ignored him or treated him with hostility. He wrote letters to Hedwig, and to his family, but received nothing in reply. His sense of isolation and dejection increased with each passing day. He was becoming unhinged.

In early November 1946, an investigative judge, fastidiously dressed in a tailored suit and smoking a cigarette in a jade holder, walked into his cell and introduced himself as Jan Sehn, Krakow's lead investigator in the Polish war crimes trials. He had been tasked with collecting materials for Rudolf's forthcoming hearing.

Sehn explained that he wanted Rudolf to make a list of the documents that had been destroyed before the Red Army had liberated Auschwitz. He left him with a few pieces of thin paper and some sharpened pencils. At first Rudolf refused. He didn't see why he should remember. But then he reconsidered. After all, he had nothing better to do and, on the whole, he had been favourably treated by the Polish. Soon he was enjoying the task, becoming 'thankful . . . for the present assignment of writing . . . which brings me great satisfaction.'

A few days later Sehn returned to the cell, collected Rudolf's notes and, observing the prisoner's helpful inclination, suggested that he next write some character sketches of the senior leaders of the SS: Himmler, Eichmann, Maurer, Pohl, Glücks. A week or so later, Sehn again visited the Kommandant. Having told Rudolf that his notes would be entered into the official record at his trial, Sehn asked him to write about the camp's operations: the transports, the selections, the gas chambers. This took more time, with Rudolf recalling the inner-workings of the camp in a tiny, marginless scrawl across the thin prison paper.

In between interviews, Rudolf kept up the one-sided correspondence with his family. On Christmas Eve, he wrote another letter to Hedwig, his words growing increasingly nostalgic and bitter:

> The eyes of expectant, glad, blissfully happy children, under the tree with its lights, used to be our reward for all the cares and troubles of the past year. For the sake of those happy children's hearts, all troubles, grief and anxieties were forgotten at that comfortable, quiet hour. We saw our children growing up healthy and happy, and they showed us what it was we lived for . . . But the ill-starred war has destroyed our happiness too, just as it destroyed millions of families, tore them apart and spread unspeakable suffering throughout the world.

But Hedwig again failed to reply. A few weeks later Rudolf sat down to write another letter:

> My dear good Mutz, my dear children
> Another month has passed, without any news of you. The last news I had was your dear letter of 23 June, which I received on 7 September. I draw all my hopes for you from that letter. But it is so long ago — I

wonder how you are today, my dear ones, how may it be going with you now?

How much more calmly I would face everything if I knew you were all in good health and provided with the necessities of life, if I knew whether you have good people helping you, whether you are allowed to live in peace? If I knew what your sad lives are like in general? Questions upon questions, and they give me no rest. I have to answer them for myself. But no amount of sad thoughts can do any good. All our lives are like this – it is Fate, and we can do nothing to alter it.

I am always with you all in my thoughts, and I wait – I go on waiting uneasily for news of you, for some sign of life from you, confidently hoping and wishing that you are all in good health, that all is well with you, that your lives are bearable. I myself am still healthy.

This is my third letter from here. I wrote the first on my birthday, the second at Christmas time. I hope that both those letters have reached you.

Finally, I wish you all well, my dear ones, I sent you my heartfelt greetings, all my good children, my Mäusl, my Burling, my Püppi, my Kindi and my Klaus. And my fervent greetings to you, dear, good Mutz.

For ever and always

Your Vati

Two months after Rudolf's arrival in Krakow, Jan Sehn continued to encourage him to write; not just about the war years, but also about his family, his background, his own story. At first, Rudolf resisted – he did not want the world to know the details of his private life – but Sehn was persistent. It was a way to pass the time, and more, might even bring relief. But perhaps what finally persuaded Rudolf was a desire to set the record straight, to make meaningful all that he had done, and to challenge the lies and cowardice displayed by his former colleagues in Nuremberg: Göring the Luftwaffe commander, who had claimed that he was just a military man; Rudolf's own boss, Oswald Pohl, who had argued that the extermination camps were the responsibility of his underlings, and particularly of Richard Glücks; Rudolf Hess, secretary to the Führer himself, who had pretended to be amnesic; Ernst Kaltenbrunner, who claimed no knowledge of the Final Solution, despite supervising the construction of at least one concentration camp. None had told the truth, and all had cared only about saving their skins. Little good it did them. Rudolf's confession was also a final act of distorted loyalty. Unlike those senior Nazi figures who had denied the past, he felt compelled to share his recollections. To do otherwise would have betrayed what they had all believed in.

In the end, Rudolf picked up the pencil and wrote the title for the opening section about his formative years – 'My psyche, growing up, life and experience.'

> In the following pages I shall try to write about my innermost personal life, drawing on my memories in an attempt to give a faithful account of all the essential features, all the highs and lows, of my psychological life and experience. If that account is to be as full as possible, I must go back to incidents in my earliest childhood.
>
> Until my sixth year, we lived some way outside the town of Baden-Baden, where there were only a few farms in the neighbourhood. I had no playmates at all at this time, since the neighbours' children were all much older than me . . .

As he wrote, he reviewed his life's decisions:

Today I deeply regret leaving the path I had so far trodden. My life, my family, everything would have been different, although still we would have no home and no farm. But we would have had years of satisfying work in the interim. However, who can foresee what will become of those whose lives are linked together? What is right, and what is wrong?

On the last page of his memoirs, written in February 1947, Rudolf revealed why he had chosen to be so honest:

> I would never have brought myself to give such a frank account, revealing my most secret self, but for the humanity and understanding that I have encountered here [in prison]. It was something that I could never have expected, and it disarmed me entirely. It is because of this humane understanding that I have done everything in my power to contribute to casting light on circumstances that are as yet unexplained.

Rudolf was aware that his prison memoirs might gain a wider audience beyond those gathered for his own trial. He asked that whoever was going to evaluate his notes did not publish those parts relating to his family, nor his 'softer emotions', nor his 'secret doubts', believing that the general reader would be incapable of looking beyond his murderous acts:

> Let the public go on thinking of me as a bloodthirsty brute, a cruel sadist, the murderer of millions — for that is the only way that the vast majority will be able to imagine the Kommandant of Auschwitz. They would never understand that he, too, had a heart, and was not a wicked man.

With a final line stating that his writings had been voluntary and unforced, Rudolf put down his pencil.

By the spring of 1946, the Polish government had established its own war crimes process, overseen by the *Najwyższy Trybunat Narodowy* (NTN), the Supreme National Tribunal. Its task was to prosecute those 'fascist-Hitlerite criminals' who had committed murder and ill-treatment of civilians and prisoners of war in occupied Poland during the Second World War. Seven trials were held in total, of forty-nine defendants, of which Rudolf was the most high profile.

Rudolf's trial began on 11 March 1947 in the auditorium of the Polish Teachers' Union in the Powiśle district of Warsaw, a hall large enough to hold five hundred. The court was composed of a presiding judge, Alfred Eimer, and four assistant judges, along with a panel of four members of the Polish Sejm — the lower house of the Polish parliament — who were there in a symbolic capacity to represent the people. Rudolf was represented by a Polish lawyer. Attending the trial were observers from the Soviet Union, France, Germany, Czechoslovakia and Britain. At least eighty former inmates were present during the hearings. According to a journalist from *The Times*, when Rudolf first walked into the court the crowd let out a 'slight murmur'; other than that the proceedings were marked by 'an almost complete lack of expressed excitement'.

The state was represented by a team of prosecutors, headed by Tadeusz Cyprian, a forty-nine-year-old lawyer and sometime photographer from Sniatyn, today situated in Ukraine. Cyprian had some experience of war crimes trials, having sat through proceedings at both Belsen and Nuremberg as part of an official Polish delegation. To near total silence in the court, he read out the indictment, which ran to ninety-eight pages. Rudolf was charged with the deaths of 300,000 Polish and Russian prisoners and four million Jews. Rudolf sat in the dock with black headphones, listening to the simultaneous translation of the Polish prosecutor's opening statement. Cyprian argued that Rudolf was a 'willing link' in a system designed to destroy the Slav race and argued that he should hang for his crimes. Over the next few days, the state called sixty-six witnesses, of which forty-eight were Polish and eighteen were foreign. Rudolf's expression changed little as he heard the accounts provided by a long line of Auschwitz survivors who now filed in and out of the courtroom to take the stand.

Finally it was Rudolf's turn. He petulantly answered the prosecutor's questions on logistics, arguing unapologetically that only one and a half million could have been killed in Auschwitz, not four million as the prosecutor had claimed, due to the physical limits set by the crematoria. He admitted, on cross-examination, that on one night a trainload of Gypsies and Jews was taken on arrival and thrown into a large pit where they were burned alive. Forty thousand people had been killed this way.

But his most vehement defence came from his memoirs, written while in Montelupich prison, and which were inserted verbatim into the court record. In the end, he too attempted to dodge culpability. 'I never mistreated a prisoner myself, let alone killed one,' he wrote. Regarding the atrocities that took place at the camp, he claimed that 'Much happened at Auschwitz, allegedly in my name and on my orders, of which I knew nothing. I would have neither tolerated nor approved of it.' Then he insisted that, when he subsequently learned about the 'monstrous tortures' in Auschwitz, he got 'cold shudders'. He blamed his staff for abusing the prisoners, saying that they did so outside his command and maintained that, until he heard the disclosures at Nuremberg, he had been unaware of the systematic brutality that had prevailed in Auschwitz.

He went on to concede, almost by default, that he was accountable for what had taken place at the camp because of his title, rather than his plan: 'All these things did happen at Auschwitz, and I am responsible for them. For according to the regulations of the camps: The camp Kommandant is fully responsible for everything that goes on in his camp.' And Rudolf did admit to overseeing the building of the gas chambers, the selection process and the crematoria. But, crucially, he argued that it had been a mistake, not because this mass murder was immoral or monstrous, but because 'it was that very policy of extermination that brought the hatred of the whole world down on Germany'.

The prosecutors found it easy to discount Rudolf's assertion that he had only recently learned about the atrocities, presenting mountains of evidence collected from camp survivors. Similarly, his claims that his orders were disobeyed were also disproved by witness statements showing that Rudolf was in clear control of all that had taken place in the camp. And in response to Rudolf's attempt to equate the Allied bombing of Dresden and other German cities, in which tens of thousands of civilians had been killed and millions left homeless, to the murders he had overseen in Auschwitz, the prosecution pointed out that though the bombing of Dresden was indeed tragic, the aim of these attacks were military targets, while the gassings in Auschwitz were the result of the purposeful genocide of a specific ethnic minority, and therefore a crime against humanity.

Finally, in one last effort, and by now displaying loyalty to no person or idea beyond saving himself, Rudolf argued that he had been simply executing Himmler's commands. However, this argument was promptly thrown out by the court, since a fundamental premise of all the war crimes trials held in the post-war period was that SS guards and officers could not protest that they were merely following orders.

Two weeks after the trial's start, on 27 March, Rudolf stood as the jury's verdict was read out: Guilty. He showed no surprise. He had told the reporter from *The Times* that he had been expecting this outcome. On 2 April, Rudolf returned to court to hear his sentence. He looked healthier than he had at the Nuremberg Trial, his face no longer gaunt, his hair neatly combed, his grey woollen jacket clean and pressed. Again he stood, black headphones once again in place, two armed guards standing behind him, their white-gloved hands holding rifles. The president of the tribunal, Alfred Eimer, read out the sentence: 'Death by hanging in a non-public manner within the territory of the Auschwitz camp.'

This upset Rudolf greatly, who believed that it was dishonourable to die on the gallows, an execution method which he believed to be more suited to a common murderer than a man of his military standing. Eight days later the highest court in the land upheld the decision and shortly after that a letter arrived from the president of the Polish republic saying that he had 'decided not to use his power to reduce his sentence'.

On 11 April, five days before he was due to be executed, Rudolf wrote a last letter to his wife. It was a final goodbye, and a confession. In it he declared that his principles had been founded on incorrect assumptions, and that it was inevitable that they would one day break down. He said that he now realised that he had been 'a cogwheel in the monstrous German machinery of destruction', an 'automaton who blindly obeyed every order', one who had 'followed a very wrong path, and thereby brought destruction on myself'. As a result he had become 'the greatest of all destroyers of human beings'. He acknowledged that for these crimes he must die: 'With calm and composure, I see my last moments approaching'.

Enclosing his wedding ring, he reminisced about their wedding, and the 'spring of their life' on the farm in 1929. He urged Hedwig to move to a new location and to take back her maiden name, arguing that 'it will be best for my name to die with me'.

He then completed the letter with these words: 'With a heavy heart, my dearest Mutz, my poor unfortunate wife, so very, very dear to me, I send all my love to you. Remember me with love. I am with you, until my last breath'.

Within the envelope he also included a last letter to his children:

You, my dear, good children!

Your daddy has to leave you now. For you, poor ones, there remains only your dear, good Mummy. May she remain with you for a long time yet. You do not understand yet what your good Mummy really means to you, and what a precious possession she is to you. The love and care of a mother is the most beautiful and valuable thing that exists on this earth. I realized this a long time ago, only when it was too late; and I have regretted it all my life.

Klaus, my dear boy! You are the oldest. You are now going out into the world. You have to now make your own way through life. You have good aptitudes. Use them! Keep your good heart. Become a person who lets himself be guided primarily by warmth and humanity. Learn to think and to judge for yourself, responsibly. Don't accept everything without criticism and as absolutely true. Learn from life.

Kindi and Püppi, you my big girls!

You are yet too young to learn the extent of the hard fate dished out to us. But you especially, my dear good girls, are specially obligated to stand at your poor unfortunate mother's side and with love assist her in every way you can. Surround her with all your childlike love from your heart and show her how much you love her . . .

My Burling, you dear little guy!

Hang on to your happy child disposition. The cruel life will tear you, my dear boy, soon enough away from your child's world . . . You poor little guy have now only your dear good Mummy left who will care for you. Listen to her with love and kindness and so remain Daddy's dear Burling.

My dear Annemäusl!

How little was I permitted to experience your dear little personality. Your dear good Mummy will have to take you, my dear Mäusl, for us into her arms and tell you of your daddy, and how very much he loved you. May you, with your sunny ways, help your poor dear Mummy through all the dreary hours.

Once more from my heart I ask you all, my dear good children, take to heart my last words. Think of them again and again.

Keep in loving memory,

Daddy

Originally scheduled for 14 April 1947, Rudolf's execution was postponed because of fears that the residents of nearby Oświęcim would attempt to lynch him when he was being transferred from the jail in Wadowice to the site of the gallows. The execution was rescheduled for two days later. At dawn on 16 April, a team of

Letter from Rudolf to Hedwig

German POWs erected a wooden gallows with a trapdoor a few steps from the old crematorium in Auschwitz, two hundred feet from the villa where Rudolf and his family used to live. No one was admitted to the grounds without a special pass, and armed Polish military guards had been posted at the entrance to the now-deserted camp.

Rudolf arrived by army truck at 8 a.m. and was taken to the building that had once been his office; less than twenty-five feet from his old house. He asked for a cup of coffee, and once he had drunk it, he was led to a cell in the 'bunker', the camp jail in Block 11, also known as the 'Death Block'. This was the building where Zyklon B had first been used on the prisoners six years before.

Led out at 10 a.m, Rudolf appeared calm. He was marched along the cobblestones of the main camp street, past the infirmary where children had been injected with Phenol under Dr Lolling's orders, and through the courtyard where the inmates had to stand for hours, in sun or sleet, as roll call was taken.

As he turned the corner round Block 4 he saw a crowd of about a hundred people, who had gathered in a semicircle next to the old crematorium. The group comprised some former prisoners, officials from the Polish Ministry of Justice, members of the State Prosecutor's

Office and the Security Bureau. The Polish state had decreed that the execution be conducted in private, so unlike the hangings that had taken place at Belsen and Nuremberg, no journalists were present. It was a cold day and most people wore overcoats, hats and gloves.

As Rudolf approached the gallows, the crowd parted. Since his hands were cuffed behind his back, a soldier helped him climb onto the stool positioned above the trapdoor. Father Tadeusz Zaremba, a local priest whose presence had been requested by Rudolf, now approached the Kommandant and a few last words were exchanged.

After the prosecutor read out the sentence, a black-hooded hangman placed a noose around Rudolf's neck, which Rudolf adjusted with a movement of his head. At 10.08 a.m., after a nod from the prosecutor, the hangman pulled the stool out from under the former Kommandant so that he hit the trapdoor beneath. The priest then began to recite a prayer.

At 10.21 a.m. Rudolf Höss was pronounced dead.

A few minutes later his body was cut down and placed in a simple wooden box. The corpse was later transported to a hospital in Krakow where doctors performed an autopsy. The next day it was taken to a local cemetery where it was buried in an unmarked grave.

EPILOGUE

The families of the Nazi leaders reacted to their legacies in many different ways: pride, shame, fear. The Höss family chose denial. It was almost as if their family history had started in May 1947. Given a clean slate, new myths were created, the foremost being one of heroic survival, particularly on the part of the head of the family, Hedwig Höss, who, so the story went, managed to feed and protect her family against all odds in the harsh years after the war.

And there was truth in that, for life was indeed harsh. After Rudolf's execution, Hedwig and her five children continued to live in the small apartment above the sugar factory in St Michaelisdonn. They walked around with rags tied to their feet, and subsisted on vegetables grown in their patch of garden. People in the village shunned them. It was now dangerous to be associated with such a high-ranking Nazi family.

But they survived, and when Klaus found a job in Stuttgart, three hundred miles south, the rest of the family joined him. Over the years, the five Höss children moved away – to the Baltic Sea, to Australia, to America – but Hedwig remained in Germany. Unlike other widows of German soldiers, Hedwig was not granted a state pension, nor did she receive any other income from the government.

In 1965, Hedwig was called as a witness at the Frankfurt Trial, the German government's belated attempt, after twenty years of procrastination, to deal with some of the Nazis who had lived unabashedly in and among German society. Hedwig's only role here was to confirm that one of the defendants had never visited Auschwitz. Her appearance lasted approximately two minutes, just long enough to be sworn in, and to deny that she had ever seen the man in her husband's camp. It was the last time Hedwig Höss appeared in a courtroom.

After returning from their honeymoon on the Scilly Isles, Hanns and Ann moved to north London. The Alexander family was reunited once again, and began to grow. In 1948, Ann gave birth to their first child, Annette, and then to Jackie, in 1950. Elsie and Erich had three children, Frank, Michael and Vivien. Bella remarried soon after the war and spent the next years bringing up four boys: Peter, Tony, Julian and Stephen. Paul, meanwhile, found it harder to settle down. He jumped from job to job, eventually becoming a freelance builder and moving to Canada, only to return a few years later. He married twice and had two children, John and Marion.

Hanns' father was never able to replicate the medical practice that he had established in Berlin, but he was well liked by his patients and he and Henny lived comfortably enough. A man who had always loved the sweet things in life and had never given up his cigars, Alfred died of a heart attack in 1950. His death sent shock waves through the family. Henny was of course most affected, but she was nothing if not stoic, and for another twenty years she wore the badge of matriarch with grace.

In 1948, the Czech government announced their wish to honour Hanns with their Medal of Merit Second Class for 'recognition of exceptional merit in regards to the Czechoslovak Army and Czechoslovak people forcefully held in Germany'. A year later, the

Luxembourg government announced its intention to award him their National Order of the Oaken Crown, the equivalent of a British knighthood. However, the British government had ruled that its soldiers were forbidden from accepting honours from foreign governments for services rendered after the end of the Second World War, and the honours were declined. Hanns did not receive either award; in fact he never knew about them.

Hanns did not seek the excitement or adventure that he had experienced during the war years in later life. His work – at Japhet & Co., the company he joined before the war, and later at S. G. Warburg – his family and his community were enough for him. Hanns began to spend more time at the synagogue that his family had helped to found. Housed at first in a series of temporary accommodations – the dining room of the boarding house, then a hall borrowed from another congregation – the synagogue finally found a permanent home in the vicarage of an old church in Belsize Square in north-west London. Made up entirely of German Jewish refugees, and led by a rabbi who had survived a concentration camp, the synagogue drew upon the *Liberale* traditions of German Jewry. From the start, the Alexander Torah was the synagogue's first and most important asset. Later there would be other scrolls, but for years the Alexander Torah was the congregation's workhorse, brought out for every Friday-evening and Saturday-morning service, for the High Holy Days and all the other religious events.

Hanns and Paul were to become the unofficial caretakers of the synagogue. For the next forty years, first in top hats and tails, and later in blue pinstriped suits, they attended every religious event, making sure that the services had been well prepared, that the tables had been set up, that glasses were filled, and that prayer books and shawls were in the right place. Though they continued to play pranks and tell inappropriate jokes, much to the joy of the many children in their lives, they became a mainstay – perhaps even *the* mainstay – of this progressive and social community.

As he aged, Hanns never forgot the debt that he owed the British nation for taking him and his family in. So it was that in 1986, at the age of sixty-nine, and fifty years after his arrival in London, he and Ann threw a 'Thank You Britain Party' at the Croydon Aerodrome, the spot at which he had first stepped onto British soil. At the end

of the meal, Hanns stood up with a glass in hand, and said: 'Some of you were yourself refugees from Nazi oppression. We are most grateful and we are here by the grace of God. I would like you to be upstanding and to join me in the toast to Her Majesty the Queen.'

Although Hanns remained grateful and appreciative of his adopted home, his feelings about Germany never changed. When he and his siblings went through their father's possessions after his death, they found his Iron Cross First Class. Knowing how much it had meant to him as a boy, Bella offered the medal to Hanns. But he told her he wanted nothing to do with it, or with Germany. The anger that he felt in 1945 remained: 'The number of murderers I had to dismiss made me sick. They made fools out of us. You know, the Russians were more efficient. When they heard such stories they found the accused and shot them. We could not do it. We did not do it.' The war, for him, was never a topic for discussion. 'I would not talk to children about it because they should not be brought up to hate. I, however, am full of hatred.'

When, in his eighties, Hanns was invited by the museum established at the old site of the Belsen concentration camp to receive an award for his wartime efforts, he declined, keeping his oath that he would never return. And in this way – because of his silence, and because of his hate – Hanns' efforts went unacknowledged.

Over the next few years, Hanns attended the funerals of those closest to him: his sister Bella in 2000; his dear brother, Paul, who died in 2003; Elsie in 2004.

On 22 December 2006, Hanns – aged eighty-nine, after a long week of dinner parties and theatre-going – woke up in the night struggling to breathe. Although he insisted he was fine, Ann called an ambulance, and an hour or so later they were taken the short journey to the Royal Free Hospital. Neither slept well that night. In the morning the doctors informed Ann that Hanns had contracted pneumonia, but that the condition was not life-threatening, and told her to go home and rest. A short while later their daughters, Jackie and Annette, arrived at the hospital. Hanns removed his oxygen mask and they chatted happily. On her way out of the door, Annette kissed her father and said 'We will be back soon'.

Later that afternoon Hanns' condition deteriorated rapidly. The hospital was unable to reach Ann, who was at home, having taken some sleeping pills, but did get through to Jackie and Annette. By the time they reached their father's side, he had died. The two returned to their parents' flat, but chose not to wake their mother. When she saw her daughters in the morning, she immediately guessed what had happened. She was not surprised. They were glad that he had not suffered. He had presented a positive face until the very end.

At the funeral, the true story of his life was revealed to many for the first time. Hanns' nephews ended the eulogy as follows:

In short, Hanns was a man, a mensch . . . we can be sure that he left this world having done his duty in all respects, having left it perhaps a better place, and us, who have known and loved him, rather better people. I will end by quoting from his nephew little Benji, aged six, who on hearing of Hanns' death asked, 'Has he packed his bags because he can now go and play with Grandpa Paul in heaven?' I am sure he will. We hope that he now finds his soulmate, his brother Paul. I should like to think that they are both looking down on us now rather embarrassed by what is being said of them, but meanwhile having a good laugh at our expense and probably planning something as they did when, throughout their lives, they emulated Dennis the Menace – or was it *Max und Moritz*?

After the memorial celebration, Hanns' ashes were taken to the Jewish Cemetery in Willesden, north London, and sprinkled at the Alexander family plot. This was where his father, Alfred, had been buried years before, later to be joined by the ashes of his mother, Henny, and brother, Paul.

At the head of this family plot, rarely visited and covered with ivy, stands an impressive headstone, upon which reads the legend: 'Service before self'.

POSTSCRIPT

It is a cool November morning, the air is crisp and clear, but the clouds overhead threaten rain. I am standing at the entrance to Auschwitz below the massive black wrought-iron words that read '*Arbeit Macht Frei*', along with a man my age and his elderly mother.

The man is Rainer Höss, forty-four, wearing an orange stripy sweater covered with knitted snowflakes. Rainer is the grandson of Rudolf Höss. Having grown up in a family who refused to talk about the past, Rainer wants to know more. For years he has gathered information on his own, spending hours in the library, talking to family friends, browsing through old photographs, and reading his grandfather's autobiography. When he first started asking questions, his father, Hans-Jürgen, cut him off. More recently Rainer was accused of attempting to sell some of his grandfather's artefacts – an ornately carved wooden box donated by Himmler, an SS dagger, colour slides from the family's time in Auschwitz – and Rainer is still upset about the rebukes he received in the press.

Rainer's mother, Irene Alba, is a round-faced and chunkily built woman in her mid-seventies, with long silver hair swept back in a ponytail. Born and bred into the conservative Swabian culture of south-west Germany, Irene has lived by herself for the past twenty years, having divorced Rainer's father.

Over a million Jews were murdered here, as well as hundreds of thousands of political prisoners, Gypsies, and Catholics. This will be the first time that any of Rudolf's family has visited the camp since Hedwig and her children left their luxurious villa in 1944.

We take photographs of each other at the entrance: Rainer looks stern, Irene looks scared. We walk past the three layers of barbed-wire fence into the camp itself.

Rainer takes out his video camera and starts filming everything, as if trying to separate himself from the experience. I take out my video camera, trying to do the same. The grandson and daughter-in-law of Kommandant Rudolf Höss are back in Auschwitz, with a Jewish descendant of a family who only narrowly avoided the devastation that took place here. It is all too weird.

We walk along the uneven stony road, past the low red-brick

buildings, and then turn right down an alley towards the centre of the camp. Here, we stop in front of two black metal poles between which hangs a third pole. It was from here that the Auschwitz guards hanged prisoners for crimes such as moving during assembly or making eye contact.

This is my second visit and I am thankfully not feeling the same inner turmoil as I did during the first. Rainer is still filming – the red-brick barracks, the '*Achtung!*' signs, the electric fence upon which prisoners threw themselves to commit suicide – but when I turn to Irene, I realise that she is not doing as well.

'This not good, I am so sad,' she says, as she starts to cry. She hugs herself in her dark grey fur coat. 'I did not know any of this when I married Hans-Jürgen. He did not tell me. I find out only when my sister shows me an article from *Der Stürmer* magazine.' She is crying so hard now that it is difficult to understand her.

'Your husband was the son of the Kommandant. When he lived in the villa next to the crematorium, did he not know about the gassings?' I ask.

'He said there was a bad smell in the air. Not all the time. But oh so bad.'

'And the mother, Hedwig. Did she know about the killings?'

'Of course, of course. She lived here for all these years.'

'Why did you stay married to Hans-Jürgen for so long if you knew about this?' I ask.

'When I was getting married in church, I said until death, with sickness, with health, I stay with him for twenty-seven years. He no happy.'

I am not sure if she is crying because of the terrible crimes that have happened here or because she is feeling sorry for herself. I try to give her the benefit of the doubt.

I look round to see Rainer walking into Block 11. This is where the prisoners were interrogated, tortured and shot, and where

Rudolf's men first experimented with Zyklon B. I stay outside with Irene.

'Did Hans-Jürgen talk about this when you were married?'

'He talked about it only when he was sad. And then he would say it was a terrible time.'

I join Rainer in a barracks dedicated to the memory of the Jews deported from France, following him as he walks from room to room and studies the walls filled with hundreds of photos of Jews during better times: dressed in their finest clothes, carrying musical instruments, dancing in clubs, riding bicycles, sitting with their families at their dinner tables. All are now gone.

Rainer starts to cry. 'This is so terrible,' he says. 'What my grandfather has done. It is so bad. It is so bad. I have read so many books, I have studied this over the years, but to be here, it is much worse. What a horrible place.'

We walk out of the barracks, and head towards the far side of the camp. This is the moment I have been waiting for above all else. We walk through a short passageway made out of barbed wire.

'Here it is,' I say.

In front of us stand the gallows upon which Rainer's grandfather was hanged, next to the old crematorium. Rainer walks up to the wooden structure. He stops, stares at it for a few moments. 'This is the best place here,' he says. 'This place that they killed him.'

Irene is still having a hard time. She cannot stay close to the gallows for very long and walks away. Turning, she sees me taking a photograph of Rainer by the gallows. 'Don't do that,' she yells. 'Do not take a photograph here.'

When she asks why I have been taking so many pictures, I tell her I have been researching the story of my great-uncle, Hanns Alexander.

'He arrested Rudolf,' Rainer explains.

'I heard about the arrest,' she says. 'Rudolf was sleeping when they found him. They beat him when they caught him.'

'It was Hedwig who confessed to my uncle,' I say. 'She said that Rudolf had adopted the name Franz Lang, and told him where he was hiding in a farm nearby.'

'Is this true? It was Hedwig who told about Rudolf, not her brother?' Irene looks at me hard. 'I cannot believe it. Hedwig always told me that it was her brother Fritz who denounced him.' I tell her that I have a copy of the arrest report proving it. 'Oh my God, oh my God,' she says, hugging herself even tighter. She appears genuinely shocked.

Rainer walks over to a metal door with a small hole in it. This is the back door to the old crematorium. This is where his grandfather looked through the peephole and watched the prisoners being gassed to prove to his staff that he could cope with the mass murders taking place under his watch. Rainer shakes his head.

'Mutti, you should not come in,' he says. 'It will not be good for you.'

'I will, I will,' she said, her arms shaking, her breath short. She appears to be having an asthma attack.

When Rainer shrugs and walks on, his mother follows. I am close behind.

Rainer walks through the first concrete hall and into the next chamber. 'Look up there,' he says, pointing to a small square opening in the ceiling. 'That is where they dropped the Zyklon B.' He continues to the next room, which contains the blackened ovens where the bodies were burned. His mother stalls at the doorway, unable to move any closer.

'My God, my God,' she whispers.

'This is awful,' says Rainer. 'Awful.'

Irene has somehow shuffled forward and is standing next to the black wrought-iron doors of the furnaces. Her whole body is shaking as she sobs. '*Nein, nein, nein,*' she mumbles.

After a few moments we walk outside to sunlight and fresh air.

There, Rainer turns to me and says, matter-of-factly, 'If I knew where my grandfather was buried, I would piss on his grave.'

I set about finishing this book when I returned home from Auschwitz. It had been six years since my uncle's death, and six years since I started my research. I now had a better understanding of how Hanns Alexander came to meet Rudolf Höss. I could see the steps that had led to Rudolf becoming Kommandant of Auschwitz, and why Hanns chose to face his persecutors at the war's end.

What was less clear to me were the details. Through the research process I came to learn that history – like the story of the blind men describing the elephant – differs depending on the point of view, and is never as clear as you would expect.

As I continued my investigations, I was also struck by the importance of the texts. There was the Alexander Torah, which had miraculously survived the Nazi era. There were Hanns' letters, discovered in a small box among Ann's possessions. There was also Rudolf's memoir, a critical piece of Holocaust evidence, preserved so that future generations will never forget.

'What Hanns Alexander did was remarkable,' I was told by Whitney Harris, the man who had summoned Rudolf to the Nuremberg Trials. 'Yes, most of the leaders got away. But the important thing is we got some of them, and we were able to record their stories, for history's sake, so that people would know what really happened. That is what he accomplished.'

I also learned that the same recorded history endures in different ways. When I visited Rudolf's daughter I noticed a copy of her father's memoirs lying on her bedside table; she told me she had barely read it. In Hanns' apartment, in the week after his death, I found the same book on his living-room table, well thumbed, and with his name pencilled on the inside front cover.

As for the Alexander Torah, it is still used to this day. On 16 March 2013 my family gathered at the Belsize Square Synagogue in London to hear my daughter, Sam, and my niece, Sipan, complete their bat mitzvahs. As they finished their reading the congregation called out approvingly: '*Skoiach, skoiach*', and, in the process, the two girls passed into adulthood.

As ever, we all cried.

NOTES

Chapter One

1 'ALEXANDER. Howard Harvey . . .' The *Daily Telegraph* obituary incorrectly lists 23 December 2006 as a Friday, and misspells Hanns' middle name.

11 'On 1 August 1916 . . .' From the time that he enlisted, Rudolf told everyone that he had been born on 25 November 1900, contradicting his birth, baptism and marriage certificates. Rudolf had his official SS personnel file altered so that the last digit of his birth year, 1901, was rounded out into a 'o', thus retrospectively covering up the lie about his age. A copy of this document is held in the US National Archive in College Park, Maryland. His birth and baptism certificates are available at the Baden-Baden town hall in Germany.

12 'When Rudolf and his comrades . . .' This conflict, known as the Mesopotamian Campaign, was made up of two opposing forces: the Central Powers, mostly represented by Turkish troops but with some limited German support; and the Allies, represented by the British Empire, involving mostly Indian troops and under Indian command. The Mesopotamian oil wells were strategically critical, for both sides relied on oil to fuel their global war effort.

14 'In early 1917. . .' The battle for Jerusalem went on for two months, and resulted in significant casualties for both sides – 18,000 for the Allies and 25,000 for the Central Powers. Jerusalem was finally captured by the Allies on 9 December 1917. The victory was marked by the commander-in-chief of the Allied forces, Sir Edmund Allenby, when, according to his own reports, he walked into the holy city on foot and was greeted warmly by the inhabitants.

16 'Over the course of the next few . . .' Rudolf Höss was wounded three times in the First World War according to the notes later added to his SS personnel record held at the US National Archive in College Park.

16 'Battle of Jordan . . .' To the Allies, this battle was known as the First Attack on Amman.

Chapter Two

20 'Although he came from a comfortable . . .' Alfred Alexander wrote about the death of his mother in his *Little Red Book*, an unpublished series of remembrances about his life. After graduation he went on to study medicine in Munich, determined to find a cure for leukaemia. He had qualified as a general practitioner with top marks and was offered a prestigious job at Frankfurt's city hospital, but only if he agreed to convert to Christianity. While Alfred was not particularly religious, he was also unwilling to compromise his identity for the sake of professional advancement. Instead, he accepted a lower-paid training position in Berlin. The following year Alfred's mother had been struck down by severe heart and asthma attacks. Arriving at her bedside, he was told that there was no way to prolong her life, 'which to me was the most precious thing on earth'. He 'begged' her doctors to administer morphine to put her out of her misery. One doctor was 'outraged at this damaging suggestion', but the other consented. Her last words were, 'Thank you, dear boy.' Heartbroken after his mother's death, Dr Alexander gave up the search for a cure and returned to Berlin to start up a general practice.

23 'This book inspired the boys . . .' As Hanns and Paul grew up their pranks became more ambitious and elaborate. One day, for instance, they were fighting on a tram on the way to school and broke the glass partition behind the driver, damage for which their father had to pay. On another occasion, and rather more seriously, they unhooked a tram while the driver was having tea in a little hut nearby, and then pushed the car up the line, derailing it. Nobody found out who was responsible for the vandalism. When Hanns recalled this incident seventy years later he thought it amusing, clearly unconcerned about the inconvenience, not to say danger, that he and his brother had caused.

28 'The production of the Torah . . .' The nineteenth verse of Deuteronomy, chapter 31, states: 'Now write down this song and teach it to the Israelites and have them sing it.' Accordingly, the 613th and final commandment dictates that each Jew should write or have commissioned a Sefer Torah during their lifetime, and that producing a Sefer Torah is considered a holy task or *mitzvah*. As such, the commissioning of the Alexander Torah brought a blessing upon Moses Alexander and the entire Alexander family, including Alfred and his son Hanns. When he had first arrived in Berlin, Dr Alexander had offered to lend the Torah to the Neue Synagogue, but had been told that they would not accept it on loan. Hence, it was stored in a cupboard in the doctor's library.

Chapter Three

30 'A little later . . .' Under the armistice, Germany had agreed to remove its forces from the Baltic region, but the British government had proven willing to delay the withdrawal if it meant stopping the Russians from taking control of Latvia, a bulwark against any westward spread of Bolshevik power.

31 'Rossbach quickly recognised Rudolf . . .' While in his memoirs Rudolf remembers going straight from Mannheim to East Prussia, Rudolf probably first met up with Rossbach in Berlin, as it was here that Rossbach was amassing his men before they set off for the Baltic Coast. It is possible

he served first with the East Prussian Volunteer Corps, as is recorded in his SS personnel file.

34 'After being pushed out of Riga . . .' The Freikorps also turned their attention to domestic politics, for instance when Rossbach and his men occupied the Reichstag in support of Wolfgang Kapp's failed putsch, which for four days overthrew the government. Rudolf's role in this uprising is not clear.

34 'During the party, Rossbach . . .' Robert Waite describes Rossbach's celebration in his book *Vanguard of Nazism*, p.196, and is sourced from a *Munich Post* newspaper.

35 'As the group walked through the doors . . .' This description of Hitler's Kindlkeller speech and the beer hall comes from Ernst Franz Sedgwick Hanfstaengl. This speech is most likely the same one that Höss heard, as it coincides with his membership day as well as with Rossbach's anniversary.

36 'Martin Bormann . . .' Martin Bormann was a twenty-two-year-old with a stocky build and a mouth that seemed permanently downturned. He had dropped out of school to become a supervisor on a farm in Mecklenburg, which is where he had met Rudolf in 1922. Following Rudolf's suggestion, Bormann had joined the Nazi Party soon after.

37 'Rudolf, Bormann, and the others joined Kadow . . .' This description of Kadow's murder was revealed in court and described by the *The Times*, 17 March 1924.

38 'Rudolf had been unworried . . .' Höss' assumption about the 'unspoken agreement' between the government and the Freikorps, which he hoped would result in the shortening of his prison sentence, was actually misguided. The Bavarian government may have accelerated the release of some right-wing supporters, but this was not the case for the Prussian government (who had jurisdiction over his crime).

38 'On 9 November, Hitler . . .' This description of the Munich beer hall incident and Hitler's quote comes from *The Times*, 10 November 1923. Since his speech at the Munich Kindlkeller, Hitler had had great success in growing the party: more than 35,000 new members had been recruited

between February and November 1923, bringing the total to 55,000. He had also built up the military wing of the party, the *Sturmabteilung* or SA, which was filled with former First World War soldiers and veterans of the Freikorps. Yet despite Hitler's fundraising and recruitment trips around the country, including to Berlin, the party's core membership had been limited to Munich and its surrounding areas.

39 'He studied English, so that . . .' According to his SS personnel records, Rudolf could speak English fluently.

Chapter Four

46 'The family used the cottage . . .' Another favourite summer pastime was climbing one of the garden's cherry trees and then competing as to who could spit the pips out the farthest, or who could hold the most pips in their mouth. No matter how much he tried, Hanns always lost to his eldest sister. Bella was the champion at both efforts, with an unbeatable record of thirty-four pips stuffed into her cheeks. Well into old age, Hanns and his siblings often kept a pip tucked under their top lip, only to realise that it was still there when they ate another cherry or when they visited the dentist.

46 'In terms of their studies . . .' 'They didn't do very well at school, the darlings,' remembered Bella many years later. 'I don't think they ever worked very hard.'

47 'Throughout his childhood . . .' The Alexanders kept a record of their famous visitors, with Henny asking each to add their name to a guest-book. For Dr Alexander's fiftieth birthday party in 1930, many attendees added sketches and publicity photographs along with their good wishes. The names included: Hanns Purrmann, Hans Joachim Pagels, Emil W. Herz, Albert Einstein (thanking Alexander for his human kindness following the death of Einstein's uncle), James Franck, Leonhard Frank, Rudolf Kayser, Alfred Polgar, Walter Hasenclever, Fritzi Massary, Max Pallenberg, Paul Hartmann, Sybille Binder, Alice Nikitina, Molly Wessely, Erik Charell, Paul Wegener, Max Reinhardt, Grete Scherk,

Olga and Bruno Eisner, Sabine Kalter. There was also a photo of retired colonel Otto Meyer, Alfred's commander in the First World War.

47 'or Albert Einstein eating at their dinner table . . .' One evening, for example, Hanns looked through the dining room door and saw Albert Einstein and his wife eating with his parents – the professor absent-mindedly still sporting his house slippers. After dinner Alfred escorted his guest to the salon to take coffee, intending to quiz him about the theory of relativity on Henny's behalf. But when Alfred returned to his wife later that evening, he failed to produce an answer: the two had become so engrossed in discussing the latest detective novels, a passion they both shared, that he had forgotten to ask.

47 'Hanns also mixed with his parents' friends . . .' Hanns was well used to fancy dress. As an infant, and then later as a young man, he had been forced to wear the same costume as his brother. In order to obtain a crisp image, they had to hold their pose for many minutes, as their father – who fancied himself a photographer – fiddled with the camera equip-ment. The tedium of these photo shoots was not helped by Henny, who walked around telling the boys that they looked '*sehr schön*', very beau-tiful. When they were very young they had been dressed in brown rabbit costumes, with pointy silk-lined ears, soft woollen mittens and stubby silken tails. A few years later, they had been photographed wearing lederhosen, white shirts and little black boots. When they were in their teens, they had worn matching sailor outfits, with long woollen grey coats, leather gloves and a round hat with a ribbon strapped around its rim and hanging off to one side. This delight in costumes did eventually rub off on Hanns; many years later, he would organise his own fancy-dress parties, where he would greet his guests wearing a nurse's uniform, complete with starched white hat, white dress, black canvas belt around the waist, stockings and black buckled shoes.

50 'Their bar mitzvahs now complete . . .' To hear Hanns' tape recorded account of his bar mitzvah is to hear an echo of his thirteen-year-old self: one can still hear a boy, less than thrilled that he had been forced

to perform in the ceremony and completely unaware that his world was about to be turned inside out.

Chapter Five

54 'After the ceremony the newly-weds posed . . .' When I visited Brigitte in her home in Virginia, USA, I noticed her parents' wedding photograph — Rudolf and Hedwig Höss — still hanging on the wall above her bed.

56 'At this time the SS was made up of only a few . . .' According to the historian Peter Longerich, the number of SS members may in fact be lower as this 'few hundred' figure comes from Himmler and he may have been inflating his achievements in building up the organisation.

60 'Like a nursery gardener . . .' This quote on the qualities that Himmler was looking for in an SS member is taken from his speech given on 19 January 1943.

60 'The SS officer reviewing this application . . .' Peter Longerich provides a good description of the formation of the SS and the application process in his biography *Heinrich Himmler*.

69 'Although it was no longer the romantic . . .' Rudolf's daughter Brigitte remembered the family's time in Dachau as 'wonderful' and 'very pleasant'.

69 'He had mastered a new skill . . .' Hedwig knew that Rudolf was a senior camp officer and that the inmates were political prisoners. But the oath of silence that all SS soldiers pledged would have insulated Hedwig from the more disturbing incidents taking place inside the Dachau camp walls.

Chapter Six

72 'The boycott of Jewish businesses . . .' On 26 March 1933, Hitler had met with Joseph Goebbels, the newly appointed propaganda minister, and talked to him about what he saw as the greatest remaining threat to

national security: the German Jews and their international supporters. According to a note made in Goebbels' diary, Hitler said that the solution was a large-scale boycott of all Jewish businesses in Germany. Hitler added that 'Perhaps the foreign Jews will think better of the matter when their racial comrades in Germany begin to get it in the neck.'

74 'The Reichstag fire . . .' Bella would return to Berlin a few months later for her wedding celebration. But the move out of the house and overseas had been made.

78 'That night the rabbi . . .' Hanns later said that the rabbi was being 'theatrical', realising the impact that his delayed arrival would have.

78 'To protect themselves . . .' In an interview Hanns said: 'We were trained on how to give answers to the Nazis when they attacked us as "dirty Jews". What one should say and what one should do. There was a book called the *Anti Anti*. They were the anti-Semitics and we were the anti anti-Semitics.'

79 'Regardless of the new laws . . .' In a taped interview with his nephew John Alexander, sixty years later, Hanns remembered this small act of resistance with satisfaction: 'I was very keen on ice hockey. We just went, nobody took any notice. It was not for the public, but we managed to get in somehow. It wasn't done, one knew when one was not wanted. There was probably a notice saying *"Juden raus!"* ("Jews Out!"). We shouldn't have gone, but we were a law unto ourselves.'

81 'The first step was to secure . . .' Prior to obtaining an entry visa to a new country, Hanns had to secure an exit certificate from the German authorities. Hanns' document cost 10 RM and was signed by the Berlin chief of police. The certificate reads: 'The official document Homeland certificate (for a stay abroad). Mr Hanns Hermann Alexander, born 6th May 1917 in Berlin. Holds German nationality. This certificate is valid until 31st December 1936. Dated Berlin, 10th June 1936. Signed by the Chief of Police. The holder of this certificate must sign himself before he presents it to a foreign authority.' It is a mystery, at least to me, why the Berlin exit certificate is dated on 10 June 1936, eight days after Hanns arrived in Croydon.

82 'The next day, Hanns woke early and walked to the British . . .' The British consulate was run by Frank Foley, who had built a good reputation within the Berlin Jewish community. Indeed, between 1936 and 1939, Foley's office would enable more than 10,000 Jews to leave Germany. In 1999 he was honoured by Yad Vashem as one of the Righteous Among Nations.

83 'Individuals with significant assets . . .' The original Reich Escape Tax was only levied on individuals with assets exceeding 200,000 Reichsmarks, or had a yearly income of over 20,000 Reichsmarks. At the time, the RM was set at a rate of 6.7 RM per pound sterling, therefore 200,000 RM was equivalent to £30,000 (or approximately £440,000 in today's money). These figures were lowered in 1934, resulting in a much larger number of people having to pay the tax and creating a larger impediment to departure. The new asset threshold figure was now only 50,000 RM (equivalent to about £100,000 today). In the 1950s, the West German government passed a law to repay Jews whose assets had been confiscated by the Nazis. The Alexanders never received funds for the clinic since they had sold it (rather than abandoning it), despite it being under duress and for non-market value.

84 'Hanns arrived at Croydon airport . . .' Imperial Airways blazed the trail of early commercial flight, having established the first daily flight from London to Paris a little over a decade before in 1924. However, flying Imperial could also be dangerous. By June 1936, seven of their planes had crashed, including one accident when a plane caught fire shortly after taking off in Croydon, killing the pilot and all seven passengers.

87 'as the Nazis were still keen . . .' The Nazi government expedited the Jewish exodus by increasing pressure through restrictive laws and violence (particularly Kristallnacht), approving exit visas, and even negotiating with the authorities in Palestine to accept Jewish refugees. The view of the Nazi leadership at this time was that if there were fewer Jews in the country then there would be fewer Jews to take care of later. In January 1933, there were 523,000 Jews in Germany, a third of them in Berlin. By

September 1939, more than 202,000 Jews remained in Germany, most of them elderly.

87 'Hilde took Henny at her word . . .' When the boxes were unpacked in their new home in London, the Alexanders found all their belongings intact, Dr Alexander's First World War uniform among them. Later Hanns and Paul worried that a Kaiser outfit might not make such a good impression with their new English neighbours. So one night the twins crept out of their rooms and discarded the uniform piece by piece in rubbish bins up and down Kensington High Street: the shiny pike helmet went in one bin, the tasselled jacket in another, the boots in another. The one thing Dr Alexander would not let the twins throw away was his Iron Cross First Class. He kept it in its green box, tucked away in a desk drawer.

91 'At the camp he witnessed . . .' One of the atrocities Paul Graetz may have witnessed during his time in Sachsenhausen was the deaths of twelve Jewish men who had refused to follow a guard's orders. They were beaten to death with sticks.

91 'As soon as Ann's father made it home . . .' According to his daughter-in-law, Antonia Grey (or 'Tonny' as she is known by her family members), Paul Graetz was haunted by his eighteen days in Sachsenhausen for the rest of his life. Even in his last few days – fifty years later, in a London hospice – Paul Graetz called out in terror, pleading for a camp guard not to beat him.

92 'Then, one month later, on 24 July 1939 . . .' The *Ausbürgerungslisten* were published in the *Reich Gazette*, the official newspaper of the German government under the Nazis. Over 390 lists were published with over 39,000 names. The final list was published in 1945.

Chapter Seven

98 'One of these guards was Josef Kramer . . .' At the end of his prison memoirs Rudolf describes many of the men he worked with over the years – Himmler, Glücks, Maurer, Pohl, for example. But he does not

discuss Josef Kramer in any detail, even though he worked closely with him for many years. However, Rudolf had sufficient respect for his former adjutant to approve Kramer's appointment as Kommandant of Belsen.

100 'In November 1940 . . .' This meeting between Rudolf Höss and Heinrich Himmler was likely to have taken place in Berlin, for there is no record of Himmler having visited the camp at this time.

102 'The children transformed the villa . . .' Much of the material from this section concerning the life of the Höss family in Auschwitz comes from a series of interviews I conducted with Rudolf's second daughter, Brigitte. It took me more than three years to find her, persuade her to talk, and eventually meet.

103 'Angel of Auschwitz . . .' This praise for Hedwig was echoed by Anieli Bednarskiej, a young woman who lived in the town of Oświęcim. Though not a prisoner, Anieli worked in the Höss villa from 1940 to 1943. In testimony provided after the war, she said, 'Frau Höss behaved towards me in a very decent manner. She tried to persuade me to sign the "*Volksliste*" [in which a non-German citizen could declare themselves German]. When I refused she didn't try to persuade me further.'

104 'She could expect, he said, her guestbook . . .' Hedwig, like Henny Alexander, also kept a guestbook – hers filled with the names of various Nazi luminaries who visted the Höss family from early September 1940 through to March 1945. The guestbook was found at the Old Sugar factory in St Michaelisdonn by FSS92 officer Karl Abrahams in 1946 and donated to Yad Vashem.

105 'Heinrich Himmler, or "Uncle Heiner" . . .' Ever since a boy, Himmler had frequent stomach trouble and may have abstained from meat at times but, unlike Hitler, he was not a vegetarian. Rudolf Höss' second daughter, Brigitte, told me that she called Himmler 'Uncle Heiner'. This is somewhat different from the nickname given by others, who somewhat sarcastically called him 'Heini', meaning 'little boy who is scared' (Himmler had never seen action during the First World War).

106 'Each week Rudolf had his hair cut . . .' I interviewed Jozef Paczynski,

the 'Little Pole', in his apartment in Krakow, Poland. He remembered cutting Rudolf's hair each week and how, the first time, he was very nervous as he had only just started cutting hair. 'He did not speak to me,' Jozef recalled. 'He just looked disgusted that a prisoner was cutting his hair. My hands were shaking, but I had seen his hair cut before, it was not too difficult.' Over the next three years, Jozef cut Rudolf's hair every week and during this time the Kommandant never spoke a word to him. 'He was always pleasant to his family and children. If you didn't know about the killings you wouldn't have thought he was a bad man; he seemed normal.' Jozef had also seen Rudolf at the entrance gates to the camp when the prisoners went off to work. 'When they came back, exhausted and carrying the bodies of corpses, he just looked on; he never interfered.'

107 'Yet other prisoners had less favourable experiences . . .' The memories of prisoners who came into contact with Rudolf Höss during their captivity in Auschwitz have been captured in video testimonies collected by Steven Spielberg's Shoah Archive. It is possible to download video testimony from this at various sites, including the University of California in San Diego, as well as Royal Holloway, University of London.

109 'He also said that he wanted to build . . .' By 1941 IG Farben was the largest chemical company in the world, with more than 100,000 employees. It had close ties to the Nazi regime, funding the party's rise to power and participating in its war machine. IG Farben owned 42.5 per cent of Degesch, the company that owned the patent for and manufactured Zyklon B, the chemical used in the gas chambers. IG Farben also built a huge oil and rubber factory called Buna, four miles from the Auschwitz II/Birkenau camp. There, tens of thousands of prisoners worked under brutal conditions. Later, a new concentration camp, known as Monowitz, was built specifically to house IG Farben prisoner labourers. Thirteen of IG Farben's twenty-four directors were sentenced to prison following the Nuremberg IG Farben Trial, but almost all went on to enjoy long and successful careers after the war.

111 'Including hundreds of children . . .' According to the Auschwitz

Museum, of the 1.3 million or more people deported to Auschwitz-Birkenau approximately 232,000 were children under the age of eighteen. Immediately upon arrival, the vast majority of these children were selected and sent to the gas chambers. A few boys and girls were selected for work. From the middle of 1943, some children were kept alive for 'medical' experiments supervised by Josef Mengele. When the Red Army liberated Auschwitz it found around seven hundred children amongst the seven thousand surviving prisoners.

112 'Molotov–Ribbentrop Pact with the Soviet Union . . .' Russia became known as the 'Soviet Union' in 1922. It was officially recognised as such by Britain in 1924. I have left Rudolf Höss' references to 'Russia' after 1922 – for example when he talks about 'Russian prisoners' in Auschwitz, even though they may well have been Ukrainian or from Belarus – to ensure authenticity.

113 'In the summer of 1941 . . .' In his memoirs, and in interviews conducted before the Nuremberg Trials, Rudolf insisted that this meeting with Heinrich Himmler in which he was ordered to carry out the Final Solution took place in the summer of 1941, before Germany's attack on the Soviet Union, and that soon afterwards, he visited Treblinka, where he saw Jews from the Warsaw Ghetto exterminated. This version of history is supported chiefly by Richard Breitman, Washington DC Holocaust Museum historian and chairman of the US Congressional Commission for the Declassification of Nazi Documents. But many scholars have disputed the claim, arguing that Rudolf Höss misremembered the dates. They point to the fact that the Warsaw Ghetto was not liquidated until the summer of 1942 and Treblinka was not operational until the same time. What is likely is that Rudolf met Himmler more than once about this sensitive matter and, given the consistency of his testimony (to the British, Americans and Poles), the date for this historic meeting is entirely possible.

Chapter Eight

122 'When it was finally their turn to go . . .' When the time came, Hanns and Paul's departure from France was further delayed while their commander, Major Gordon Smith, was given orders to destroy the bridge approaching St Malo.

122 'Hanns did not view . . .' Hanns' name change had been officially registered, and later on in life Hanns would regret this, viewing it as yet another loss that he had suffered at the hands of the Nazis. Ironically, the obituary in the *Telegraph* spelled his name incorrectly as 'Harvey' rather than 'Hervey'. The British were not the only ones to make mistakes. Many of his German documents also include inaccuracies. For example his German passport has his name as 'Hans' rather than 'Hanns'.

124 'who had adopted the name Harding . . .' Erich and Elsie changed their name to Harding after the war, with Erich also shortening his first name to Eric. The name change was poorly handled. To this day, and to much hilarity, their son Michael is known as Michael Harding Harding.

129 'With Paul nowhere to be seen . . .' Hanns recalled the story in which he chatted up the French girl in an interview given many years later with his nephew, John Alexander.

Chapter Nine

135 'Usually Rudolf would let the junior officers . . .' Rudolf included this recollection in his signed witness statement that he gave to the British on 14 March 1946 (certified by Captain Cross): 'I remember one particular incident . . . When I arrived there I gave the immediate orders to close all the doors and continue with the gassing of the two-thirds which had entered the chamber. After this was finished I proceeded together with the sentries into the dressing room using hand searchlights. We succeeded in pressing the prisoners into a corner and then let them

out individually. They were then shot in another room of the crematorium with small arms ammunition on my orders.' I found an original carbon copy of this statement in a file at the Intelligence Museum in Chicksands, UK, another at the US National Archive in College Park. A copy is also hung on the wall of the Holocaust exhibit at the Imperial War Museum in London. This incident is also described in a report by Jerzy Tabau that was smuggled out of the camp and later entered into the Nuremberg Trials ('The Polish Major's Report', L-022). It is also included in Martin Gilbert's book *The Holocaust*.

140 'Their father would drive them across the fields . . .' Even in her later years, Brigitte still savoured the moments that she had shared with her father: 'He was the nicest man in the world,' she told me. 'He was kind and was only ever good to us.' She remembered them eating lunch and dinner together, playing in the garden and, sometimes, while sitting in the living room, yards from the camp's crematorium, he would tell them the story of *Hansel and Gretel*. Brigitte was convinced that her father was a sensitive man and had guessed that he was involved with something bad. 'I'm sure he was sad inside,' she recalled. 'It is just a feeling. The way he was at home, the way he was with us, sometimes he looked sad when he came back from work.' But, she was also aware of another side to her father: 'I have been reading his book. I cannot read much of it. I'm not sure what to believe. There must have been two sides to him. The one that I knew and then another . . .' Brigitte struggled to reconcile her father's dual nature. When asked how he could be the 'nicest man in the world' if he was responsible for the deaths of at least one million Jews, she said: 'He had to do it. His family was threatened; we were threatened if he didn't. And he was one of many in the SS. There were others as well who would do it if he didn't.'

142 'While the Höss children may not have noticed the gas chambers . . .' When I interviewed Rudolf's daughter Brigitte, she was clear that she had no knowledge of the gas chambers. Rudolf's daughter-in-law Irene also said that her husband, Hans-Jürgen, claimed he had no knowledge

of the gas chambers nor of the murders that took place in the camp. However, Brigitte said that she was aware that her father had supervised a camp and that she herself had seen prisoners working in the villa's garden as well as in the house itself. 'We didn't know what he did,' Brigitte told me. 'We were only ten, eight, seven, five years and one-years-old. We did not know what he did, even if it was close by. We didn't see smoke, we didn't see what people now write and say. We didn't know anything. We maybe knew that there was something there, but not what.' Brigitte claimed that all she knew was that her father ran some kind of prison and that her only exposure to it was the zebra-striped prisoners who worked in the villa, whom she describes as always 'happy and kind'.

142 'Indeed to a certain degree . . .' Stanislaw Dubiel remembered Hedwig discussing her views on the Jews from his time working as a gardener at the Höss villa. His testimony was recorded as part of the evidence submitted for Rudolf's trial in 1947.

142 'Hedwig stopped having sex . . .' Anieli Bednarskiej – a young woman from Oświęcim who worked as a servant in the Höss villa – said that Hedwig was having an affair with a prisoner. Bednarskiej's testimony was collected after the war. Hedwig's lover was Karola Bohnera, a German Kapo who cleaned boots and fried fish for them in the villa. Since he didn't have a number or a prisoner designation, he was allowed to move around freely. One day, Rudolf returned unexpectedly and found Hedwig and Bohnera in the greenhouse. He quickly understood what was going on and 'made a scene'. Hedwig was able to pacify Rudolf, but on the condition that Bohnera never return to the villa. However, she continued to see him when her husband was away.

142 'In the spring of 1942 . . .' This remarkable story of Eleanor's time with Rudolf was captured in detailed testimony that Eleanor provided two years later to SS investigative judge Konrad Morgen. After the war it was included in the report *SS Dachau* and entered into evidence by the Americans during the Nuremberg Trials.

Chapter Ten

148 'Receiving alarming reports stating that . . .' This telegram from 1942 describing the Nazi plan to exterminate the Jews is quoted in *Blind Eye to Murder* by Tom Bower and *Holocaust Encyclopedia* by Walter Laqueur.

151 'By the start of 1945 . . .' The lack of resources and preparation in support of the war crimes effort didn't have to be this way. 'In sharp contrast to the ill-prepared war crimes efforts, high priority *was* being given to tracking down the German scientists. Even before the end of the war, the Allies had focused considerable efforts on locating nuclear scientists and transporting them to the UK and US. One earlier OSS mission, codenamed 'Alsos', was designed to locate and when possible interrogate German nuclear physicists. By March 1945, a new initiative codenamed 'Operation Paperclip' was proposed. It involved the dispersal of over three thousand specialists across Europe to pick up engineers, technicians, and rocket scientists. Once found, these scientists were transported to Britain and America, in the process denying the Soviets their knowledge. Operation Paperclip would be a spectacular success, giving the British and Americans a significant advantage in their post-war military efforts.

151 'The British were even less ambitious . . .' One of the causes for the investigators' lack of resources stemmed from the policy vacuum back in England. War crimes had fallen under the purview of the Foreign Office, and in particular forty-nine-year-old Viscount Bridgeman. Upon taking up his command Bridgeman had been told that the war crimes efforts should be limited to only what was absolutely necessary. One of the main reasons given was that they didn't want to repeat the 'Hang the Kaiser' campaign that had been so unpopular after the First World War. Furthermore, they expected that most of the war criminals would be gathered in the American Zone and therefore would not be the responsibility of the British occupying forces.

152 'In early 1945 . . .' A few weeks earlier, in December 1944, Hanns and Paul had been approached by a certain Captain Harvey from the Intelligence Corps to see if they wished to become interpreters. They had to complete a series of linguistic tests and interviews. In a letter to his parents, dated 9 December 1944, Paul explained why he was not interested in this position: 'As they don't pay or promote us they can stick their lousy specialist jobs in any case. I have been for three months with prisoner-of-war prisoners and now when they promote the officers they say "sorry no aliens". So as far as I am concerned they can stick their jobs. All I want is a cushy job in a safe nice area.' Hanns was keener on accepting the new position, seeing it as an opportunity to take on more interesting work.

153 'Paul also thought that Hanns was being unfair to Ann . . .' In this same letter, Paul wrote to Elsie asking her to help find him a wife: 'The following conditions must be adhered to: she can be impossibly ugly or old, if she gives me freedom to satisfy my own feelings somewhere else. She must get me out of the army, and into a good business, which must be a reserved occupation for the next war. She can be any nationality she bloody well feels like. If not, English is an asset. She should or must be Jewish (easier for the holidays). If she lives in Whitechapel she must move. Otherwise I leave the details to you. (One more point about nationality if she is French, she must be a good whore, otherwise not interested in that sort of nation.)'

Chapter Eleven

155 'Morgen immediately visited . . .' Konrad Morgen described his investigation during a series of testimonies and affidavits provided to the Nuremberg Trials.

157 'He also discovered that Maximilian Grabner . . .' In his paperwork to Berlin, Grabner had misleadingly stated that the prisoners at Auschwitz had died from disease and malnutrition.

165 'At the end of the month . . .' Upon his return to Berlin, Rudolf once again became the focus of Konrad Morgen's inquiry. The SS judge had met Eleanor Hodys in Dachau in the autumn of 1944, and she had told him about her affair with Rudolf. Konrad immediately initiated criminal proceedings against Rudolf Höss, along with the other top SS officials tasked with what he called the 'blood orders,' including Adolf Eichmann, Hans Loritz and Oswald Pohl. Morgen later told the Nuremberg Trial that he was surprised to realise that Himmler had been playing him all along. 'It just seemed to be unthinkable, in view of the education of the SS and its values of sincerity, frankness and honesty, to think that the Reichsführer-SS was capable of such insidious activities and of being two-faced, the hidden face bearing the characteristics of a common criminal.' Sometime in late autumn of 1944, the Reichsführer then told the judge to cease the investigation into Rudolf Höss and others. Morgen was taken off the case and reassigned as Breslau's chief judge.

Chapter Twelve

174 'Nonetheless he agreed to help . . .' At the end of the war the Germans had evacuated some of the Belsen inmates to the nearby Hermann Göring factory. When the British had arrived the Germans had attempted to relocate these prisoners once again, but their train had broken down and the prisoners had instead been placed in a camp outside Wolfsburg, near Hanover.

174 'Hanns drove the child and the nurse . . .' According to Hanns, reuniting that child with her mother was the most cherished achievement of his six and a half years in the army. He recounted this story to another member of the Belsize Square Synagogue, Herbert Levy, in a recorded interview in 1995.

174 'On 16 May . . . Leo Genn . . .' Leo Genn had grown up in a Jewish family in Stamford Hill, north London. He had studied law at Cambridge and, after qualifying as a barrister, had worked as a lawyer in a London

theatre. While never giving up his legal practice, he had also become a professional actor, performing Horatio to Laurence Olivier's Hamlet at the Old Vic in 1937. He was a man of immense charisma, with a smooth but authoritative voice and a calm demeanour. At the outbreak of war he had joined the British Army's Judge Advocates Office.

175 'In the three weeks since the camp's liberation . . .' In a memo written on 21 May 1945, Leo Genn updated Brigadier H. Scott-Barrett at the War Crimes Commission in London, on the 'unsatisfactoriness of the position'. He wrote, 'I am very far from complete as to personnel and the work, which in any case could only proceed at slightly better than its somewhat pedestrian speed up to now, will now be very little accelerated.' At this time hundreds of thousands of Germans were held in displacement camps across Europe. Many were disorientated and identified themselves without any attempt at deceit. This would have been the perfect time to focus efforts on catching and prosecuting the war criminals. Instead, the vast majority weren't even identified, let alone seriously interrogated. For example, Gustav Wagner, the 'Angel of Death' from the Sobibor concentration camp, and Ernst Heinrich-sohn, who supervised the deportation of Jews in Paris, were both held in internment camps, but went unquestioned and were soon after released. Another example was Adolf Eichmann, who was held for a brief time in an American POW camp before escaping. He was never identified even though he was on the CROWCASS watch-list. It would be decades before he would face justice in an Israeli courtroom.

175 'Beyond this, however, they were on their own . . .' According to *The Times,* in an article published on 18 June 1945, there were 'many complications' hampering the war crimes investigators, including the fact that many of the witnesses had already left the camp and those who remained spoke numerous languages. Perhaps most importantly, according to the article, the British were simply unprepared to carry out the required investigative and legal effort: 'The full horror and chaos of Belsen took us [the British] unawares.' Nevertheless, by the publication of this article,

86 SS guards, including 28 women, had been taken into custody and 300 affidavits had been collected.

176 'The British wartime policy on interrogation techniques . . .' During the war Colonel Robin 'Tin Eye' Stephens ran a London-based detention centre that held German spies; after the war he ran an interrogation centre for war criminals in Germany. Stephens' 1945 report, entitled *A Digest of Ham*, was the British Army's interrogation bible at this time and provides a snapshot of the techniques that Fox and Hanns would have used. In 1948 Colonel Stephens faced a court martial, with three others, for the abuse that took place at a British interrogation centre in occupied Germany. Two prisoners had died during interrogations, while others would claim to have been tortured with lighted cigarettes, doused in cold water and threatened with execution. Britain, it would be said, had established 'concentration camps' similar to those of the Nazis. One soldier would be found guilty, the others, including Stephens, were cleared.

177 'Hössler responded . . .' This and the other interrogations by Hanns and Fox come from the transcripts of the Belsen Trial available at the National Archive, London.

182 'Hanns had by now developed two sides to his personality . . .' Then in her eighties, Lucille Eichengreen talked to me about her experiences with Hanns during a telephone interview. She had grown up in a Jewish family in Hamburg before being deported to the Łódz ghetto in Poland, then Auschwitz and finally Belsen, which is where she had first met Hanns, just after the Belsen Liberation in May 1945, and stayed in touch with him after the war. 'He always had a smile,' she said. 'He wanted to be liked. He wanted to be charming, he was very good looking and he knew it. He was popular, almost easygoing, with a smile and a joke. In a sense he could be very funny and with a fast response. He rather lived life on that basis rather than show his real side.' When I asked her what this 'real side' was, she said: 'He was a Jew; he was very, very angry at what he saw. He saw it firsthand. He had grown up with it.

And then he saw the camp when we were in terrible shape. Well he would call Germans "krauts" as a matter of course. He spoke to them in a rather harsh voice. There was no kindness showing. He judged them the same way I did because they were Germans and that was very unusual for a British officer.' I asked her then why Hanns left the camp to go looking for Nazis: 'Because he felt the injustice of what had been done to us. And as many as he could catch he caught. He felt compelled to do this.' But other people didn't? 'No, because there were not many people in this British unit that were Jewish, could speak German, and had an understanding that it could have happened to them.'

184 'Driving around northern Germany . . .' Hanns was not only looking for war criminals during these tours, he was also looking for survivors, or at least word of their fate. His sister Elsie had written to him asking about friends and family members, and he was trying to track them down. In a letter dated 25 June, Hanns wrote that he had been able to find only one of the names, which had been published in the Netherlands on the Red Cross list of 'saved people'. He encouraged her to write to a contact in Eindhoven in the Netherlands, a Red Cross worker who 'is reliable (Dutch underground!)'.

184 'With Paul by his side . . .' Paul did not look forward to supervising German prisoners of war. In a letter to his parents he wrote: 'It is now the third day that I am doing this new job, of which I was so afraid, as I thought I could not manage my temper. It is a most important job, the most important I have done since joining the army. For once we are somewhere useful. It has taught me some very useful lessons for a lifetime, as far as Germany is concerned. I always imagined that these bastards seen in this terrific quantity would make me hate them, but it does not. I thought I might feel pity, but it does not. I thought I might find some happiness to see them behind wire, but nothing of the kind. They make me feel physically sick, they smell, they stink . . . They still believe that Germany will win and must win. They are stubborn idiots but utterly useless for the world. There is only one way out in my opinion. Labour

gangs in Bavaria for life. I am sure there is only one good German and that is one who is 6ft below ground. You should see the German officers. Arrogant bastards. The SS and SA is a shocking crowd. I wonder what they would say if they would know I am a German Jew. They would die in their coats.'

188 'Despite her repeated requests that he apply for leave, Hanns was too preoccupied . . .' At the end of July, Hanns, Captain Fox and the rest of 1 WCIT had been pulled from Belsen to help with a case involving the deaths of thirty-one SAS soldiers in the French Zone in the small town of Gaggenau. Yet when the WCIT tried to lend a hand, offering to deploy the skills that they had built up in Belsen, their help went unwelcomed. The man in charge of the investigation, a Major Bankworth, criticised them for their lack of experience and dismissed their efforts in Belsen, saying that the only war criminals that should be prosecuted were those who had perpetrated crimes against members of the British Army. As a result, Hanns and his colleagues were marginalised and spent most of the time playing cards and drinking tea. When three weeks passed, Leo Genn decided enough was enough and brought the team back to Belsen.

189 'Hanns' first task was to ensure that the number one defendant, Josef Kramer . . .' Like the other SS prisoners, Kramer had lost considerable weight in captivity, but he had retained a certain swagger and presented himself as a man who could not be easily intimidated. He had already provided an account of his life in his original affidavit: he had been trained as a guard in Dachau and Sachsenhausen before being moved to Auschwitz in 1940; in 1941 he briefly ran Natzweiler-Struthof, the only concentration camp on French soil; in 1942, he had returned to Auschwitz to run the Birkenau camp; and finally, in 1944, on the recommendation of Rudolf Höss, he had been appointed Kommandant of Belsen by Richard Glücks.

192 'a total of at least four million had been gassed . . .' Over the years there has been much controversy concerning the numbers killed in

Auschwitz. This has not been helped by the fact that Rudolf Höss himself changed his estimate in his various testimonies. The figure of four million originated with the Soviet Union after its liberation of Auschwitz in January 1945. This number was repeated in the prosecutor's opening statement at the Belsen Trial in September 1945. This figure was quickly modified as additional information came to light. Since the war's end, and despite the lack of records kept in the camp, it has been possible to make estimates based on witness statements, interviews and contemporaneous documents. According to many historians, including those at the Auschwitz Museum, the most likely figure is that 1.3 million people died in Auschwitz, of whom 90 per cent were Jewish.

192 'For the next few weeks, the world was transfixed . . .' Some of the headlines during the Belsen Trial included: 'SS Killed 4,000,000 at Oświęcim prosecutor says at Kramer Trial', *New York Times*; 'Blonde Beastess has confessed her guilt', *Daily Mirror*; 'Gas chamber survivor describes horror: We were dumped liked potatoes', *Winnipeg Evening Tribune*; 'Tell how Nazis experimented on nude women', *Chicago Tribune*; 'Irma Grese makes three confessions', *Daily Express*; 'Kramer trial to get story of massacre', *Washington Post*; 'Inferno on Trial', *Time Magazine*; 'Kramer cross-examined: I gassed prisoners on orders of Himmler', *The Scotsman*; 'Mass murder, I'm guilty. Belsen head girl admits', *Toronto Star*.

193 'The defendants' lawyers had a hard time . . .' When the lawyers attempted to defend the accused, they were reproached by the press for being insensitive to the witnesses and of disloyalty to the British cause of justice. Letters were written to the papers, saying that the court was being too fair to the defendants and, given their crimes, that the typical rules of the British legal system should not apply. But the Belsen Trial had been established upon the foundations of this very legal system, and it was believed to be critical to allow the defendants to have a chance to protest their innocence. By giving them their day in court, it was argued, any guilty verdict would carry a greater sense of gravitas and finality.

193 'When it came to Josef Kramer's turn . . .' *The Times* ran a story on 9 October 1945, under the title 'Discrepancy explained', on why Kramer had retracted his first affidavit claiming no knowledge of the Auschwitz gas chambers: 'He had given his word of honour to Obergruppenführer Pohl of the Oranienburg headquarters of the concentration camp system [*Amtsgruppe D*] that he would say nothing about them. When his first statement was made the war was still being fought: at the time of the second statement Hitler and Himmler, to whom he felt bound to honour, existed no longer.'

193 'At 9.34 on the morning . . .' When he heard that the Belsen defendants had been hanged, Hanns wrote a letter to Ann: 'I heard tonight that the Belsen thugs were hung yesterday. I am glad of that, so they cannot escape any more and I do not have to start looking again.'

195 'He had been promoted to the rank of captain . . .' Hanns was not happy with how long it had taken to be promoted to captain and believed it was because he was not born in England. In a letter to his parents, written in October 1944, Hanns wrote: 'I won't get the captaincy now or at any time. Don't forget I'm still a b[loody] foreigner. And promotions are still made in the good old-fashioned way. The question is not what you know, but whom you know.'

Chapter Thirteen

202 'Over the course of that summer . . .' The details of Rudolf Höss' stay in Gottrupel come from a June 2001 *Zeit* article, titled *Flensburger Kameraden*. This article goes on to say that Rudolf left behind a few articles in the barn, including his black leather coat and his briefcase: 'The coat was later used as a painter's smock by one of the villagers, the briefcase of the mass murderer found employment as a book-bag for school-children.'

202 'Rudolf spent the rest of the autumn . . .' This information on Rudolf Höss' movements during his time in Gottrupel was given by Rudolf to his British interrogators in a statement made on 14 March 1946.

Chapter Fourteen

204 'Leo Genn had returned to England . . .' Genn's next role was playing alongside Vivien Leigh in the film *Caesar and Cleopatra*.

208 'Hanns and his driver . . .' The details of Hanns' seventeen-day odyssey come to us from the field reports he gave his boss, Lieutenant Colonel Tilling. The Luxembourg newspapers also followed his adventures with great interest, describing Hanns' journey as 'like something from a detective novel' and 'a wild goose chase'. For the past seventy years, these documents have been tucked away in files in the Luxembourg and British National Archives.

209 'Inside were documents belonging to . . .' In late 1944, Himmler had originally conceived of the Werwolfs as a clandestine force that would fight behind advancing enemy lines. Its mandate had been changed in the spring of 1945, when Nazi propaganda chief Joseph Goebbels had announced that the Werwolfs would mount an insurgency against the Allied occupation of Germany. However, despite being made up of former SS soldiers and Hitler Youth, the Werwolfs had failed to mount any serious challenge to the Allies. Nevertheless, any member of the Werwolfs might be armed and dangerous and, though only fourteen years old, 'Gustav Henning' would have to be approached with great care.

214 'Hanns collected all of Simon's possessions . . .' Later, this same landlady, Frau Berhorst, would lodge a complaint with the British authorities against Hanns for stealing seven thousand marks worth of items from Gustav Simon's rooms. This accusation resulted in a stern letter sent four months after the arrest, on 6 April 1946, from the head of the British Intelligence Bureau to Group Captain Somerhough, in which the War Crimes Group was admonished for failing to inform them immediately that the Gauleiter had been arrested and then asking that they be 'informed of the disposal of this confiscated property and of what it consisted'. In his response, Hanns wrote that he had passed

the confiscated items to the War Crimes Legal Department, with the exception of the clothing, which he said he distributed to displaced persons in Belsen. Given the effort that it would have taken for the landlady to complain and the tone of the letter from the Intelligence Bureau, it is possible that some of the Gauleiter's money had not made it into the War Crimes Group's evidence room, and had ended up in Hanns' pocket.

219 'There were, however, conflicting reports . . .' Recently unearthed by a number of Luxembourg historians and investigative journalists, including a long article published by *Revue* magazine, this version of the death of Gustav Simon is based on evidence discovered within the Luxembourg National Archive, along with testimony provided by many of the people involved. This alternative account is bolstered by various inconsistencies with the official version: why, for instance, if Simon had committed suicide in prison on 18 December 1945, was a death certificate not issued until 8 February 1946, a full two months after his death? Equally, how could a man who was 1.6m high possibly hang himself from a bedpost that was 1.4m high? Even if such a feat was technically possible, how could the guard posted outside his door on suicide watch, for twenty-four hours a day, not have noticed what was taking place inside the cell? Finally, if the suicide had taken place, why had so many people come forward saying that the official version was untrue? According to this 'unofficial account', the murder was motivated either by Luxembourg collaborators, who did not want Simon to reveal their identities in court, or by partisans, angry at Simon's treatment of the Luxembourg nationalists and Jews. When, sixty years later, this alternative account of Gustav Simon's death was sketched out during a meeting of Hanns' nephews, nieces and their spouses, not one person raised an objection. They believed that it was entirely possible that Hanns could have disobeyed a direct order, overseen the extra-judicial killing of a senior Nazi, led the cover-up of the story, and kept the secret hidden ever since. Hanns' nephew Peter Sussmann went further, having spent three years in Luxembourg

in the 1970s and having discussed the Gauleiter's arrest with Hanns when he had visited him in Luxembourg: 'He left me with the impression that Gustav Simon was not dead when he picked him up at the prison,' Peter recalled. 'Do I think that Uncle Hanns killed Simon himself? No. He was not the kind of man to do that. He was not stupid; he would have known about the Geneva Convention and, if found out, he would have been put behind bars. But do I think that he could have allowed it to happen? Absolutely yes. He hated those bastards. And if asked which way I would cast my vote, of the two versions? I would go with the partisan story, that Simon was killed in the woods and that Hanns then issued the other story to make it all kosher.'

224 'Lucille Eichengreen remembers it slightly differently . . .' It is interesting how two people who experienced the same event from the same point of view can have very different recollections. When I asked Lucille Eichengreen why her account of the escape from Belsen was different from Anita Lasker's – even though they were sitting next to each other at the time – she said: 'You can ask ten people who were in the same place at the same time and you will get ten answers. I'm not saying mine is right or hers is wrong or vice versa. I can't tell you really why.' When I asked if Hanns would have invented a story or stuck to the truth, she answered: 'He would have told the truth. But he would have used some curse words and some humour in between.'

Chapter Fifteen

226 'Leo Helger, for many years . . .' The story about Himmler giving Rudolf various artefacts, and how they came to be returned to Hedwig, comes from Rainer Höss, Rudolf's grandson. These items are now stored at the IFZ institute in Munich, Germany.

227 'But if Rudolf were to flee . . .' When I met Rudolf's daughter Brigitte, she said that Rudolf struggled with this decision. He wanted to protect himself, and believed that the best way to achieve this was to escape to

South America. At the same time he did not want to abandon his family, who he knew would face tremendous obstacles in post-war Germany. But if he stayed, and was caught, it would be in nobody's interest. In the end, he decided to leave and to bring his family to South America later.

231 'Hanns next went to the Red Cross offices . . .' A letter written to the author, on 1 April 2010, from the Czech Republic Red Cross Tracing Service, said that on 2 September 1942, Cäcilie Bing was in fact put on a transport XII/2 from Frankfurt to Theresienstadt (serial number 37); and then on 29 September 1942 she was put on one of the Transport Bs from Theresienstadt to Treblinka (serial number 1473). Sara Graetz, Ann's grandmother, was put on the same transport. This letter concluded: 'Nobody survived the Transports Bs.'

233 'Punctilious as ever . . .' Three months later, on 27 May 1946, Oswald Pohl was arrested by these same Haystack investigators. He had taken on the identity of 'Ludwig Gniss' and was working on a small farm near the village of Armsen, only thirty miles west of Belsen. Following a lengthy trial, Pohl was sentenced to death on 3 November 1947. He was executed in 1951, following a series of protracted appeals and counter-appeals. To the last he denied responsibility for the Nazi death camps, claiming to be only a bureaucrat.

234 'Since May 1945 . . .' To this day we do not know what happened to Richard Glücks. In his unpublished memoirs, *Don't You Know There's a War On*, British Field Security Section agent Fred Warner says that he found Glücks' body in another Flensburg grave. However, there is no independent confirmation that Warner did in fact find Richard Glücks' body. Indeed there are stories that Glücks died many months after the May 1945 meeting with Höss and Himmler. For example, a classified cable held in the US National Archive, seen by the author, states: '5 Oct 45. Suicide reported from Flensburg. Died while in custody (MI14 Report).' Not only does this memo challenge the fact that Glücks died in May 1945, which most historians believe, but it suggests that Glücks was held in British custody. This invites the question: what was he doing

during the missing months? Was he helping the British in some way? An alternative version has him escaping from north Germany after the war to South America and involved with the ODESSA network (acronym standing for *Organisation der Ehemaligen SS-Angehörigen*, or 'Organisation of Former Members of the SS'). The novelist Frederick Forsyth would later build on this rumour, making Richard Glücks the mastermind of the Nazi post-war network in his novel *The Odessa File*.

235 'Taking a vehicle from the War Crimes Group's . . .' Throughout early 1946, the War Crimes Group's Captain Somerhough kept a close eye on Hanns' activities. On the bottom of one of Hanns' typed dispatches, Somerhough had scrawled a note, dated 18 February 1946: 'Capt. Alexander due on Pohl then Flensburg re Höss and Glücks.'

235 'Hanns' first stop was at the home of Glücks' wife . . .' The details of Hanns' investigation into the whereabouts of Richard Glücks come from Hanns Alexander's field report, UK National Archives, 13 March 1946.

238 'Ran out of the room and hid under a tree . . .' Many years later Brigitte would say that she still experienced migraine headaches because of the incessant shouting of Hanns and his colleagues that day.

238 'Hanns realised that they must develop . . .' This version of the story comes from Captain Cross in an unpublished letter he wrote on 27 March 1985 to Colonel Robson of the Intelligence Corps. It is worth noting that Cross does not get all his facts right. For example, he mentions in this letter 'Frau Hoess [sic] and three sons', whereas Hedwig had only two sons. An alternative version is provided by Brigitte, Rudolf's second daughter, who remembers her mother telling her what happened: Klaus and Hedwig had been arrested and were indeed in separate cells. For days Hedwig was tormented by her son's agonised screams as he was being tortured by Hanns and the other British soldiers. Still, she didn't relent, until she was visited by her brother, Fritz, who informed her that Rudolf had managed to secure passage out of Germany and was at that very moment on a boat to safety in South America. It was only then, knowing that Rudolf was safe, that Hedwig revealed her husband's identity and location to Hanns. However,

Hedwig's version of events does not match the rest of the evidence, and it is quite possible that Hedwig told this story to her children so that they did not believe that she betrayed their father to the British.

Chapter Sixteen

240 'Over the next hour the men . . .' According to the letter written to Colonel Robson of the Intelligence Corps by Captain Cross on 27 March 1985, some of the men included in FSS 92 unit were Henshaw, Rapkins, Durkin, Kuditsch, Wiener, Roberts, Cresswell, Dobons, Abrahams and Shiffers, though some of these men had adopted alias identities. For example, 'Shiffers' was in fact Sansavrino.

241 'Hanns knew that they all wanted to be "in on the kill" . . .' Over the years, numerous people have claimed to have been involved in the arrest of Rudolf Höss. Indeed, in a tape-recorded interview with his nephew John Alexander, Hanns said, 'Lots of people were involved with the work. Some people were reading the letter to the wife, others were watching the wife.' In his field report, sent on 15 March 1945, Hanns mentions the doctor from 5th RHA, Captain Hartford from 318 FSS, as well as the men of Captain Cross' FSS 92 unit. Rudolf Höss' official arrest report has Captain Cross' name on it, though such documents were often signed by an administrator rather than the person who actually carried out the arrest. In Richard Butler's book, *Legions of Death*, Bernard Clarke, one of the members of FSS 92, says that he was involved with the arrest. (It is from this book that the quote from the doctor comes: 'Call them off . . . unless you want to take back a corpse.') At the Imperial War Museum in London, there is a file which places Charles Steven Mackay close to the interrogation of Höss. I spoke to Ken Jones, in Wrexham, a British soldier based in northern Germany during the war, who said that he slept in the cell with Höss to ensure that he didn't kill himself in the days after the arrest. The official and unpublished history of the British Army Intelligence Corps gives credit of the arrest – 'their

most important catch' they called it – to one of their members, Karl 'Blitz' Abrahams, a Liverpool-born and German-speaking Jew who was a member of Field Security Section 92. I spoke to Karl's son, Stephen Abrahams, who said that he possessed letters between his father and mother which confirm that he was involved with the Höss interrogation, but the letters do not mention the arrest and his father never spoke to him about these events, nor did he write about them in his memoirs.

242 'In ten minutes I want to have . . .' Hanns knew that he was responsible for Rudolf Höss being beaten during his arrest. In a recorded interview with Herbert Levy, he said, '[Rudolf Höss] did say that he was extremely well treated by the British, with exception of the arresting officer. I did my bit . . . guilty.' Those ten minutes of abuse, along with allegations of further attacks at British hands, would be enough for scores of Holocaust revisionists to argue over the years that Rudolf Höss' testimony was tainted. Their argument goes like this: Höss' testimony was beaten out of him and therefore his evidence at Nuremberg, and later his autobiography, could not be relied upon. This led them, supposedly logically, to argue that because the 'story' of the Final Solution relied so heavily on Rudolf Höss' testimony, the Holocaust never really happened.

243 'At around midnight the prisoner . . .' In his autobiography and his later testimonies, Rudolf maintained that the only person he had ever killed himself was Walter Kadow, back in the 1920s. This conversation with Hanns in the truck was the only time that Rudolf ever admitted that he personally killed any other people. Later, he had acknowledged *supervising* the murder of two and a half million people, but never to killing by his own hand.

Chapter Seventeen

249 'Martin Bormann . . .' After many years of rumours and unconfirmed sightings, the German government confirmed in 1998 via DNA evidence that Martin Bormann had died in May 1945 near Hitler's bunker in Berlin.

250 'Cables zipped back and forth . . .' A cable sent from BAOR headquarters on 22 March 1946 said: 'HOESS [sic] is to be tried by the British authorities and the Poles have consequently been told that we are not prepared to hand him over.' Then on 27 March, another cable said: 'Foreign Office in favour of Hoess being handed over and consider it a matter of high political importance.' Finally, on 27 April, a letter was sent to the US Army in charge of Höss' custody in Nuremberg, saying that the British had now agreed to the 'delivery' of Höss to the Polish authorities, but if the Polish government didn't sentence Rudolf Höss to death then the British government will 'request his delivery to British Authorities for a further trial'.

253 'By contrast, Whitney Harris looked dapper . . .' I met Whitney Harris in his office in St Louis, Missouri. By this time, Harris was in his nineties. He was charming and generous with his time. 'In Nuremberg we based all our efforts on written documents,' he told me. 'We wanted to prove the accuracy of the Holocaust beyond a shadow of a doubt. This would be the first time in history that war criminals would be brought to justice, and we wanted to get it right.' Harris died of cancer at his home in 2010.

254 'The first was Gustave Gilbert . . .' The inkblot test had been invented in 1921 by the Swiss psychologist Hermann Rorschach and, while popular with American psychologists, it was new to Gilbert. He presented Rudolf with ten individual 4 x 10-inch cards, each covered with different oddly shaped inkblots. The first five cards were printed in shades of black and white; the second five were brightly coloured, with reds, blues, oranges and yellows. He asked Rudolf how he felt about each card and what the pictures resembled. The prisoner said that one card looked like an animal skin, another like two people dancing, and a third was like a 'pelvic girdle of an exhumed corpse – during my activity in the concentration camp I often attended post-mortems and exhumations – a post-mortem dissection'. A recent review of the Kommandant's responses by Rorschach expert Barry Ritzler suggests that Rudolf was a sensitive man who was

more expressive than the other Nazis tested in Nuremberg and, as a result, avoided situations that might stimulate an emotional response. Ritzler also says that Rudolf appeared to be experiencing depression when he was tested in Nuremberg and that he lacked empathy. This might explain his bout of what he called 'prison psychosis' from his prison time in the 1920s, as well as his daughter Brigitte's recollection that 'he was sad when he came back from work'.

257 'The defence lawyer, Dr Kurt Kauffmann, introduced Rudolf . . .' The Nuremberg Trials were conducted in English, German, French and Russian. Everything said was instantly translated into the four languages by a panel of interpreters who worked in a long line of booths to one side of the main courtroom. To understand what was being said, participants, including Rudolf, wore chunky black plastic headphones that were hooked into an elaborate system of cables, amplifiers and transistors. This was the first time that any judicial proceeding had been simultaneously translated into so many languages. After the trial a similar sound system would be installed at the new United Nations building in New York.

260 'At lunch in the prisoner's canteen . . .' Frank's explanation that he was now willing to admit his role in the Holocaust because of Höss' testimony the day before, was reported in the London *Times*, 20 April 1946, under the headline: 'Frank declares his guilt: Part in massacre of Jews.'

260 'While Rudolf had been appearing as a witness . . .' Later that year, in October 1946, the Nuremberg judges handed down their sentences: of the twenty-four defendants, twelve were sentenced to hang, Kaltenbrunner, Göring and Frank among them. Martin Bormann, who was tried *in absentia*, was another of those sentenced to death. Seven of the remaining twelve defendants were sentenced to life in prison; the rest were acquitted.

263 'My dear good Mutz . . .' It is not clear what Rudolf meant by *Mutz*, his pet name for Hedwig. According to the Langenscheidt dictionary *Mutz* can mean a 'bear', a 'bobtailed animal', or a 'short tobacco pipe'. But as with most family nicknames, the origin of its meaning may be

more obscure. These previously unpublished letters from Rudolf Höss to his wife and children are held by the Auschwitz Museum.

265 'Little good it did them . . .' The fate of some of the key Nuremberg defendants was as follows: Ley had killed himself before the trial; Kaltenbrunner and Pohl died on the gallows; Göring escaped his sentence by killing himself in his cell the night before his execution; and Hess – Hitler's deputy – spent the rest of his life in Spandau prison, Berlin, until he died in 1987.

266 'On the last page of his memoirs . . .' There are times in his memoirs when Rudolf avoided the truth to protect others, as when he claimed that his wife didn't know about the gas chambers when she clearly did. And there are times when he is simply wrong about the facts, as when he claimed that the anti-Semitic magazine, *Der Stürmer,* was edited by Jews, or perhaps when he claimed to have received the orders from Himmler to implement the Final Solution in the summer of 1941, rather than 1942, which most historians now consider more likely. Equally, at various venues Rudolf provided different numbers for those killed in Auschwitz – to the British in Camp Tomato he had said 2 million, to the Americans in Nuremberg he had said 3 million, in his prison writings he had said that Eichmann's figure of 2.5 million was too high, while at his Polish trial he had said the figure may have been closer to 1.5 million. However, if his various testimonies are compared, they show remarkable consistencies, given the stressful context within which they were given. Most historians therefore agree, with some small qualifications, that his memoirs are reliable.

267 'According to a journalist from *The Times* . . .' The *Times* article on Rudolf's trial, published on 25 April 1947, under the byline 'from our Warsaw correspondent', was written by Joel Cang. Between March 1946 and December 1948, Cang (1897–1974) was the paper's correspondent in Poland. Between 1927 and 1948, he was also the Warsaw correspondent for the *Manchester Guardian* and *News Chronicle*. In this same article, Cang wrote that he met Höss in a side room during the proceedings, describing him as 'disconcertingly unlike any concept of one who, as witnesses

swore, had seized Jewish children and hurled them on to the death-cars and watched the SS men under his command burning other children alive . . . In appearance and manner he was the complete denial of any criminal type theory.' While they were talking, Rudolf showed Cang a copy of a letter he had received from Hedwig on the day that the trial began. When Cang asked how he could bring his children up so close to the camp, Rudolf replied: 'I kept them away from all that.'

271 'Enclosing his wedding ring . . .' According to documents supplied by the Polish Government Institute of Remembrance, Rudolf's wedding ring, which had proved so decisive in Hanns' unmasking his real identity in Gottrupel, was returned to his wife in Germany on 28 April 1947 with the words: 'I enclose Rudolf Höss' wedding ring which the Highest National Tribunal has allowed to be sent together with Höss' last letter to his wife Hedwig.' Rudolf's daughter Brigitte confirmed to me that her father's wedding ring was sent to her mother, along with the two letters to Hedwig and the children. She added that Hedwig wore the ring on her finger until her death and that it was interred with her ashes. Rudolf's death's head ring, which Klaus had carried to Hedwig in the last days of the war, is now held by Rainer Höss.

271 'letter to his children . . .' A copy of this letter is held by the Auschwitz Museum in Poland. The original, though rarely viewed, is kept in a box tucked away at the back of a crammed cupboard in the home of Rudolf's second daughter, Brigitte, in Virginia.

272 'Originally scheduled for . . .' This account of Rudolf's final days was compiled by the researchers at the Auschwitz Museum in Oświęcim.

Epilogue

275 'The families of the Nazi leaders . . .' The children of the senior Nazis reacted in different ways. Niklas Frank, the son of Hans Frank – the Nazi governor of the General Government of Poland – wrote a memoir exploring his feelings in explosively angry tones, confessing to masturbating as a child

every year on the anniversary of the execution of his father. As Frank said: 'This was to relieve the pressure from my mother and my siblings to celebrate the end of an "innocent hero" whom I hated.' But where there was hate, there was also pride. Gudrun Himmler, the daughter of Heinrich, supported a group that raised funds for Nazi veterans. Perhaps more conflicted was Wolf Rudiger Hess, the son of Hitler's secretary, Rudolf Hess, who, protesting against the unjust Spandau prison imprisonment of his 'innocent' father, refused to serve in the German military.

276 'It was the last time Hedwig Höss appeared . . .' In 1989, Hedwig travelled to Washington DC to visit her daughter. After a week playing with her grandchildren and seeing the sights, she went to bed one day and didn't wake up. Her ashes are entombed in a cemetery on the outskirts of the city. Brigitte didn't want anyone to find her mother's remains, so she gave the cemetery administrator a modified version of her name. On 3 March 1990 a short service was held in a small stone cloister. Hedwig's resting place was among the graves of Jews, Christians and Muslims.

276 'He jumped from job to job . . .' During his time in Toronto, Paul and his wife Lila were among the early active members of Congregation Habonim, a synagogue attended by other Holocaust survivors from Germany and other eastern European countires, and one established in the German *Liberale* tradition. The synagogue is still going today, located on Glen Park Avenue, Toronto.

276–7 'A year later the Luxembourg Government . . .' In a letter dated 15 April 1948, sent by the British Foreign Office to the Luxembourg Embassy in London, an official explained why Hanns – along with Tony Somerhough and Gerald Draper – would not be able to receive a knighthood from Luxembourg: 'I am afraid that the rules and principles observed by H.M. Govt. in these matters prevent us from returning a favourable reply . . . The services which the proposed decorations are intended to recognize were rendered after the termination of hostilities. Persons in the service of the Crown are not ordinarily permitted to accept foreign honours, and this rule has only been relaxed so as to allow of the acceptance of Allied awards offered in recognition of services during the war . . . I feel sure, however, that you will appreciate how extremely difficult it would be to give exceptional treatment to these cases without injustice to numerous other British subjects to whom the rules have already been applied.' With hindsight things could have been different. For though Hanns Alexander wore the British uniform at the time of his service (January 1940–April 1946) he was in fact considered stateless by the UK until his naturalization in April 1947, and therefore perhaps the Luxembourg government could have awarded Hanns the knighthood without requiring UK permission.

277 'Hanns did not receive either award . . .' While Hanns was precluded from receiving the significant awards from Luxembourg and Czechoslovakia, he did receive three more common awards from the British army for his general wartime service, including the France & Germany Star, the Defence Medal and the War Medal 1939–1945. These he proudly wore each year when he joined the annual veterans' parade down Whitehall in London.

277 'From the start, the Alexander Torah . . .' Sometime in the 1970s, a few days before the High Holy Days, Hanns discovered that one of the Alexander Torah's handles had broken. The scroll was almost two hundred years old by this point and, given its constant use as the synagogue's main Torah, it was not surprising that it needed repairing. The scroll was now Hanns' responsibility and inheritance. There was not enough time to have the scroll repaired by a trained and experienced *Sefer Torah* scribe, so instead, he chose to fix it himself. After work one day, Hanns went to the synagogue, removed the Torah from its Ark and laid it down on the podium at the centre of the stage. Carefully unwinding the scroll, he then detached the broken wooden handle to which the parchment was connected and, after a brief visit to the synagogue's kitchen cupboard, replaced it with a broom handle. Once the scroll was wound up and covered by its velvet cloth, Hanns replaced the Alexander Torah in the Ark, ready for its next religious outing.

279 'He had presented a positive face . . .' Ann died seven weeks after Hanns. After being together for so many years, it appears that she could not live without him. Her ashes were added to the family grave in Willesden.

Postscript

281 'It is a cool November morning . . .' I travelled to Auschwitz with Rainer Höss and his mother Irene in November 2009, having seen an article about Rainer in an Israeli newspaper in which it was claimed he was attempting to sell artefacts inherited from his grandfather to Yad Vashem. When I spoke to Rainer he denied the article's accusations, saying that he had been willing to donate the items, and invited me on the trip to Auschwitz. Rainer later returned to Auschwitz as part of a documentary called *Hitler's Children*.

286 'There was also Rudolf's memoir . . .' Four years after Rudolf Höss died on the gallows, Sehn would facilitate the publication of Rudolf's memoirs in Polish in 1951 as *Wspomnienia* ('Memories') by Wydawnictwo Prawnicze, with an introduction by the Polish criminologist Stanisław Batawia. In 1958, Rudolf's jailhouse writings were published in German for the first time by Deutsche Verlags-Anstalt under the title *Kommandant in Auschwitz: Autobiografische Aufzeichnungen von Rudolf Höss* ('Kommandant of Auschwitz: Autobiography of Rudolf Höss'), edited by Dr Martin Broszat, the director of IFZ, Germany's pre-eminent National Socialism research institute. A year later, and twelve years after it had first been drafted, Rudolf's memoirs were translated into English by Constantine Fitzgibbon and introduced by Lord Russell – who as Deputy Judge Advocate General had been one of the chief legal advisers during the Nuremberg war crimes trials – and published under the title *Commandant at Auschwitz* by Weidenfeld & Nicolson. It was this last version, republished by Phoenix Press in 2001, that Hanns had a copy of lying on his living-room table on the day he died. A popular North American edition of the memoirs was published in 1992, under the title *Death Dealer: The Memoirs of the SS Kommandant of Auschwitz*, by Prometheus Books, edited by Steven Paskuly and translated by Andrew Pollinger. Since they were written in 1946, Rudolf's memoirs have been translated into scores of languages and, through

various editions, been read by hundreds of thousands of people around the world.

287 'As to the Alexander Torah . . .' In 2012 Hanns' nephews and nieces met and discussed the future of the family Torah. Its parchment was ripped in places; the ink of some of the characters had run; sticky tape held some of the pages together. As such it was deemed not *kosher*, unusable. After a long and emotional discussion it was agreed that the Torah held such sentimental and historic value that it should be restored. The family members pledged the funds to send the scroll to a *sofer* in east London, who would make the relevant repairs so that once again the Alexander Torah could play a regular part in the synagogue's services. The repairs are due to be complete by the end of 2013.

Hanns Alexander's Family Tree

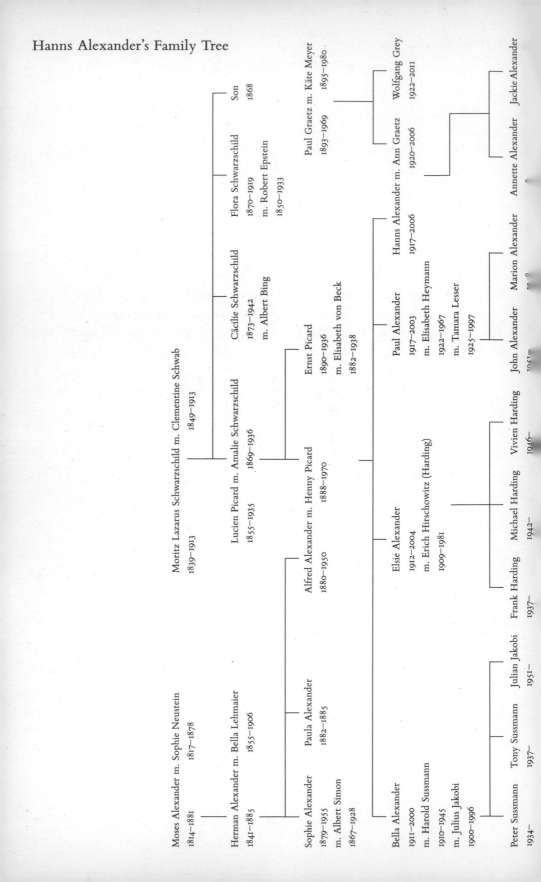

Moses Alexander m. Sophie Neustein
1814–1881   1817–1878

Herman Alexander m. Bella Lehmaier
1841–1885   1855–1906

Moritz Lazarus Schwarzschild m. Clementine Schwab
1839–1913   1849–1913

Lucien Picard m. Amalie Schwarzschild
1855–1935   1866–1936

Cäcilie Schwarzschild
1873–1942
m. Albert Bing

Flora Schwarzschild
1870–1919
m. Robert Epstein
1850–1933

Son
1868

Paul Graetz m. Käte Meyer
1893–1969   1895–1980

Sophie Alexander
1879–1955
m. Albert Simon
1867–1928

Paula Alexander
1882–1885

Alfred Alexander m. Henny Picard
1880–1950   1888–1970

Ernst Picard
1890–1936
m. Elisabeth von Beck
1882–1938

Paul Alexander
1917–2003
m. Elisabeth Heymann
1922–1967
m. Tamara Lesser
1925–1997

Hanns Alexander m. Ann Graetz
1917–2006   1920–2006

Wolfgang Grey
1922–2011

Bella Alexander
1911–2000
m. Harold Sussmann
1910–1945
m. Julius Jakobi
1900–1996

Elsie Alexander
1912–2004
m. Erich Hirschowitz (Harding)
1909–1981

Vivien Harding
1946–

John Alexander
1951–

Marion Alexander

Annette Alexander

Jackie Alexander

Peter Sussmann
1934–

Tony Sussmann
1937–

Julian Jakobi
1951–

Frank Harding
1937–

Michael Harding
1942–

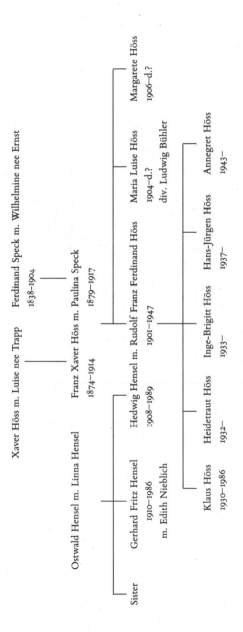

Xaver Höss m. Luise nee Trapp

Ferdinand Speck m. Wilhelmine nee Ernst
1838–1904

Franz Xaver Höss m. Paulina Speck
1874–1914   1879–1917

Ostwald Hensel m. Linna Hensel

Hedwig Hensel m. Rudolf Franz Ferdinand Höss
1908–1989   1901–1947

Gerhard Fritz Hensel
1910–1986
m. Edith Nieblich

Sister

Maria Luise Höss
1904–d.?
div. Ludwig Bühler

Margarete Höss
1906–d.?

Klaus Höss
1930–1986

Heidetraut Höss
1932–

Inge-Brigitt Höss
1933–

Hans-Jürgen Höss
1937–

Annegret Höss
1943–

RESEARCH SOURCES

Hanns Alexander was my great-uncle. He died in 2006 and I only learned about his wartime activities when I heard the eulogy given at his funeral service. The family never spoke about these things and we were told, first as children, later as adults, not to ask Hanns or other family members about what took place during the war.

To find out about my uncle's activities, I conducted research at many institutions around the world. I have relied on declassified and recently released documents held by several archives, particularly documents released by the Auschwitz Museum Archives regarding Höss' last few days in prison (the museum is also the keeper of the original Rudolf Höss memoir); unpublished and recently declassified documents in the British National Archive in Kew relating to Hanns Alexander's arrest of Rudolf Höss and of Gustav Simon, as well as files regarding Oswald Pohl and Richard Glücks, Operation Haystack, and the 1 War Crimes Investigation Team and War Crimes Group; unpublished and recently declassified documents from the Intelligence Museum in Chicksands, relating to the arrest of Rudolf Höss and to Field Security Section 92; Luxembourg National Archive reports and documents relating to Hanns Alexander's arrest of Gustav Simon; Holocaust Museum in Washington DC, particularly for video footage of the Nuremberg Trials, including Höss' testimony and photographs of Rudolf Höss in Auschwitz; recently declassified files from the United States National Archives in College Park, including material supplied by Richard Breitman, Director of Historical Research for the US Government's Nazi War Criminal Records Interagency, particularly the 'Dachau Report' and cables related to Gustav Simon and Richard Glücks; correspondence with Barry Ritzler, who found

Rudolf Höss' unpublished Rorschach test in Gustave Gilbert's filing cabinet; as well as survivor interviews, held by the Shoah Database, available at University of San Diego, California, and at Royal Holloway, University of London. In addition, I was assisted by Yad Vashem in Israel; the Dachau Archive in Munich; the Sachsenhausen Museum in Berlin; the Grand Ducal Palace and National Archive in Luxembourg; the Institute of National Remembrance in Warsaw; and the Imperial War Museum in London.

Much of the text is based on new sources, including my interviews with Rudolf Höss' daughter Brigitte; Rudolf Höss' daughter-in-law, Irene Alba; Rudolf Höss' grandson, Rainer Höss (who also allowed me to reproduce many images, including the extraordinary family photographs taken at the Höss villa in Auschwitz); Whitney Harris, the American prosecutor at the Nuremberg Trials; Anita Lasker and Lucille Eichengreen, whom Hanns helped in Belsen; Jozef Paczynski, the 'Little Pole' who cut Rudolf's hair; and Eva Schloss, Anne Frank's stepsister. I also made use of taped interviews with Hanns, Bella, Elsie and Paul Alexander recorded by John Alexander and Herbert Levy. In addition, I had access to hitherto unpublished letters between Hanns and Paul Alexander, their sisters, Elsie and Bella, and their mother Henny; as well as letters sent from Rudolf Höss to Hedwig and his children, held both by the Auschwitz Museum and the Höss family private collection.

Internet

There are numerous useful resources now available on the Web, especially the full records of the Nuremberg, Belsen and Frankfurt Trials. On the Belsen site you can find the full transcripts of the trial, including the affidavits that were recorded by Hanns Alexander. On the Nuremberg site, you can find transcripts of Rudolf Höss' testimonies as well as those of Eleanor Hodys and Konrad Morgen. However, be wary of many other sites, whose veracity ebbs and flows like the tides. One site in particular, Wikipedia, is prone to political editing, especially when it comes to the Nazi leaders. A hobby of mine during the research of this typescript has been to push the Wikipedia envelope: I would log on and, without reference, correct the birth date of Rudolf Höss and then, a few days later, someone else would log on and change it back, again without source, then I would correct it again, and so on.

A note on place names

My apologies to readers who are confused by my use of German, Polish and other place names in *Hanns and Rudolf*. I did have my own rules, which I will try and explain.

For cities, I have used the spellings I thought would be most familiar to an English-speaking audience. There, are however, a few exceptions: 'Oświęcim' and not 'Auschwitz', for example, to differentiate the town from the concentration camp. For German street names I have taken contemporary, uncompounded, spellings where possible – for example, 'Oranienburger Strasse' rather than 'Oranienburgerstrasse' – so that readers will find it easier to locate these places on maps and street signs. Where these names have changed, such as Kaiserallee (which today is Bundesallee), or where the street no longer exists (such as Achenbachstrasse), I have chosen the historically appropriate name. Belsen was perhaps trickiest of all, as it was known by different names: survivors called it 'Bergen-Belsen'; the British named their HQ next to the camp, 'Hohne'; while the displaced persons called it 'DP Camp Bergen-Belsen'. For the sake of clarity, and because it was how both Hanns and Rudolf named it, I have described the concentration camp as 'Belsen' throughout.

For more information on place names and for other background material, please visit www.hannsandrudolf.com

BIBLIOGRAPHY

I found the following texts useful:

Alexander, John. *A Measure of Time*. A self-published history of the Alexander family.

Arendt, Hannah. *Eichmann in Jerusalem*. Provides a key exploration of the 'banality of evil'.

Auschwitz-Birkenau Museum. *KL Auschwitz seen by the SS*. Includes eyewitness accounts by housemaids and gardeners who worked in the Höss villa.

Bardgett, Suzanne and David Cesarani. *Belsen 1945*. An introduction to the camp by two of the best Holocaust researchers.

Bower, Tom. *Blind Eye to Murder*. A powerful treatise on the failures of the British and Americans to bring the Nazi leaders to justice.

Browning, Christopher. *Ordinary Men*. A look at Reserve Police Battalion 101's motives for murdering the Jews. He takes a different view from Daniel Goldhagen (also included in this list of sources).

Butler, Rupert. *Legions of Death*. An excitable history of the SS, which includes a description of Rudolf Höss' arrest.

Eichengreen, Lucille. *From Ashes to Life*. A young girl's account of life in Belsen, including a description of her rescue by Hanns Alexander.

Fry, Helen. *The King's Loyal Aliens*. A great introduction to the story of the Jewish refugees who fought for the British during the Second World War.

Gilbert, G. M. *Nuremberg Diary*. The American psychologist's account of his time with the defendants as they awaited their trial.

Gilbert, Martin. *The Holocaust: The Jewish Tragedy*. Includes a description of the incident in which prisoners mounted an uprising in one of Birkenau's gas chambers.

Godfrey, Antony. *Three Rabbis in a Vicarage*. The history of the Belsize Square Synagogue, North London.

Goldensohn, Leon. *The Nuremberg Interviews, An American Psychiatrist's Conversations with the Defendants and Witnesses*. Edited by Robert Gellately, a terrific insight into the minds of the leading war criminals by the American psychiatrist.

Goldhagen, Daniel. *Hitler's Willing Executioners*. An examination of why 'ordinary' Germans perpetrated the Holocaust. He takes a different view from Christopher Browning (also in this list of sources).

Harris, Whitney. *Tyranny on Trial*. A guide to the Nuremberg Trials written by one of the American prosecutors shortly after the war.

Hoare, Oliver. *Camp 020: M15 and the Nazi Spies*. An extraordinary account of wartime interrogation techniques, and includes Colonel Robin 'Tin Eye' Stephens' interrogation manual *Digest of Ham*.

Hoess, Rudolf. *Commandant at Auschwitz Rudolf Hoess*, also known as *Death Dealer: The Memoirs of the SS Kommandant of Auschwitz*. This autobiography was written in a Polish prison cell while Rudolf awaited his death sentence. While *Commandant at Auschwitz Rudolf Hoess* was published first with a translation by Constantine Fitzgibbon and an introduction by Lord Russell, the *Death Dealer* version, which was edited by Steven Paskuly, is written in a more contemporary English. Both versions include an introduction by Primo Levi.

Kemp, Anthony. *The Secret Hunters*. A good introduction to the Allies' efforts to track down war criminals at the end of the war.

Kershaw, Ian. *The End: 1944–1945*. Explores the last days of the Reich providing tremendous insight into the Nazis' final phase.

Langbein, Hermann. *People in Auschwitz*. Perhaps the definitive account of life in Auschwitz, told by a resistance leader and inmate.

Lasker-Wallfisch, Anita. *Inherit the Truth*. A personal story of the young girl who managed to stay alive by playing the cello in Auschwitz and was saved from Belsen by Hanns Alexander.

Lebert, Stephan and Norbert (eds). *My Father's Keeper*. An excellent anthology of interviews with the children of Nazi leaders.

Leighton-Langer, Peter. *The King's Most Loyal Enemy Aliens*.

Lifton, Robert Jay. *The Nazi Doctors*. A survey of the terrible deeds overseen by the medical officials at the concentration camp, including a superb introduction.

Longerich, Peter. *Heinrich Himmler*. Perhaps the definitive account of the man who ran the SS.

Rees, Laurence. *Auschwitz: The Nazis & The Final Solution*. Research from this book became the foundation for a major BBC documentary series.

Segev, Tom. *Soldiers of Evil*. An account of some of the main camp Kommandants, including Josef Kramer and Rudolf Höss.

Shephard, Ben. *After Daybreak: The Liberation of Belsen, 1945*. An introduction to what took place in Belsen.

Smith, Bradley. *Reaching Judgment at Nuremberg*. A useful primer, especially on the politics in the USA, Britain and the Soviet Union that led up to the creation of the war crime trials.

Smith, Michael. *Foley: The Spy Who Saved 10,000 Jews*. A good description of the life of the British passport officer who saved thousands of Jews by giving them visas to escape from Berlin.

Steinbacher, Sybille. *Auschwitz: A History*. A fine introduction to the camp and its background.

Waite, Robert G. L. *Vanguard of Nazism*. The best book on the Freikorps movement.

Walters, Guy. *Hunting Evil*. An exploration of the Nazi hunters, including a look at 1WCIT and Tony Somerhough's War Crimes Group.

Wiese, Christian and Paul Betts (eds). *Years of Persecution, Years of Extermination*. Chapter 10 is a good introduction to the extraordinary life of Konrad Morgen, and provides a reading list for further enquiry.

ACKNOWLEDGEMENTS

Many people helped me with this book, to all I owe a huge debt of gratitude. In particular:

To the early supporters of the project, Farzad Mahootian and Charlie McCormick, who told me I had to do it when I didn't think I should, or could. To my fabulous readers: Elizabeth Wheeler, Hali Taylor, Dominic Valentine, David Lillard, Gillian Tett, Kate and David Harding, Gregory Kent and Gillian Stern. To the incomparable Dabney Chapman, who assisted me on many a translation without notice and with such grace, and to Anthea Bell, who did a fabulous job translating Rudolf Höss' writings. Thanks also to Marion Godfrey, Sheridan Marshall and Caroline Sloan for their help with the German text. Thanks to Darren Bennett for creating such clear and compelling maps for the book. To my interviewees: Anita Lasker-Wallfisch, Lucille Eichengreen, Whitney Harris, Jozef Paczynski, Rainer Höss, Brigitte née Höss, Victor Weitzel, Julian Mayer, Julia Draper, Noel Egerton and Freddy Mayer.

A special thanks to my cousin, John Alexander, for his superb history of the Alexander family, the Alexander Torah, and his recordings with Uncle Hanns and the rest of the Alexander siblings.

I would also like to thank the following for their help with my research efforts: Major Edwards and Fred Judge (Intelligence Corps Museum, Chicksands); Stephen Walton (Imperial War Museum, London); John Starling (Auxiliary Military Pioneer Corp Association); Helen Fry; Johanna Bleker (Berlin University); Rebecca Schwoch (University Hamburg); Iwona Kwaczala, Anna Skrzypinska, Piotr Setkiewicz and Wojciech Plosha (Auschwitz Museum, Oświęcim); Anthony Polonsky (Brandeis College); Léandre Mignon, Romain Meyer, Francois Moyse, Judith Cohen and Rebecca Erbelding (United States Holocaust Memorial Museum); Saul Ferrero (Yad Vashem); Klaus Tätzler (Bergen-Belsen Memorial Museum); Gillian Walnes (Ann Frank Center, Amsterdam); Vaclav Vochoska (Czech Embassy, Washington DC); Aaron Breitbart (Wiesenthal Center LA); Paul Dostert (Luxemburg Center for Documentation on the Second World War); Dr. Klaus Lankheit (Institut für Zeitgeschichte München); Richard Breitman (Nazi War Crimes and Japanese Imperial Government Records Interagency Working Group); Herbert Levy; Manfred Deslaers (Centro Diaglo, Oświęcim); Monika Thomsen (Gemeinde Handewitt); Bridget McGing (Wiener Library); Peter Peterlini (Bundesverwaltungsamt); Dagmar Rumpf (Baden-Baden State Archive); Karen Strobel (Mannheim State Archive) and Steven Paskuly.

Thank you to Farrar, Straus and Giroux, and to the Random House Group for granting me permission to include extracts from *Nuremberg Diary* by G. M. Gilbert and *Nuremberg Interviews*, edited by Robert Gellately. While every effort has been made to trace the holders of copyright in all text extracts and images, I would like to apologise in advance for any errors or omissions. All corrections deemed necessary can be made in future reprints.

Many family members deserve my gratitude for their support, it can be scary to open up a family's past. In particular, I wish to thank my father Frank Harding, for sharing his mother's letters; my sister Amanda, who made the crazy visit to Luxembourg so much more fun;

cousins Jackie and Annette, who generously shared stories about their parents, Hanns and Ann; Aunty Vivien who was so refreshingly honest; Julian and Fiona Jakobi for sharing their family archives; Peter Sussmann for his clear memories and for his mother's letters; cousin Judith for her account of Aunty Bing and life in Frankfurt; Marion 'Cookie' Alexander, who found the treasure trove of Hanns and Paul's wartime letters in the attic; Madeleine Hensel, for her memories of Hanns and Aunty Bing; Allan Morgenthau, who so kindly told me about his dear Helga; Michael and Angela Harding, for their courageous support; Kate (Weinberg) Harding, who was a champion from the start; and to my cousin James, whose unflinching belief in me, despite all evidence to the contrary, helped me get through my darkest hours.

To my amazing team of international English-language editors: Tom Avery at William Heinemann, who acquired the book first and has so brilliantly steered the editing process ever since, and Thomas LeBien at Simon & Schuster and Janie Yoon at House of Anansi Press, who made significant contributions to the book. To my extraordinary agent, Patrick Walsh, and his fabulous team at Conville & Walsh, it has been a privilege to work with you all. Also thanks to Ivan Mulcahy for his early work on the book. Of course, despite all the help, I take total responsibility for all aspects of the book and all and every error is my own.

To my awesome daughter, Sam, who found Hanns and Ann's letters in the storage unit and who kept me company while I tap, tap, tapped away.

Finally, almost, I would like to thank my darling wife, Debora Harding, who has supported me throughout this project, despite the many journeys away from home, and whose feedback I most appreciate. I love you more.

Most of all, I want to thank my son, whose pride in this story, and his dad, inspired me to complete this book, when all I wanted was to curl up under the covers and think of him. Thank you Kadian.

INDEX

Liebe Mami!

Ich schreibe mal wieder Mittag
ich tod müde bin und Heute nur 8 U
Bett liegen will. Ich hatte nämlich
ereignisreiche Woche hinter mir + Sen
erstag war mit Papi bei Frau von Ka
bad sehr gut und reichlich. Papi hat
Freitag Mittag bis heute nu Schicht
aber ihn noch nicht gesprochen, aber ich

De cpt. Alexandre au gespr·ch mat dem bér minister
bér J. Thorn.

Onkel Hans
Alexander 1946

...e sympathy with you, as I understand
.. placed in a similar unhappy position
...r, your above mentioned letter is
. restraint.

.to which particular Artillery Officer
.."there is always time for a letter".
..f, I somewhat resent the implicatio
..ment would be such an imbecile as to
..riminating statement.   I can only
..Officer, that he was neither in that
..ing married, but was in fact that m
..lor.

..dam, may I wish you a very happy
..dd a word of sympathy with you in
..ailing task, of piloting Captain
..h the troubled waters of married li

.. Madam,
.. Your obedient servant,

J.H. Tilling : Lt: Col:
R.A.

..s no excuse, so if I were you I'd
.. even stronger.

with ice
re, as pr
h should
t to Bru
, but at
ine to I
t was th
as just
e the ot
ting tha
yed read
aken lik
be helpe
hey were
t on lea
you will
her lett
e that w
end me,
av Simon

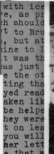

THE SANDS AT CARBIS BAY, ST. IVES CORNWALL.

that he was hiding under a different name somewhere in the Eifel
ntentions, with the O.K. of the O.C. were to spend a day or two o
have two days in Brussels and then return here, but after the fi
I saw that those who had been looking before did not try the way
d have gone about the job, and all of a sudden I put my pride in
hing that swine. And once I had started to get going I could not
r two clues to work on, and with a l
did manage to catch him, the result
come off, but I do not mind really,